Sketchbook Joy

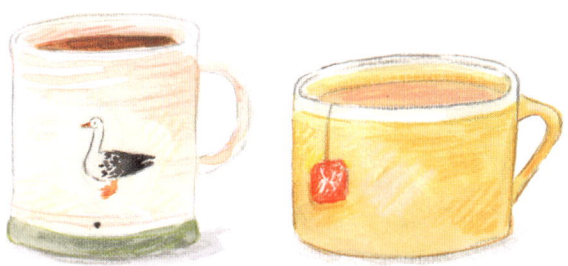

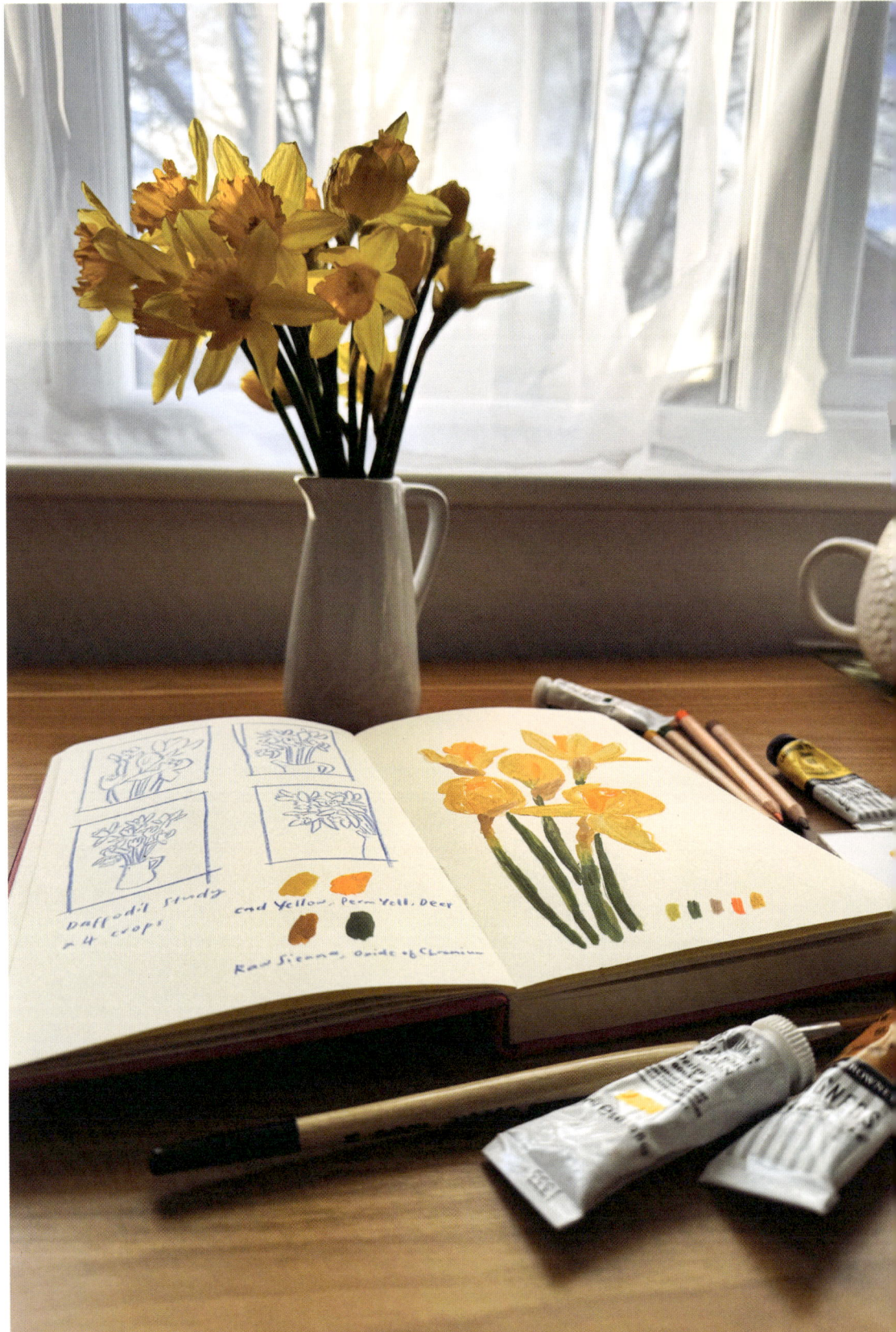

Sketchbook Joy

HOW TO EMBRACE YOUR CREATIVITY AND FILL YOUR SKETCHBOOKS WITH COLOUR

KATIE MOODY

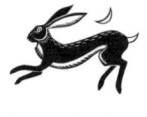

Leaping Hare Press

Contents

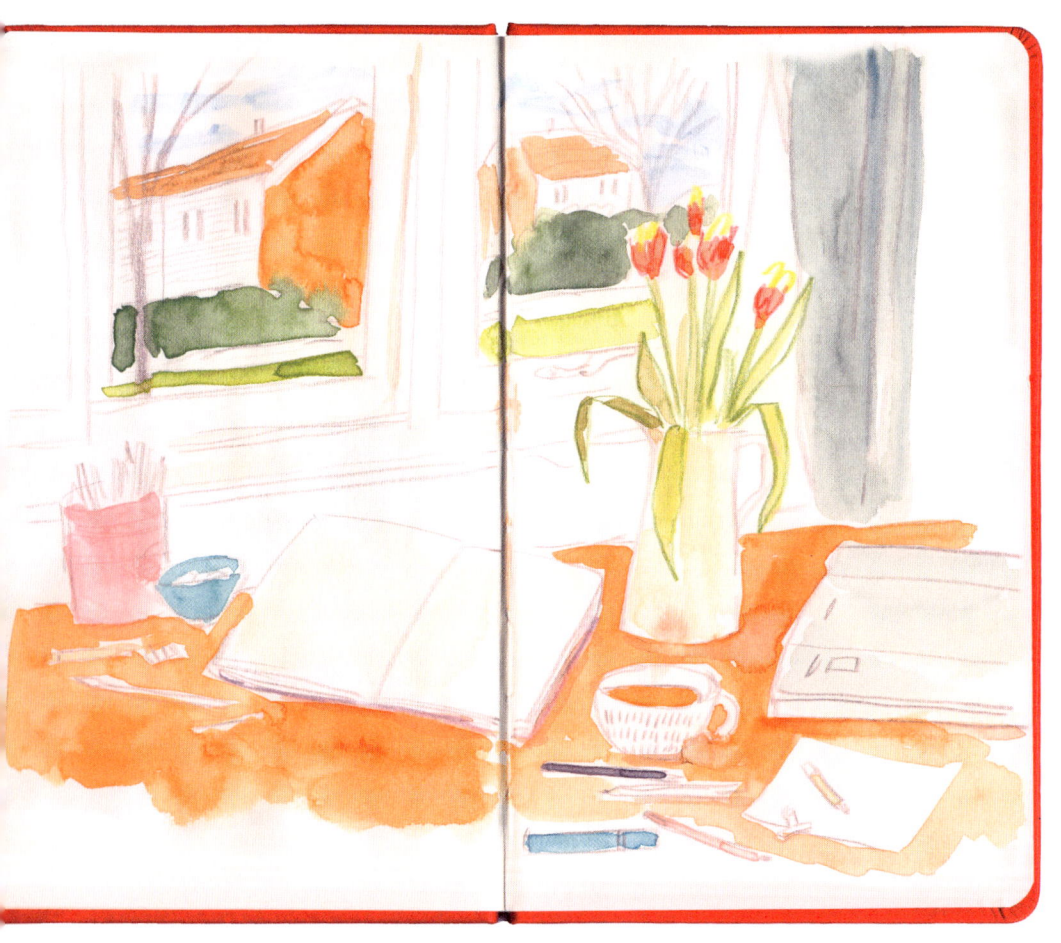

PROJECTS

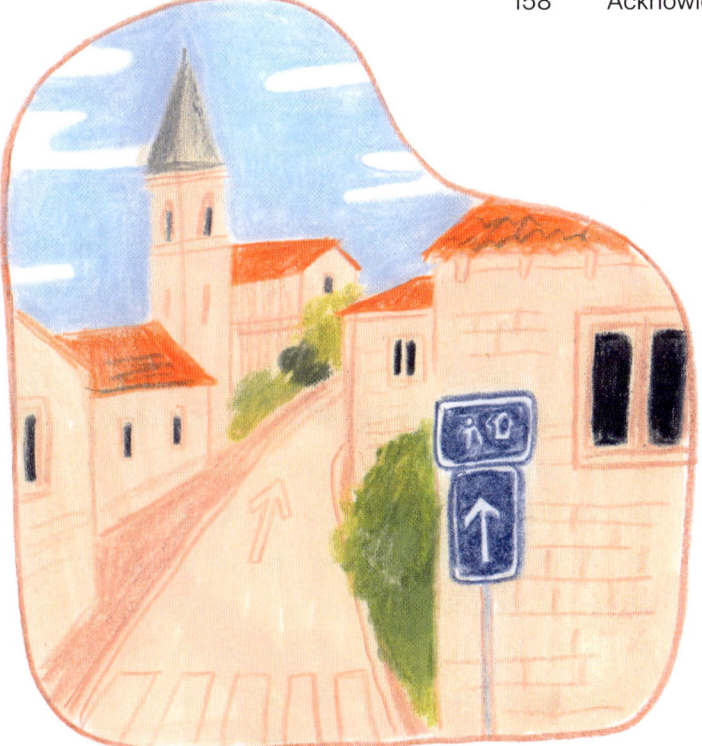

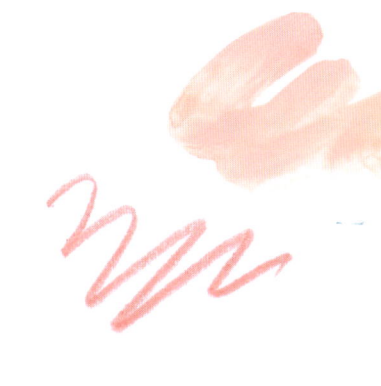

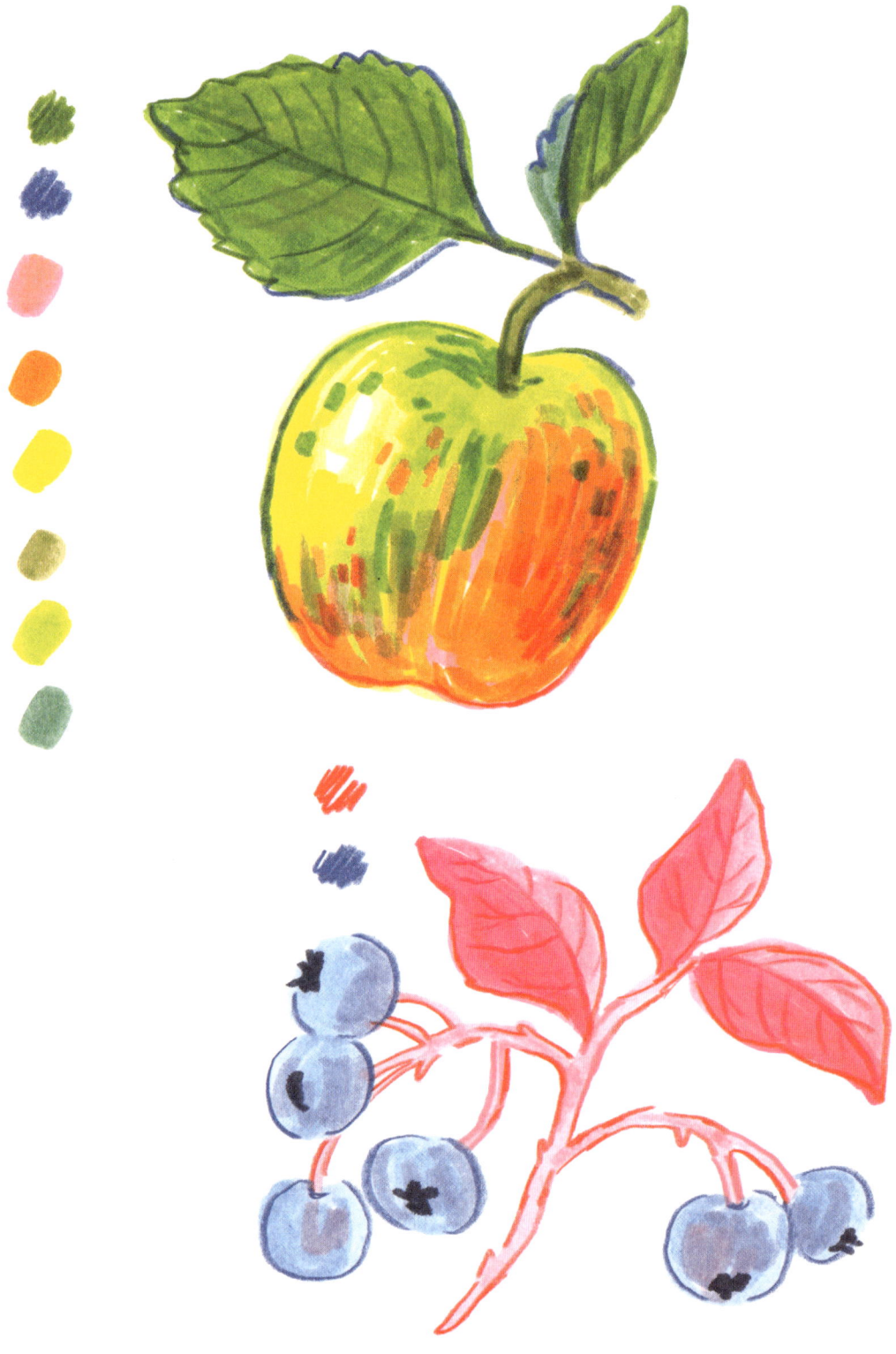

Introduction

Filling sketchbooks with my art changed my life. I know that's a pretty bold statement, but it really helped me to gain confidence and enabled me to build a career and connect with a community. Now I'm so excited to share everything I've learnt so far with you.

This book isn't about teaching you the right way to create – I don't believe that exists. There's no judgement in this book about skill level or time commitment or the level of art supplies you use. Instead, I'll be sharing various ideas, techniques and methods for filling your sketchbook, but with the understanding that these are open and can be changed to suit you. You may find a project ignites a flurry of new ideas and sketches, so take that spark and run with it. I want this book to give you the confidence to create and the encouragement to grab your materials and get excited to try new techniques.

The more you create, the more you'll discover what you love to do. You might prefer a specific medium, a particular subject matter, or maybe you'll discover that you love a bit of everything! There really is no right or wrong with art, and when it comes to this book, I hope it encourages you to embrace your own creativity. We all think in different ways and we all create differently too.

Sketchbooks are a safe space for creating; they can be shared with the world or kept hidden, for your eyes only. Style, method, technique. . . it doesn't really matter what you do as long as you're enjoying the process. As soon as you feel that little moment of inspiration, grab your art supplies and get creative – even if it's just for five minutes. It's time to find your sketchbook joy!

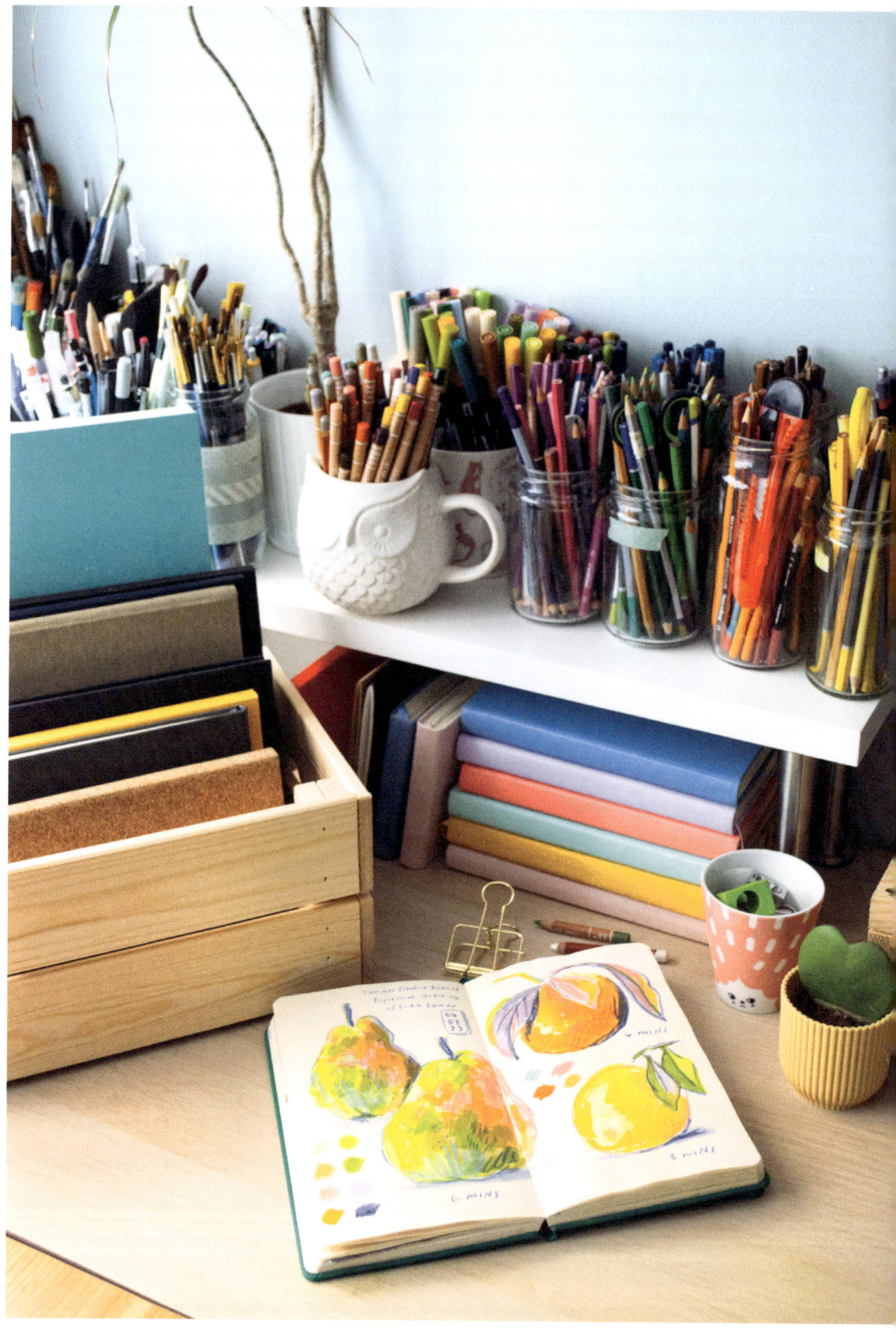

Why use a sketchbook?

Sketchbooks are where ideas are formed, low-pressure doodles happen, sketches take shape and experiments can lead to more and more creativity.

Not all artists use sketchbooks, but it can be a really great way to develop ideas. After filling your pages with experiments, composition thumbnails and pencil sketches, you can recreate work that stems from your sketchbook onto large canvases. Famous artists like Leonardo da Vinci, Vincent van Gogh, Edgar Degas and Alphonse Mucha used sketchbooks, which were filled with studies, notes and tests that stand alone, or were developed into bigger pieces.

You can also keep all of your art-making in a sketchbook! Fill various sizes of sketchbook with your paintings, your playful experiments and attempts at colour mixing. It doesn't have to lead to anything or be shown to anyone else. It can be public, private or somewhere in between, depending on what you'd prefer. And you don't need fancy art supplies, huge canvases or years of experience behind you – you can start where you are, with what you have.

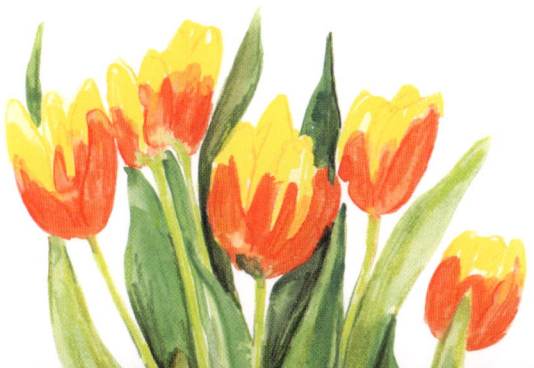

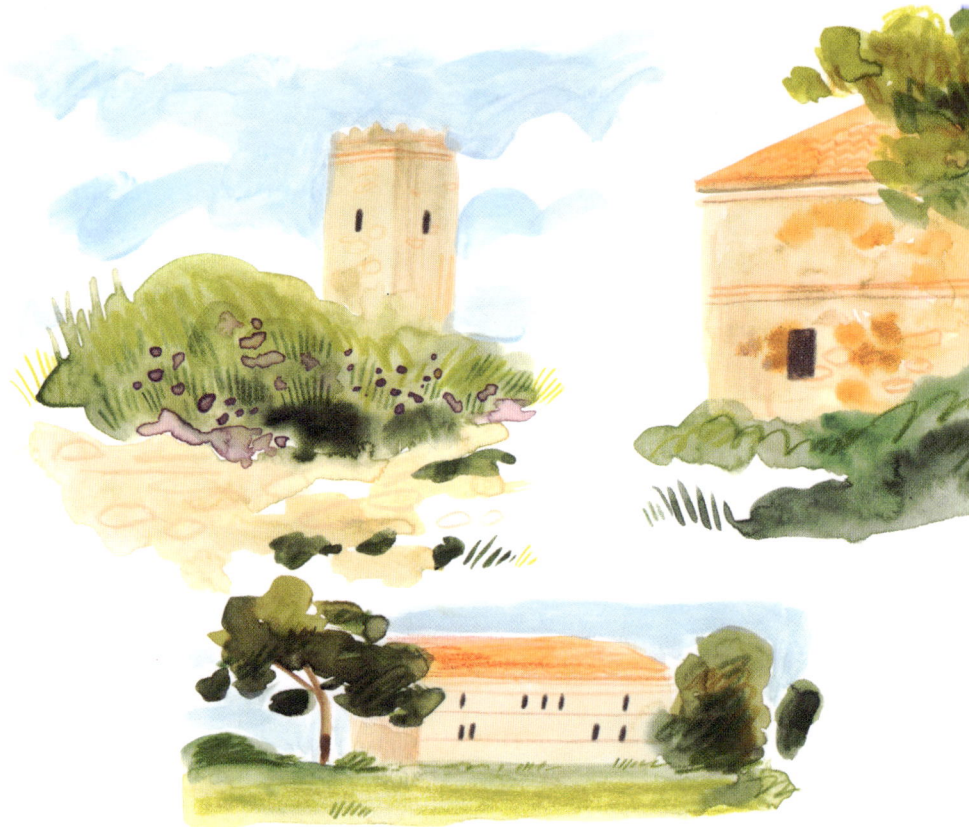

A sketchbook can also be a fantastic opportunity for mindfulness. Use it to empty your mind of clutter and to get your thoughts out onto a page, or just to save something on paper, like a to-do list or a shade of paint you've been meaning to buy. It can be filled with your notes and thoughts, as well as sketches and doodles – it can even be filled with scribbles from a ballpoint pen and still count as a sketchbook!

I think sometimes we feel that a sketchbook has to be perfect, and we have an idea in our head of what our sketchbooks 'should' look like (see page 16 for more about perfectionism). Oftentimes we scroll through social media and see these incredible, curated sketchbooks, but it's okay if yours isn't like that. I bet these artists have other sketchbooks that are messy, scrappy and rough – we just don't see them.

A sketchbook is actually a very personal object. I love that it can document journeys and events that we may not even realize we're going through, but which we discover at the end of our book. It's an amazing feeling to reach that final spread and see all these pages filled with drawings, notes or doodles, whether it took six months or six years to fill them. Flipping from that very first page and seeing the development and growth in confidence is a huge achievement.

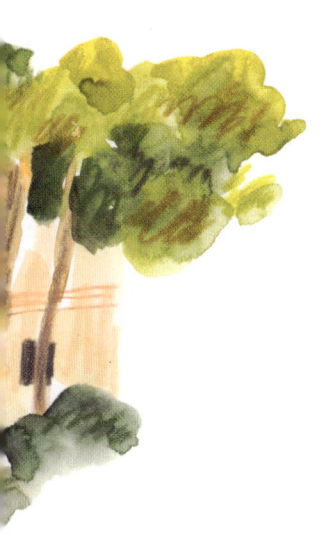

Even if you have multiple sketchbooks that are barely filled, you should look at those pages with pride instead of disappointment. Just the act of putting pencil to paper is fantastic.

It doesn't matter if you don't like it, or it didn't turn out how you'd hoped. You created something – what a wonderful thing to do!

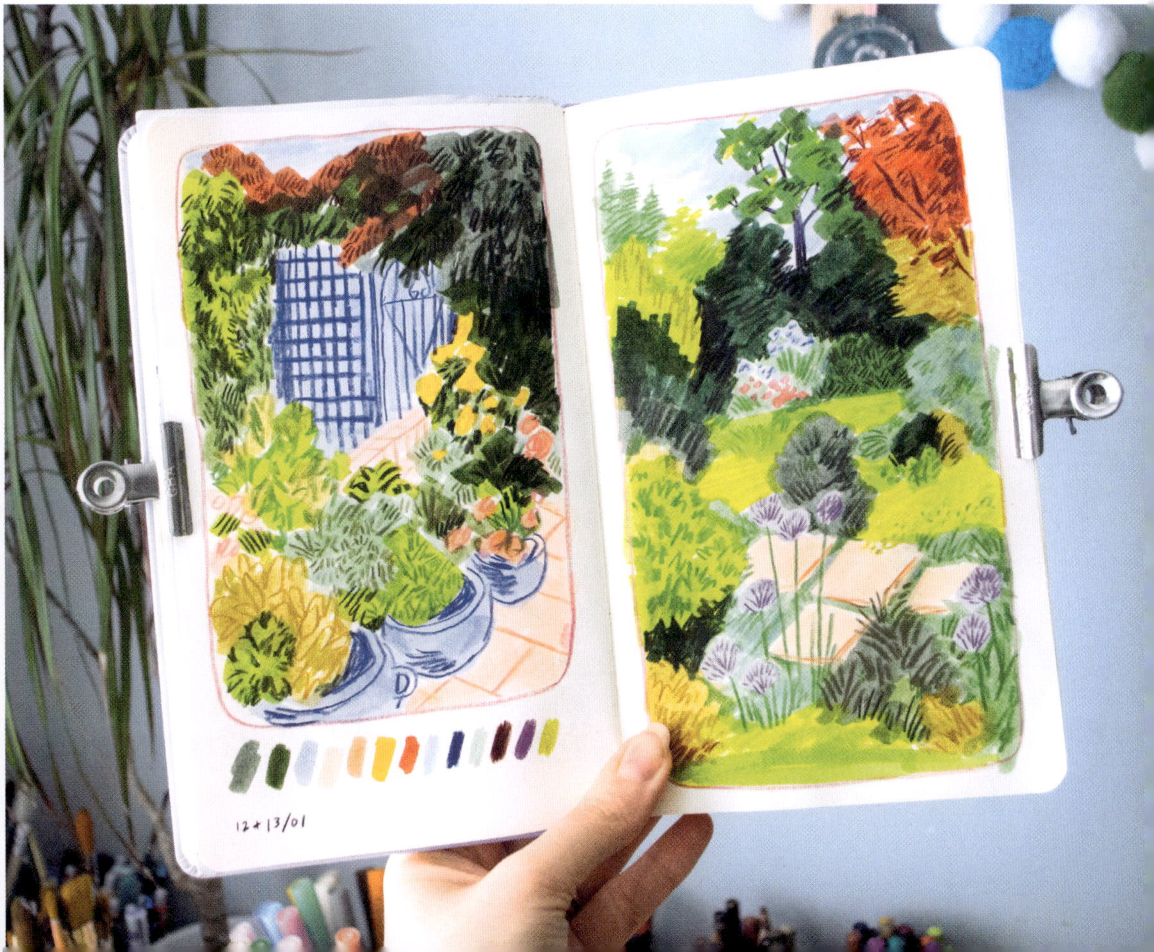

12 + 13/01

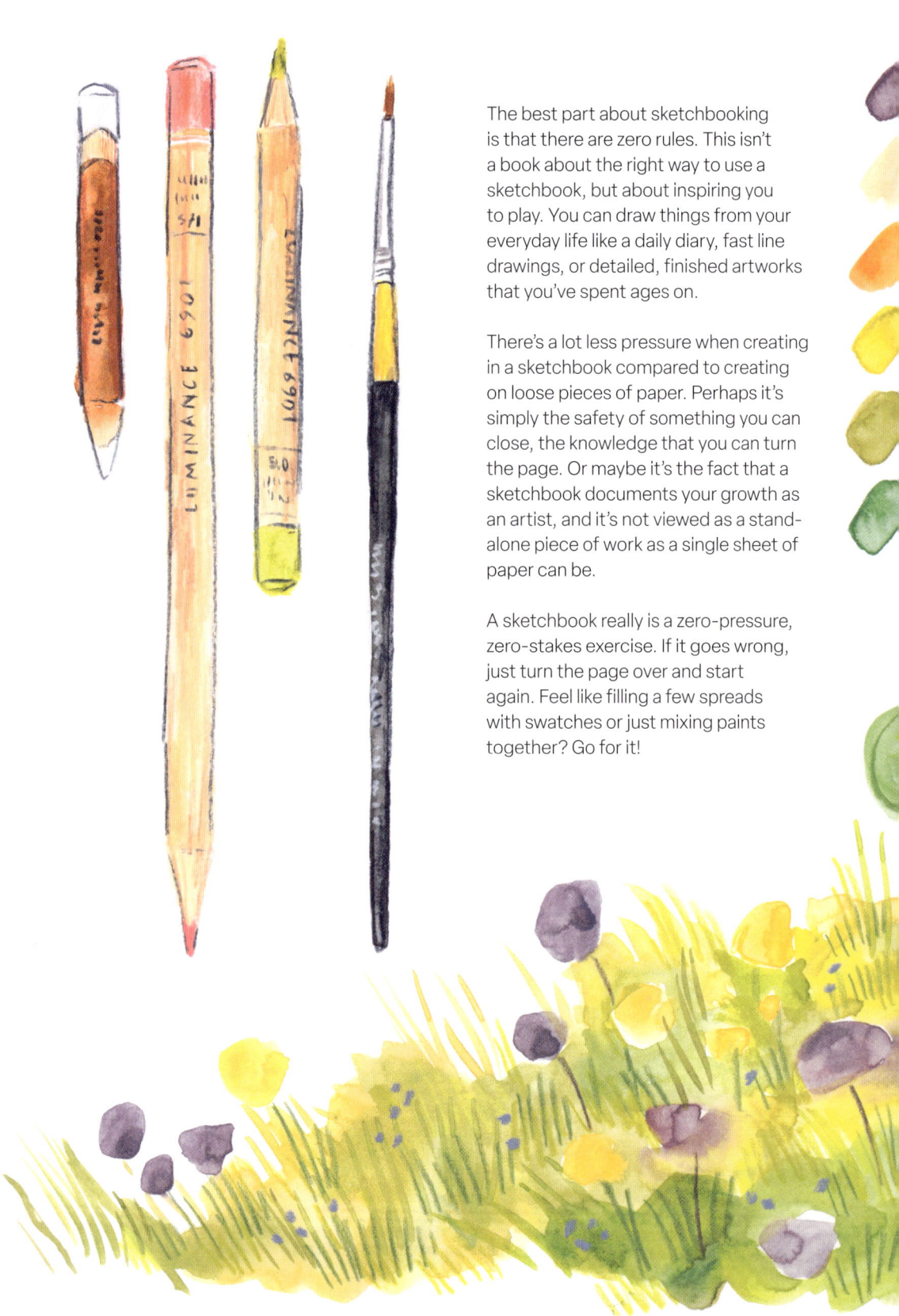

The best part about sketchbooking is that there are zero rules. This isn't a book about the right way to use a sketchbook, but about inspiring you to play. You can draw things from your everyday life like a daily diary, fast line drawings, or detailed, finished artworks that you've spent ages on.

There's a lot less pressure when creating in a sketchbook compared to creating on loose pieces of paper. Perhaps it's simply the safety of something you can close, the knowledge that you can turn the page. Or maybe it's the fact that a sketchbook documents your growth as an artist, and it's not viewed as a stand-alone piece of work as a single sheet of paper can be.

A sketchbook really is a zero-pressure, zero-stakes exercise. If it goes wrong, just turn the page over and start again. Feel like filling a few spreads with swatches or just mixing paints together? Go for it!

It's a place to play, study and experiment. It's a way to draw over and over again without worrying about what you did before, and a place to practise your style and learn your creative preferences.

So, let's get filling our sketchbooks, shall we?

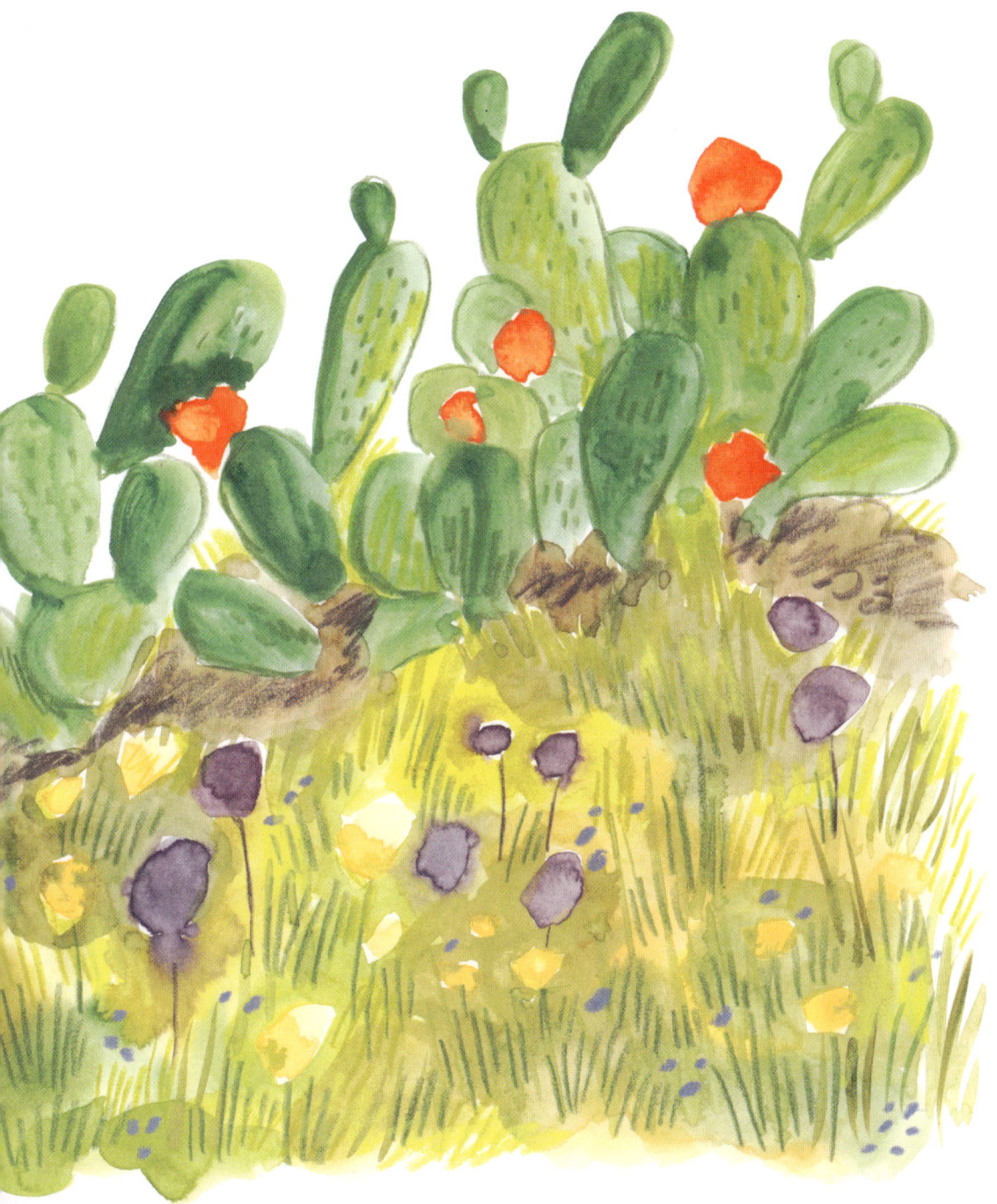

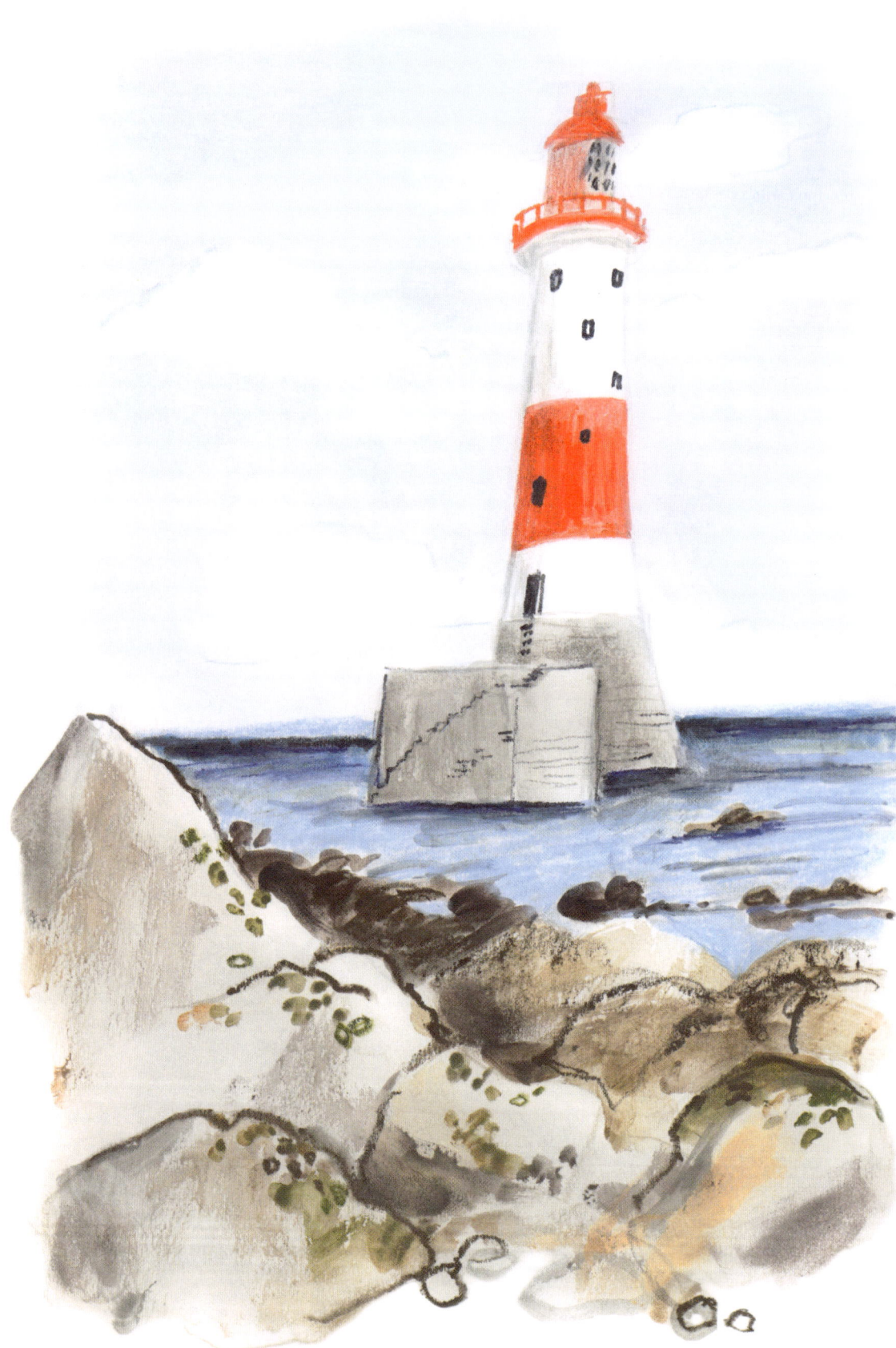

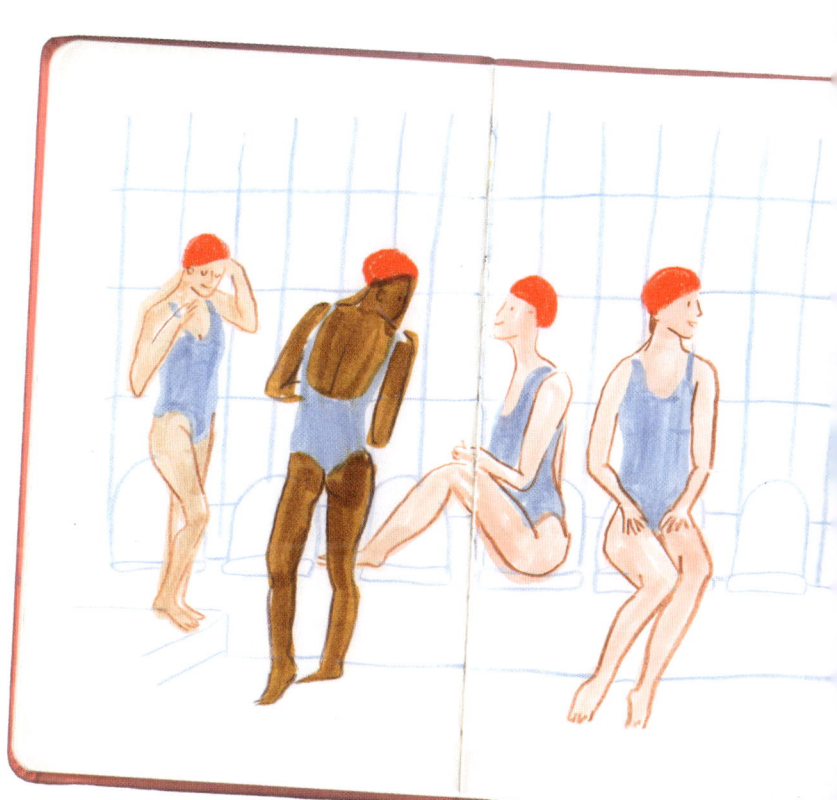

Filling your sketchbook

There are various types of sketchbook available (see page 44), yet the beauty of this creative outlet is that any type of paper can become a sketchbook, so you can start with minimal supplies and still create art that makes you happy and brings you joy.

You can fill one sketchbook with a variety of subjects, or keep multiple sketchbooks, each with a theme. There are no rules, so don't let anything hold you back!

Removing perfectionism

I think the hardest part of keeping a sketchbook is the pressure of the standards we hold ourselves to, and the perfectionistic tendencies we come up against. So often we don't create because we think our work won't be 'good enough'. It's totally normal to feel this way, but the only way to get past it is to create anyway.

Let's reframe those thoughts and remind ourselves that drawing isn't about the end result – it's about the process! And that process might lead to something you love, or it might not. Either one is okay.

We won't create our best work without putting in the effort or without creating 'bad' work that teaches us lessons along the way. I'd actually say that we want to create 'bad' work, as that's where we learn the most and discover new ideas and methods to try next time.

It's not easy, but to remove that pesky perfectionism we need to push through it. Create quickly, draw lots and paint with new materials – fill your sketchbook despite those thoughts. And if you don't like something, that's fine! Just turn the page and try again. That's the best thing about a sketchbook!

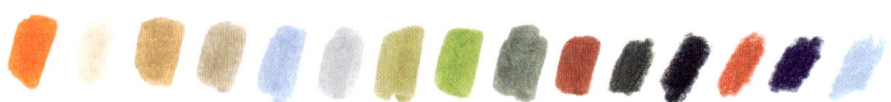

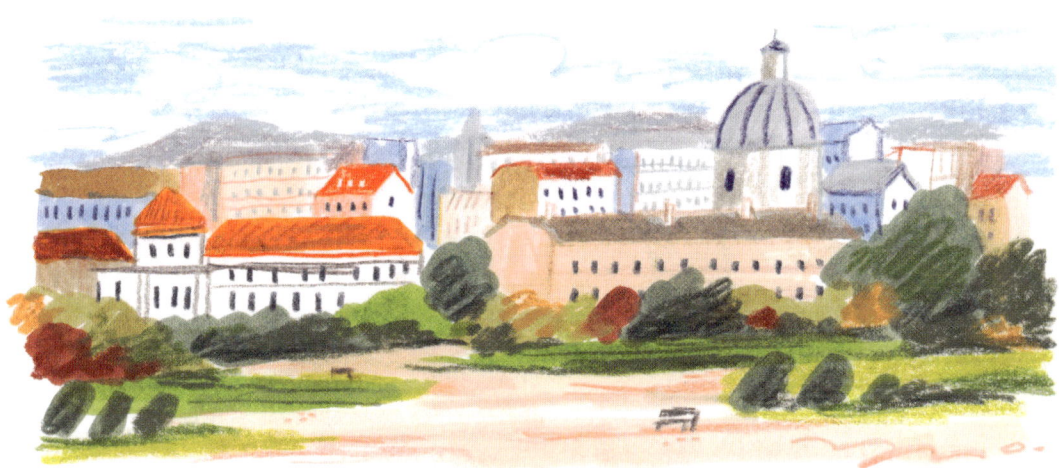

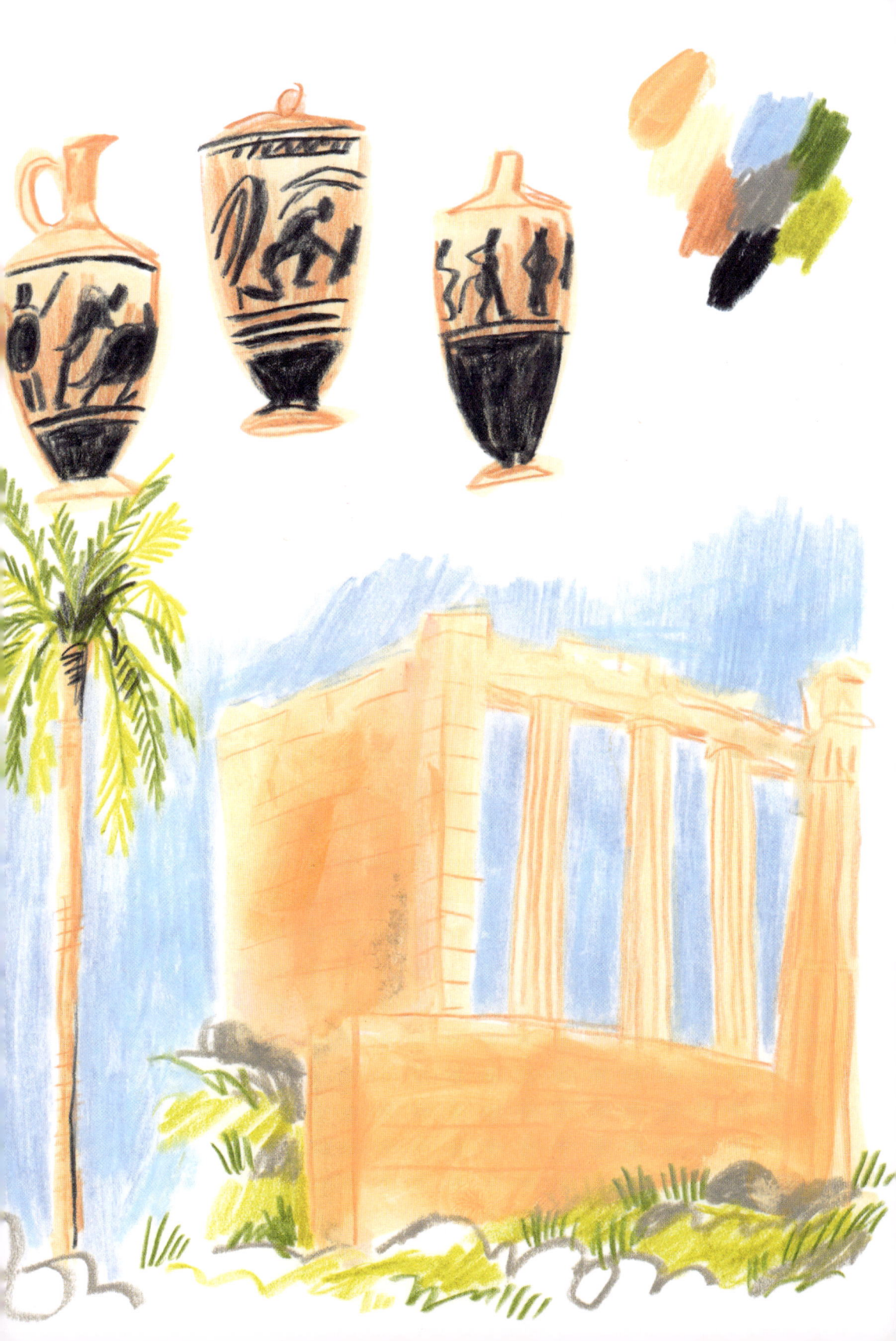

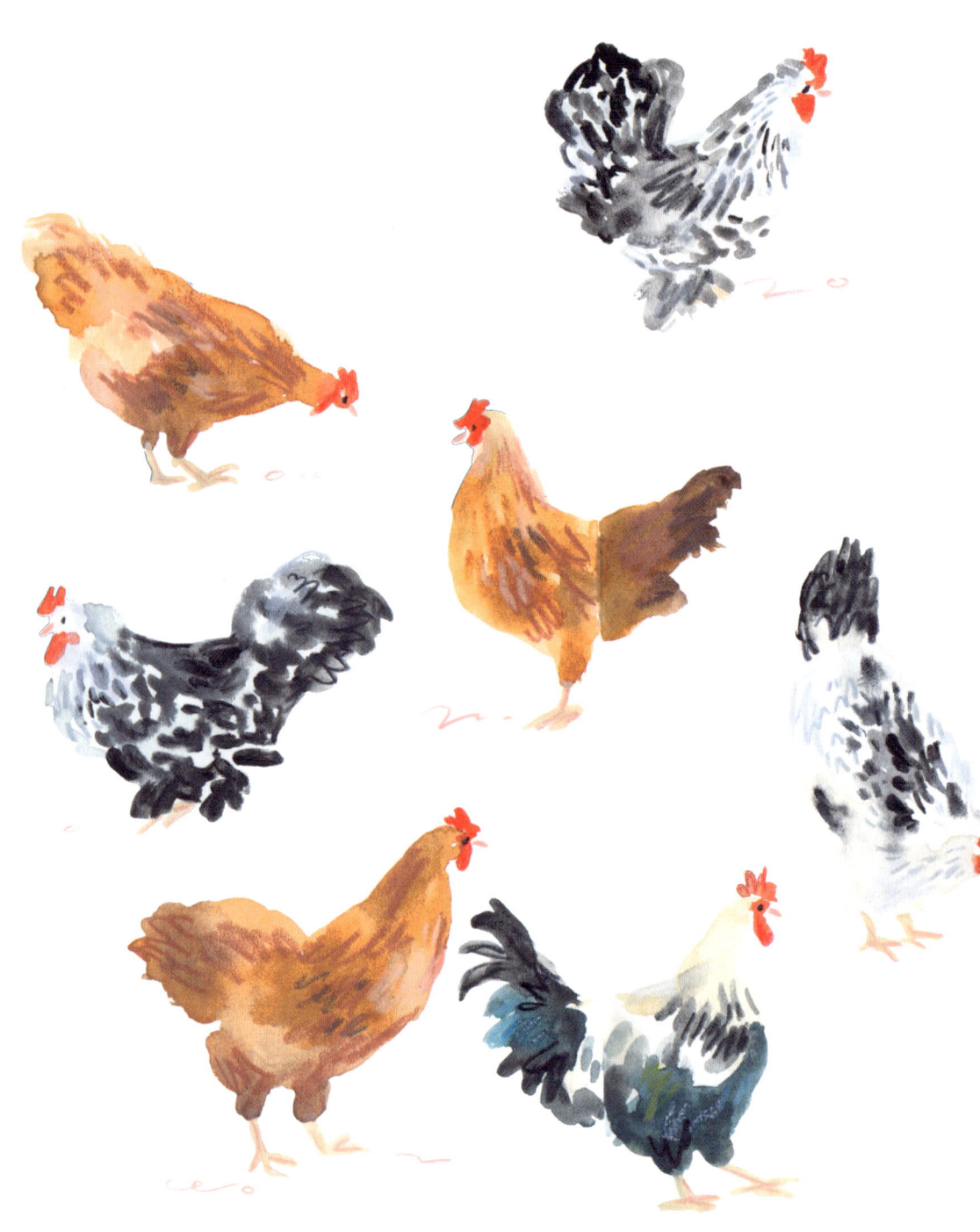

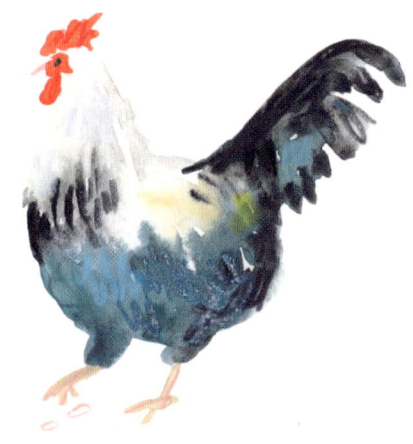

Making time

Time is one of the biggest personal barriers to creating art. We often want to make the most perfect environment to create in, and that can include a tidy space with no distractions and a lot of time at our disposal. The reality is that this golden trifecta is very hard to come by – simply because life gets in the way!

Yet making time is easy – if you change the goalposts. The amount of time you can make for your art will depend on your life circumstances, and this will vary vastly from one person to another.

Some artists will have lots of hours per week to dedicate to their sketchbook, while others will have a fraction of this. We often say we 'don't have time' to do something, but sometimes it's just about priorities. I often look at the screen-time figure on my phone and realize just how much time I've lost by scrolling social media. If I want to create more time, I just need to prioritize creating rather than distraction. I can

swap out my scrolling for my pen and sketchbook and do a quick drawing in the car instead while I'm waiting to pick up my partner.

If you have a lot of things to juggle in your life, then set short timers and find smaller pockets of time in which to create. A quick five-minute sketch, or even faster doodles, can fill a spread easily.

You don't even have to fill a spread all in one go – five minutes a day will add up to a full page within the week!

References

Some artists prefer to draw from their imagination, some by drawing the 'real life' views or objects in front of them, while others use photo references as a base for their art. There's no right or wrong way, and you can try out all three to find your preference.

There are a couple of different ways you can use references: creating a full copy of the reference in terms of composition and elements; or as a jumping off point for your own work, using references as colour inspiration or to start you off before adding your own ideas and interpretations.

The most important thing to know about references is which ones you can use. The best are photographs you've taken yourself, as this means they belong to you and you can use them or recreate them without any worries at all.

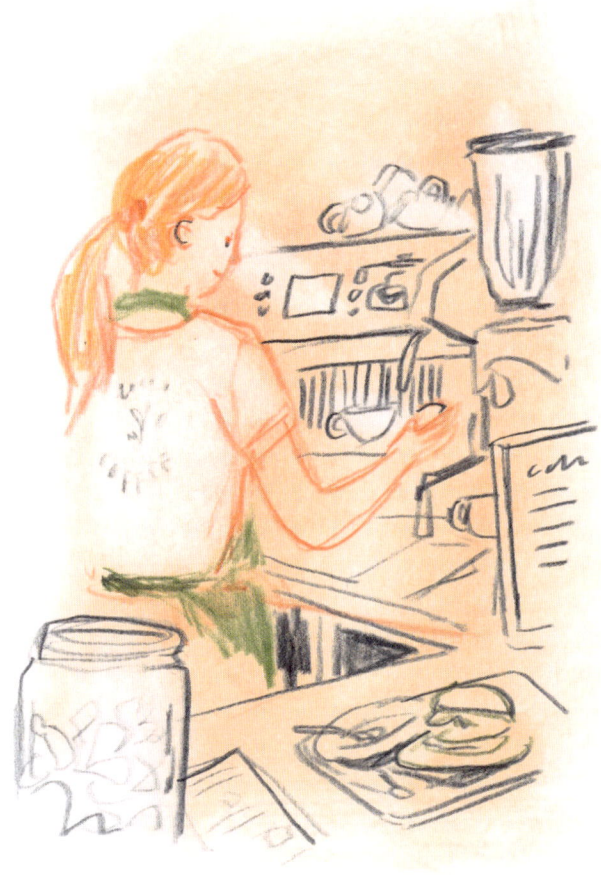

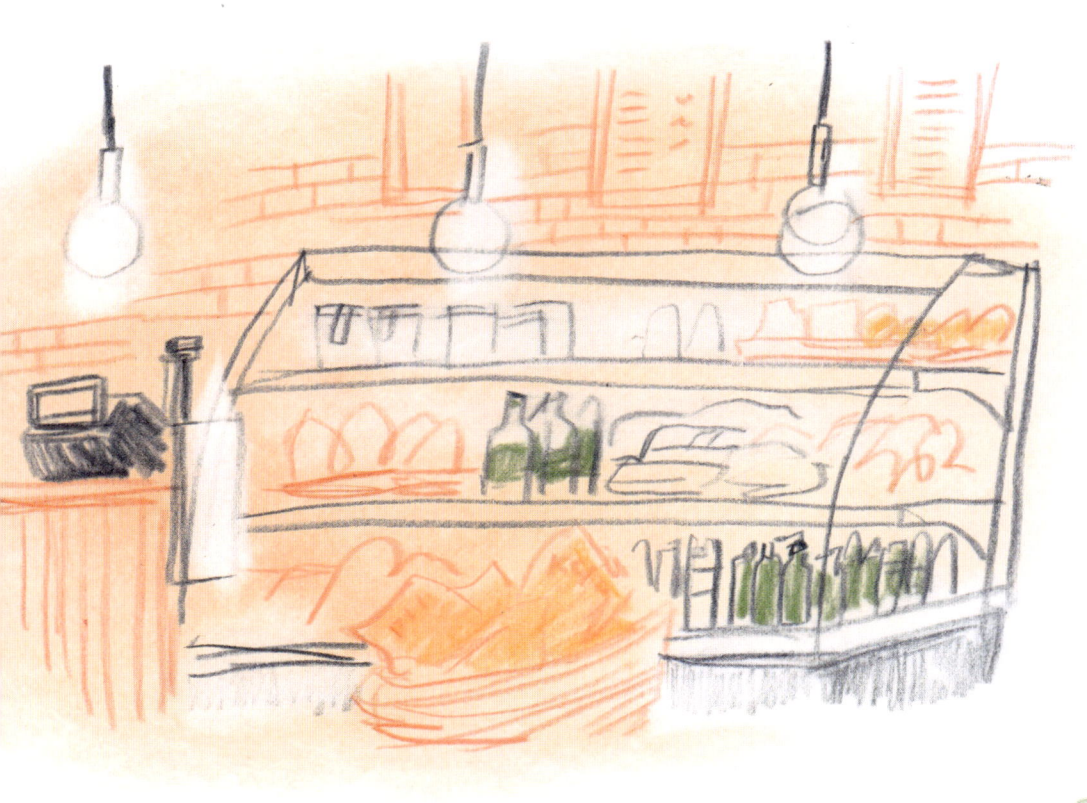

You can copy from other people's photos in your own sketchbook with their permission, but it becomes tricky if you start sharing your work more widely, and particularly if you then sell your art using references that aren't yours.

Copyright is a major element when it comes to using references. A lot of artists start by referencing images they've found online, on sites like Pinterest, but it can be hard to track down the original creator, give appropriate credit or gain permission in the first place. That's why I highly recommend using your own references, or using copyright-free images. There are a couple of websites that are my go-to for drawing from, such as Pexels.com and Unsplash.com. The images on these websites are shared under a Creative Commons licence, which means the author has allowed the use of their work without charge.

Observational drawing

Observational drawing is a great thing to practise and I really recommend giving it a go.

It can be tempting to draw from photographs all the time; after all, they generally have great lighting and composition – and nothing moves! But drawing the things in front of you is a fantastic way to develop your observational skills and really grow your creative muscle. Unlike references, you have to take a 3D object and make it 2D in your sketchbook, rather than a 2D photo to a 2D sketch. You have so many more options too, like changing the angle and drawing from above instead of from the side, switching your viewpoint for better composition, or moving objects or subjects to make things work better. It's a much more tangible and involved way of creating art.

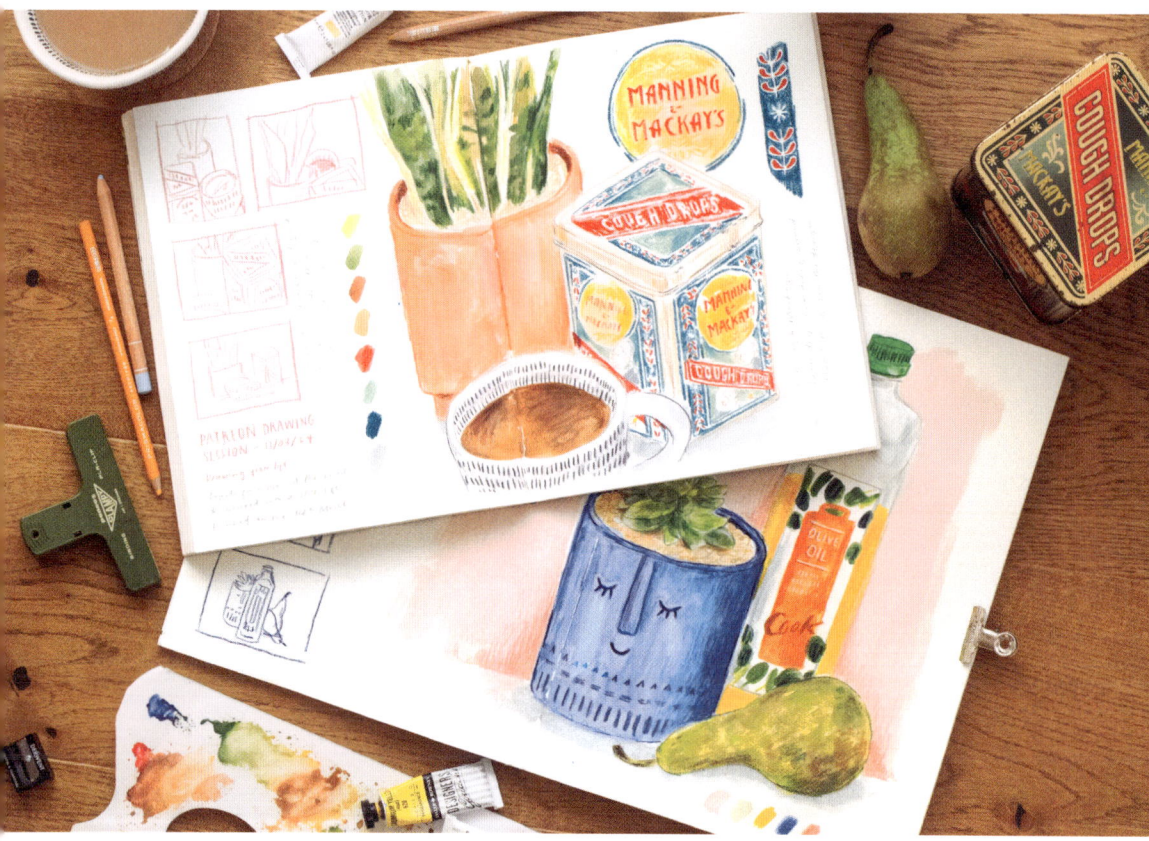

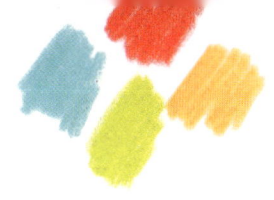

life drawing

Life drawing is another form that I would encourage you to try out in the same vein as observational drawing. Taking a 3D object (in this case the human form) and turning it into a sketch on paper is a big learning curve.

If a life drawing class feels a bit daunting, there are lots of options online. YouTube has many videos of people posing in a huge variety of ways, both with clothes and without. There are also drawing communities online that host life drawing sessions virtually, so you can be behind the screen while drawing the model on camera. It's not quite the same as drawing from a person in front of you, but it can be easier in terms of angles and positioning, so it's a fantastic way to practise.

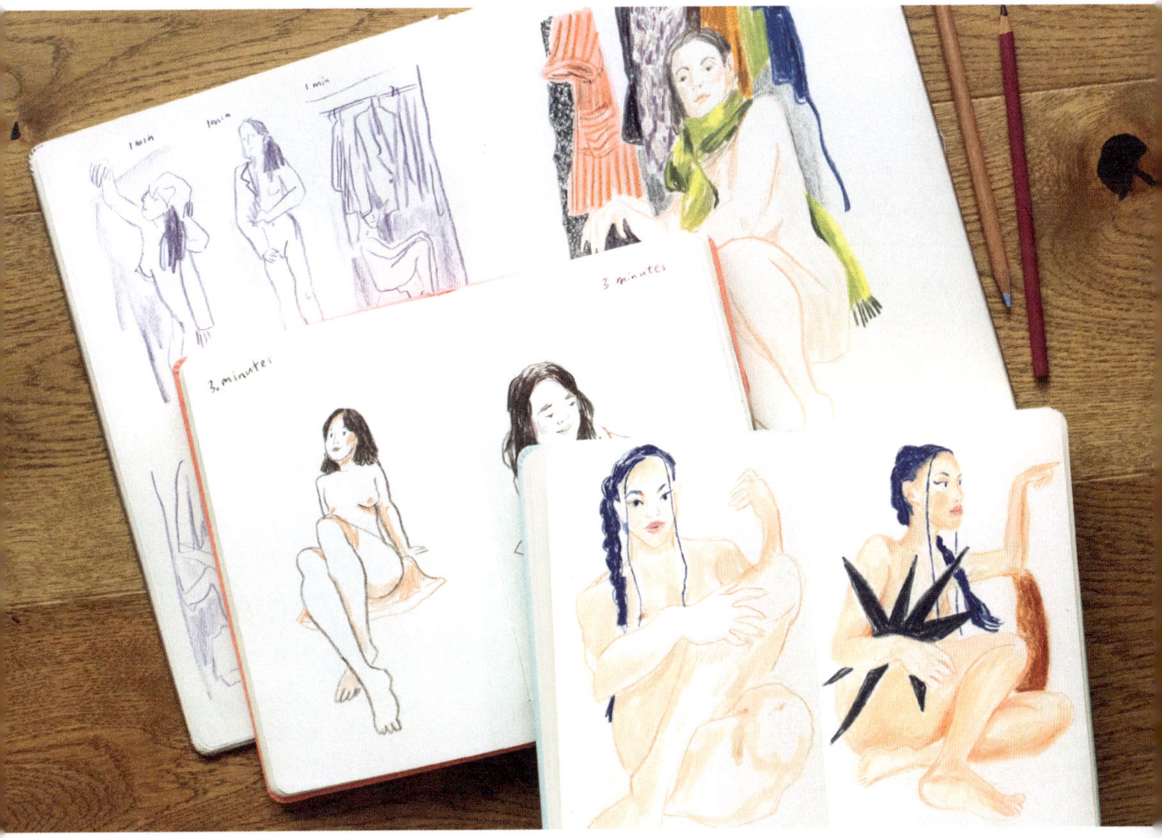

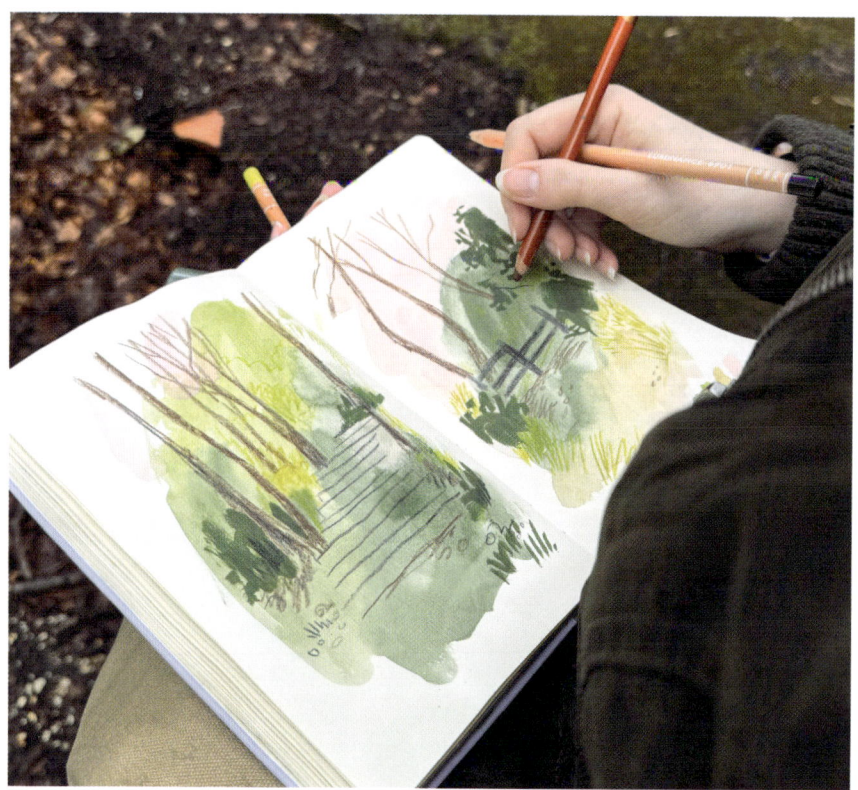

Drawing on location

Drawing outside, on location or en plein air – these are all different terms referring to the same thing. Simply put, it's taking your sketchbook with you out of the house and drawing wherever you are, whether that's in a museum, a park, at the bus stop, in the forest. . . wherever!

Once again, there are zero rules to this practice and you can approach it however you'd like. Some artists take tubes of paint and an easel when they paint en plein air (the French term for painting outside); others take a palette filled with colours and head to a specific location to fill their spreads. Alternatively, you can simply take your sketchbook and minimal supplies – maybe just a pencil or two – wherever

you go. All are valid and fantastic ways of drawing things outside.

References are a great way to see places you wouldn't normally be able to access, but drawing on location provides creative challenges. Namely the weather, your own choice of subject, and the ability to choose your own composition and angles of the view of whatever you're drawing.

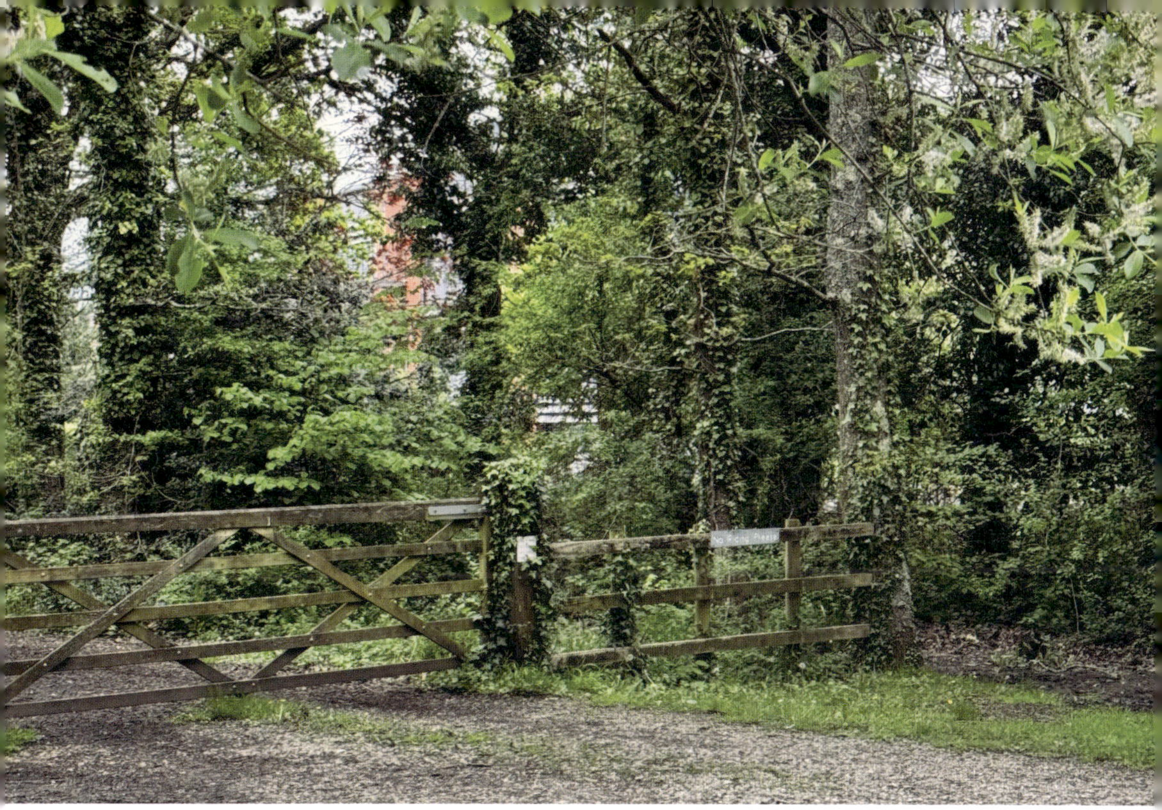

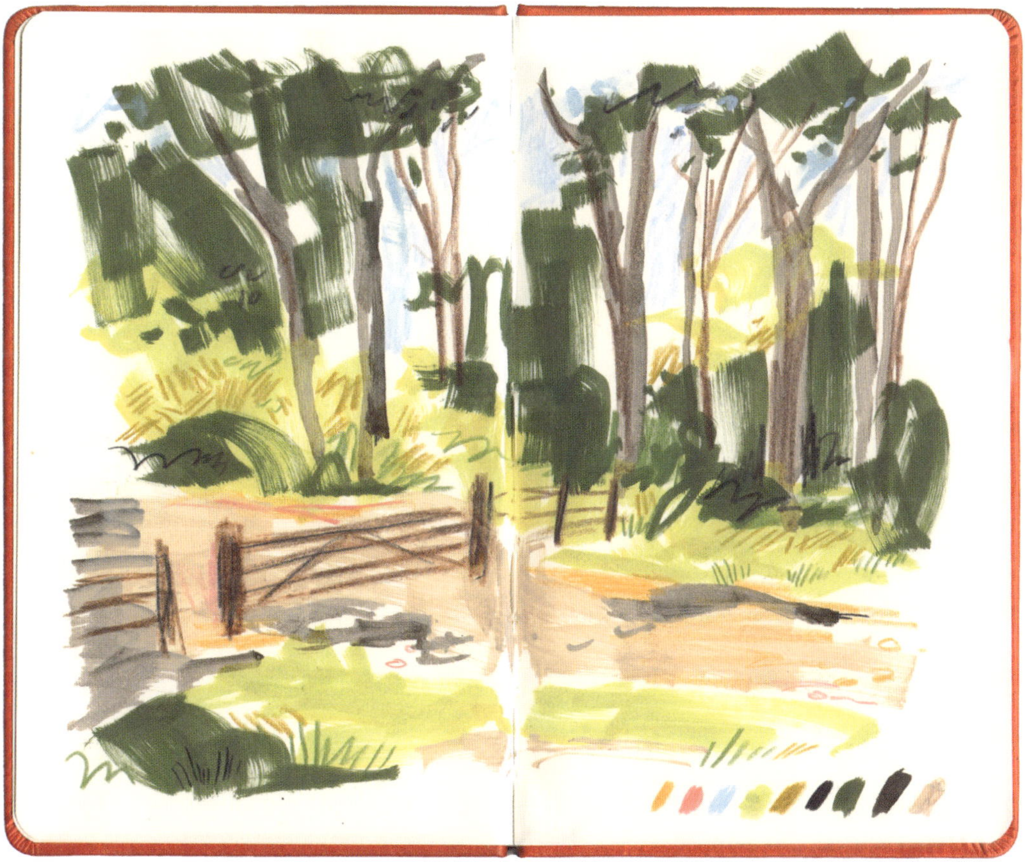

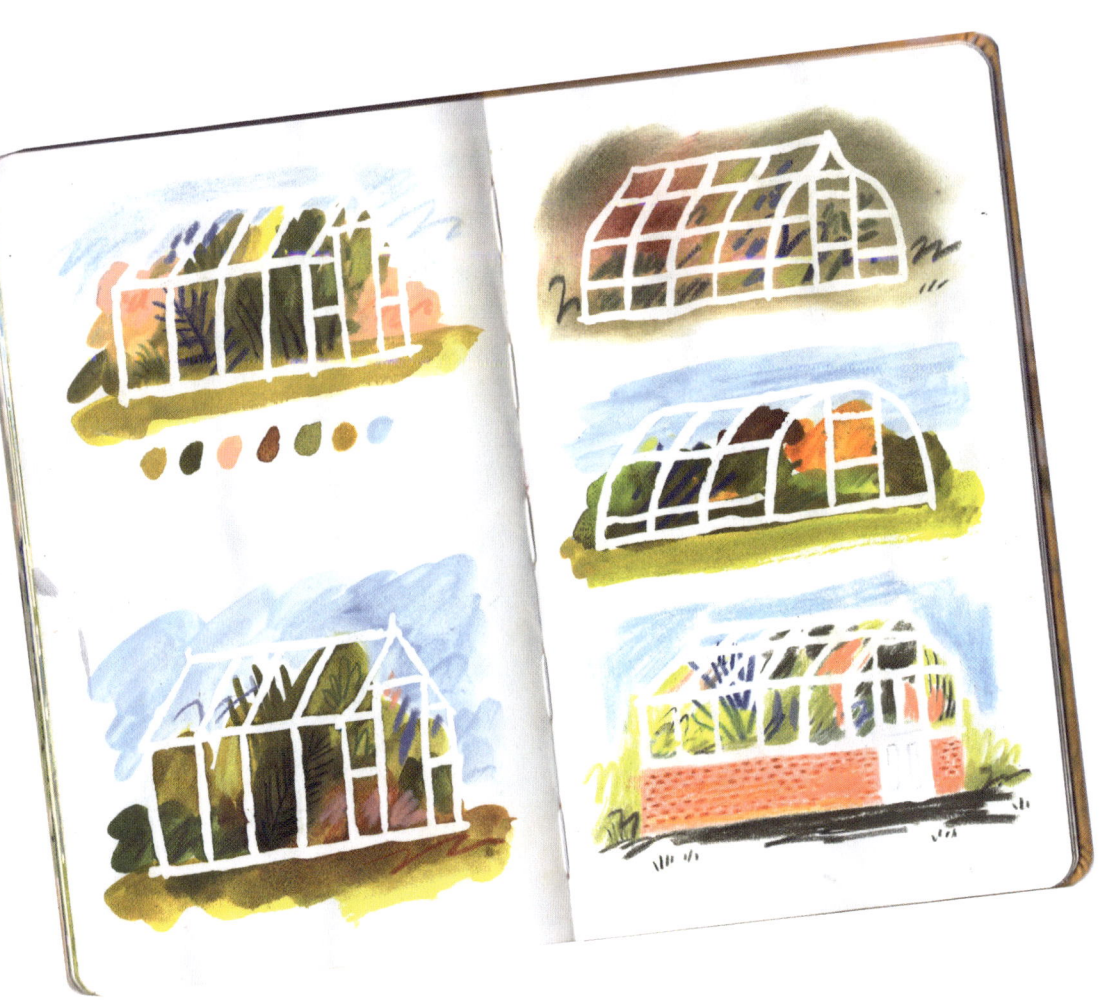

Drawing from imagination

This is one I don't do often, and I think as artists it's one we need to do more of. We used to do this all the time as children – it was rare that we would sit down and draw what we were seeing in front of us, and much more likely that we just drew whatever we wanted: monsters, mermaids, our house with the classic blue sky at the top and the sun in the corner.

Drawing from imagination has zero boundaries and opens up so many options. I think our mindset is the biggest challenge here – our desire to know if something is 'right' once it's out of our head and on paper.

But what would you draw and create if you put these limitations aside?

Creating narrative

Creating a narrative in your work is to tell a story. It can be as simple as adding a figure, an animal, or even multiple panels that tie in from one to another. The idea is that there's something that needs communicating in the work, rather than just a random image.

To create a narrative in your sketchbook spread is to illustrate your chosen story to the viewer, whether that's by evoking emotion through the lighting you create on the page, telling the story of a lone figure in the distance, or a happy little fox running through some woodland surrounded by bright colours. Colour, mark-making and subject can vary massively, but all contribute to the narrative in your art.

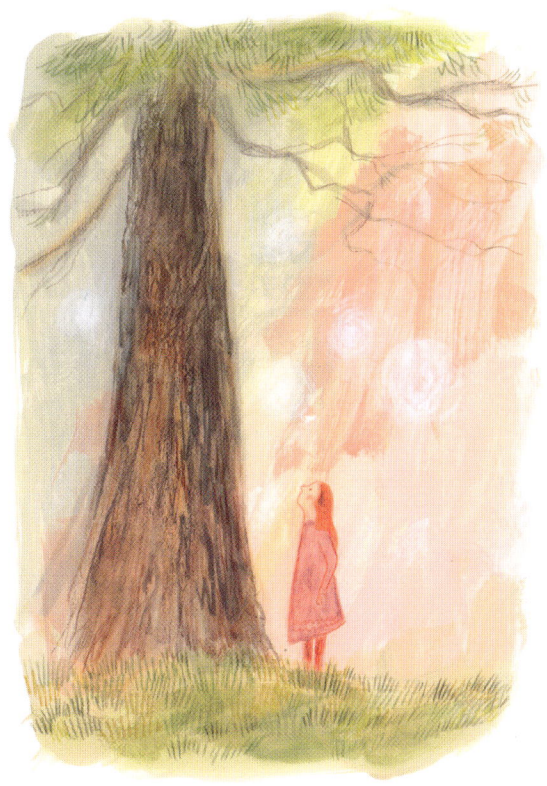

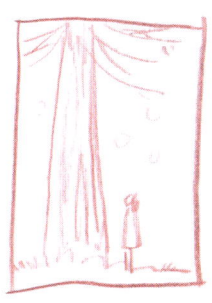

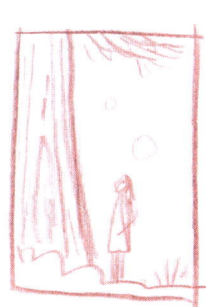

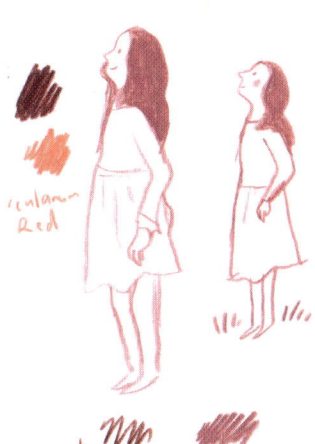

Notes and scrapbooks

A sketchbook can be a catch-all for your notes, scraps, doodles and thumbnails. My very first sketchbook is filled with scraps of paper that I taped in, hand-drawn typography and random ideas that I wanted to keep all in one place. Although my current sketchbook is very different to this, I still have separate sketchbooks for my looser, unfinished work.

You can fill your sketchbook with fast pencil sketches drawn at a museum, alongside longer notes about the exhibits or snippets torn from catalogues, simply because you love the colour palette. It could be a whole sketchbook drawn with a simple HB pencil, with doodles alongside to-do lists or articles pasted in from magazines.

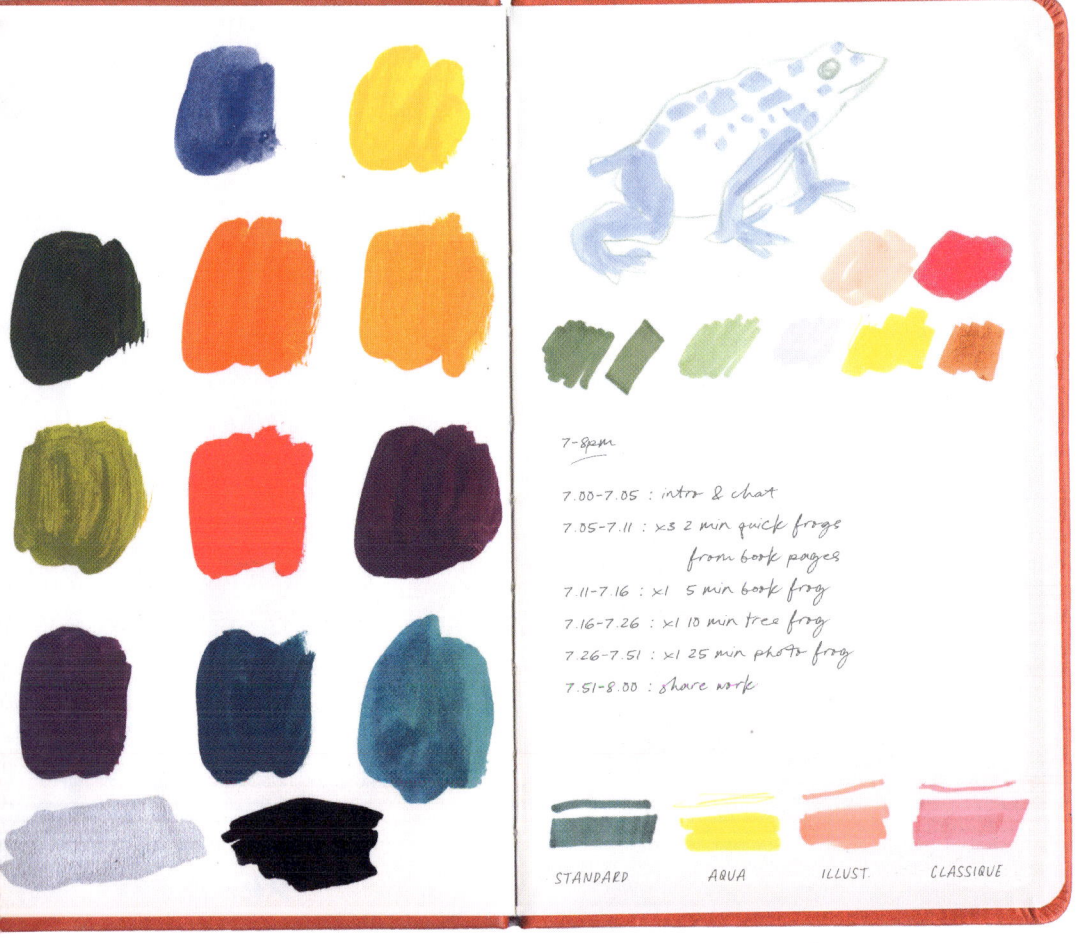

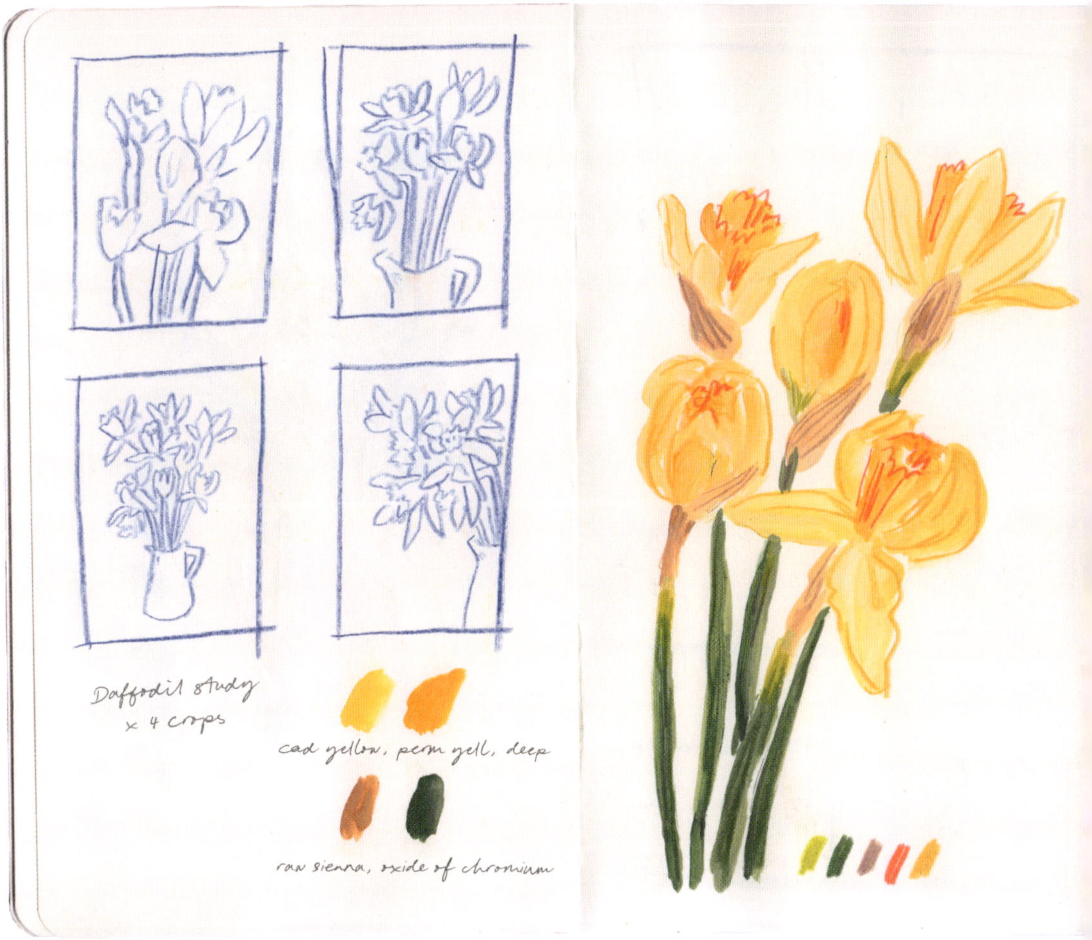

Daffodil study
x 4 crops

cad yellow, perm yell, deep

raw sienna, oxide of chromium

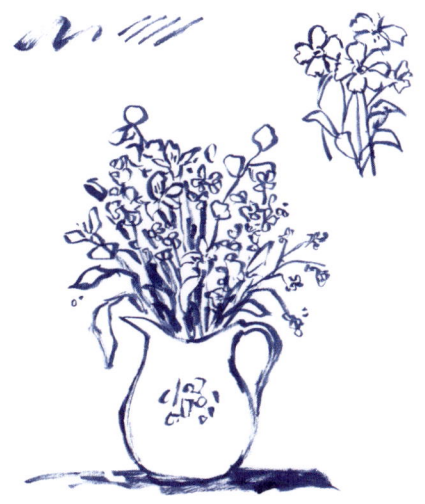

The act of commonplacing is also another way to fill a sketchbook. The idea is that you're creating a book of inspiration that you can always refer to. Traditionally this was done with writing, but I love the idea of including drawings too: a study of a shop sign that you liked the look of, notes and swatches of colour combinations you like, or drawing a scene you visualize while listening to a chapter of an audiobook.

Master studies

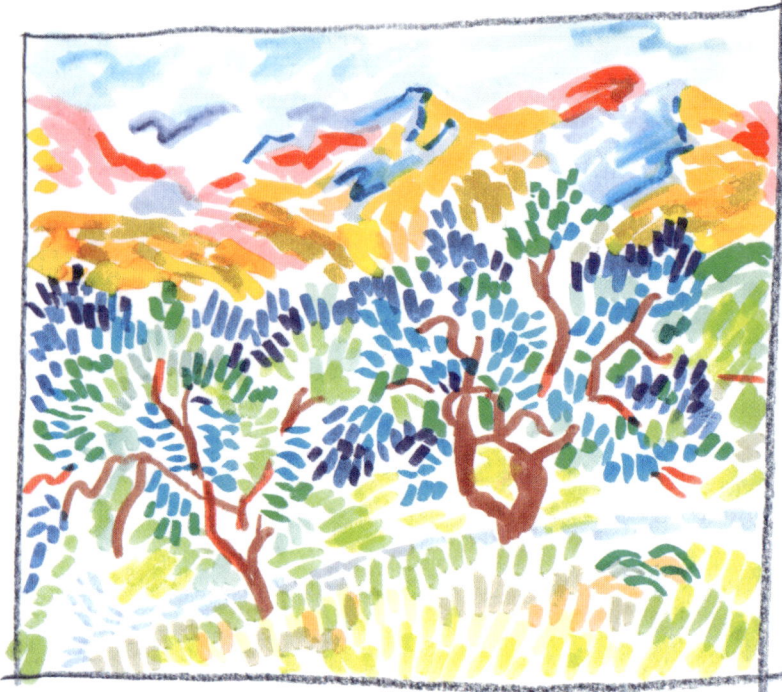

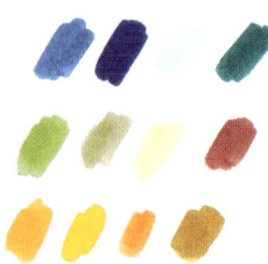

MOUNTAINS AT COLLIOUR
1905
ANDRÉ DERAIN

- BRUSH PENS

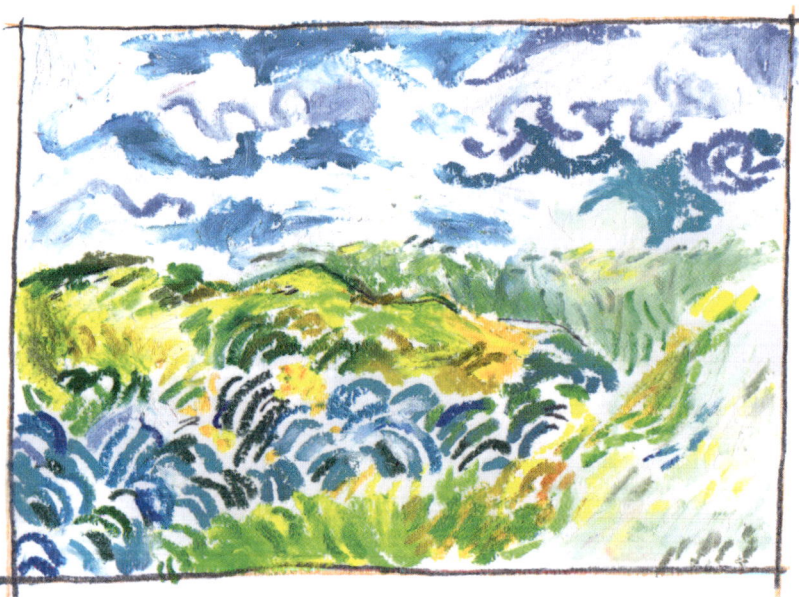

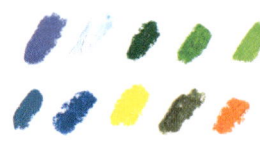

GREEN WHEAT FIELDS,
AUVERS, 1890
VINCENT VAN GOGH

- OIL PASTELS

You may have done these in art classes at school – and for good reason! Master studies are an age-old drawing practice and a great way to study technique, colour and composition.

Studying an artist's work helps you to understand more about their process and the choices that created the artwork as a whole. It really forces you to look at a piece of artwork, to see the techniques used, to notice the smaller details, and to understand the composition more than if you were to give it a quick glance.

It may inspire you to try out colours that you perhaps wouldn't have put together yourself, and help you to gather ideas about a subject that you can use as a jumping off point for your own project. As well as visiting art galleries and museums in person, a lot of galleries have collections you can look at online, and there are some fantastic resources for referencing art in the public domain.

There will be some artists' work that connects with you more than others, so I recommend doing master studies of work that really excites you. Pick a painting that inspires you and you want to learn more about, rather than one you feel you 'should' look at, or that has been done by so many before. Your sketchbook should be fun and enjoyable, not full of work that you're trying to tick off a list.

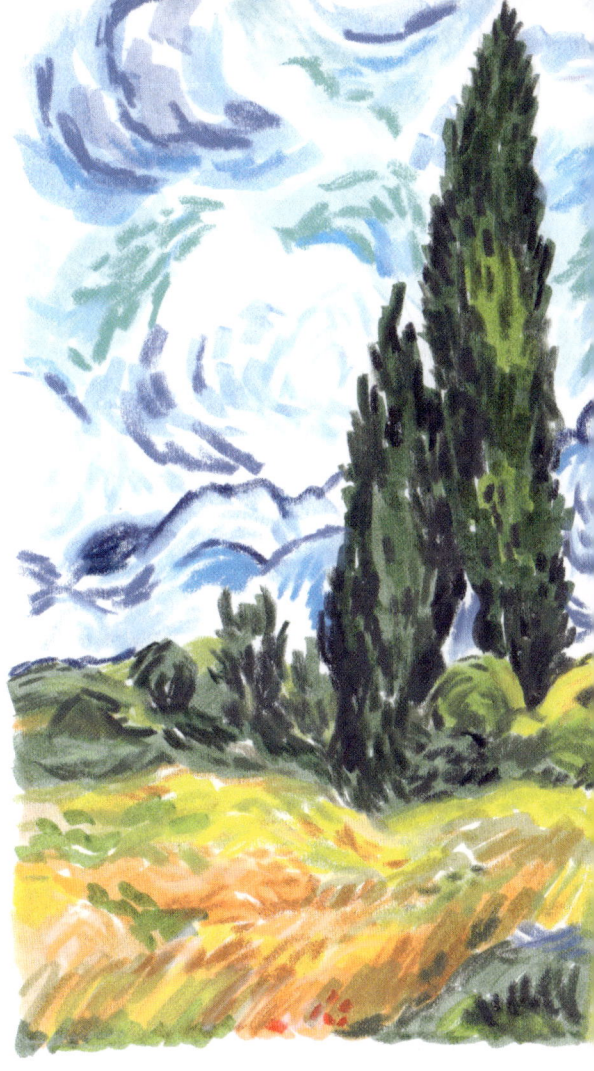

WHEAT FIELD WITH CYPRESSES, 1889
VINCENT VAN GOGH

Don't forget to write down the name of the artist and the piece you're studying! You can also write notes alongside your study, about things you've learnt or perhaps want to apply in your own art.

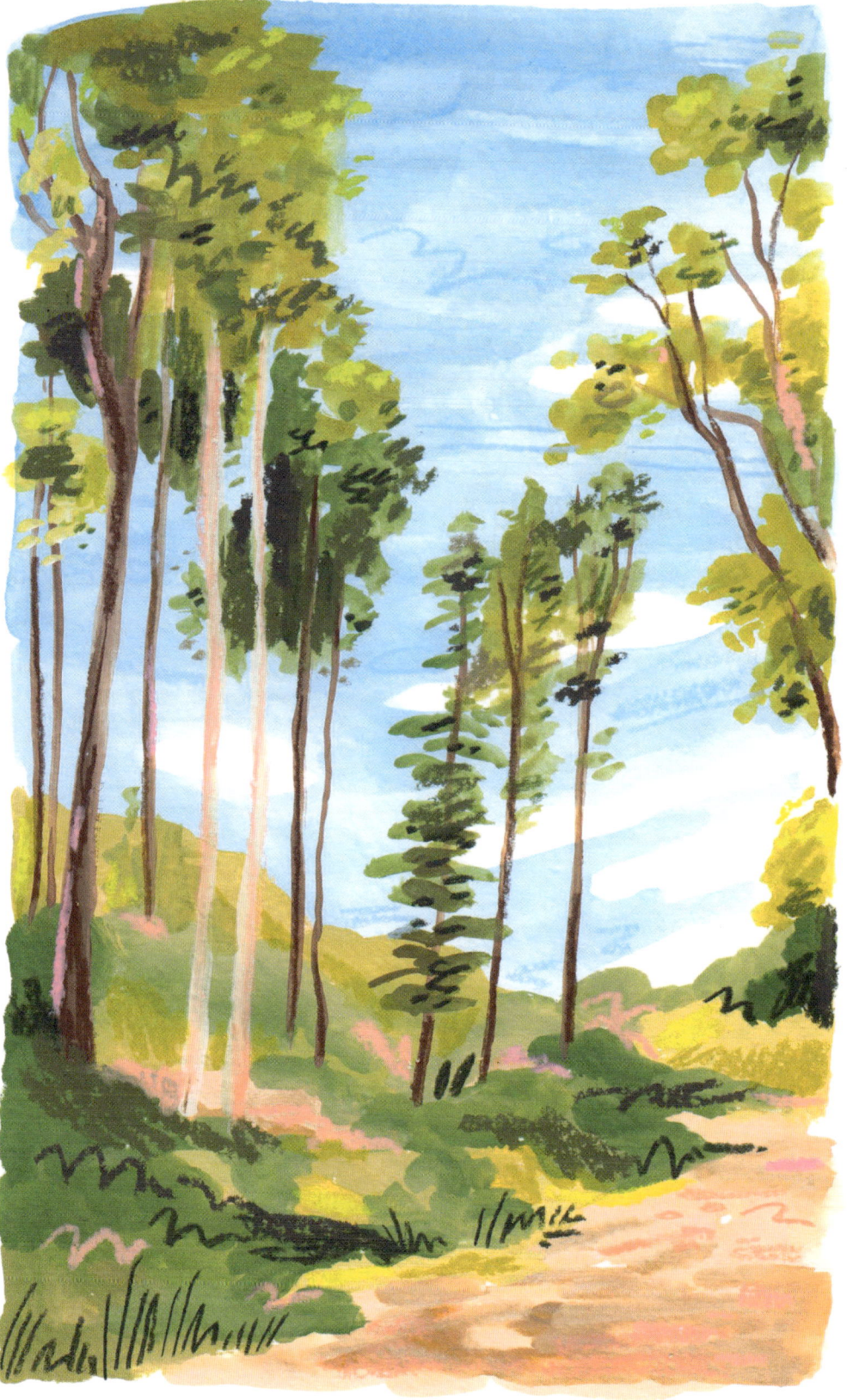

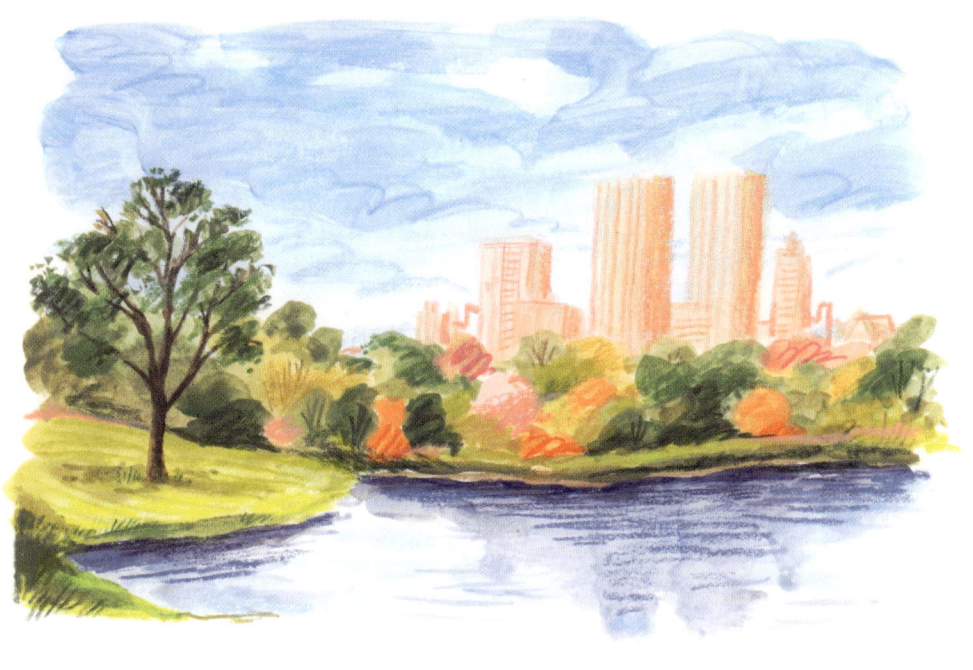

Daily habits and routine

I've already mentioned making time for art, but another way to prioritize your art is to make it part of your routine. If it becomes second nature to pick up your sketchbook, or if you've slotted it into part of your everyday routine, you're more likely to fill it!

You could grab your sketchbook at a particular time during the day: perhaps doodling or drawing in it while sipping your morning cuppa; or take it with you on your lunchtime walk and draw some of the views you see every single day. Slotting in your art practice around your daily life is a wonderful way to document things you may not have thought of, and an opportunity to practise your observational drawing skills at the same time, too.

If you want to draw daily, again it's about managing expectations. You won't be able to create a full, painted masterpiece in your sketchbook every day, but exploring ideas or doing quick sketches is much more achievable.

I've done several daily drawing challenges (spanning thirty days to a whole year), and I've learnt so much each time. Committing to a habit like that (whether personally or publicly) will definitely speed up your practice and you'll find your skills improve really quickly. Just remember that it's okay to skip a day or change things up to make it manageable for you, if needed.

Drawing prompts and challenges

With so many subjects and topics surrounding you, it can sometimes feel a bit overwhelming and tricky to know what to draw. That's why I love prompts and challenges, whether they are specific drawing prompts or just used as starting points.

You can find lots of monthly and weekly drawing challenges on social media and in online drawing communities. These range from specific subjects to broader prompts, which are more of a vibe or feeling and much more open to interpretation. You can choose whichever one suits how you are feeling at a particular time – there are great options for both.

I often find limitations from prompts or challenges actually make me more creative – having fewer options (for example a limited colour palette prompt, or being instructed to use specific materials) can produce surprising and fun results.

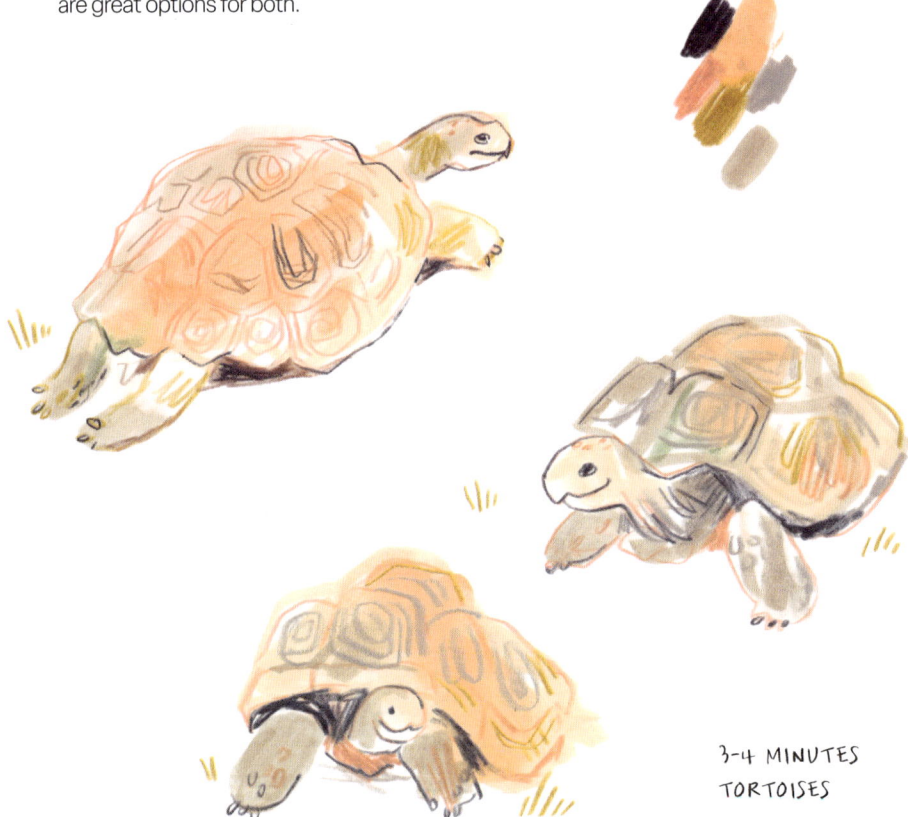

3-4 MINUTES
TORTOISES

20 MINS

Communities and drawing sessions

One of the best parts about being an artist are all the communities that come with it! They span both the online and 'real life' world, and cover all types of creatives, materials and topics.

Joining a community is a fantastic way to learn from other artists, sharing tips, techniques and art supply recommendations, as well as the connection and support that comes from being with likeminded people who share a passion. Thanks to social media, they're easy to find, whether online or local, and the friendships that come from these groups can be really special.

Platforms like Patreon, Substack and Ko-fi are a great way to connect with other artists and join drawing sessions with their communities too. Plus when you're all drawing the same reference, you can really see how others tackle it differently. One of my favourite things about hosting these sessions myself is seeing how each artist creates such varied work, despite referencing the exact same image – I always find it so inspiring and I learn so much every time.

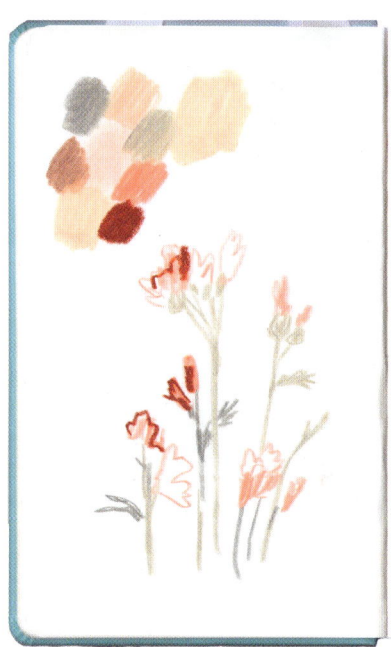
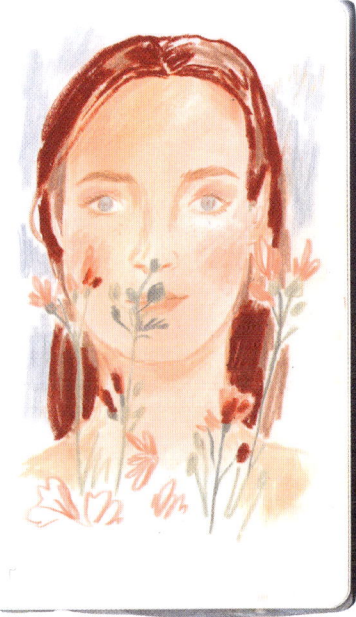

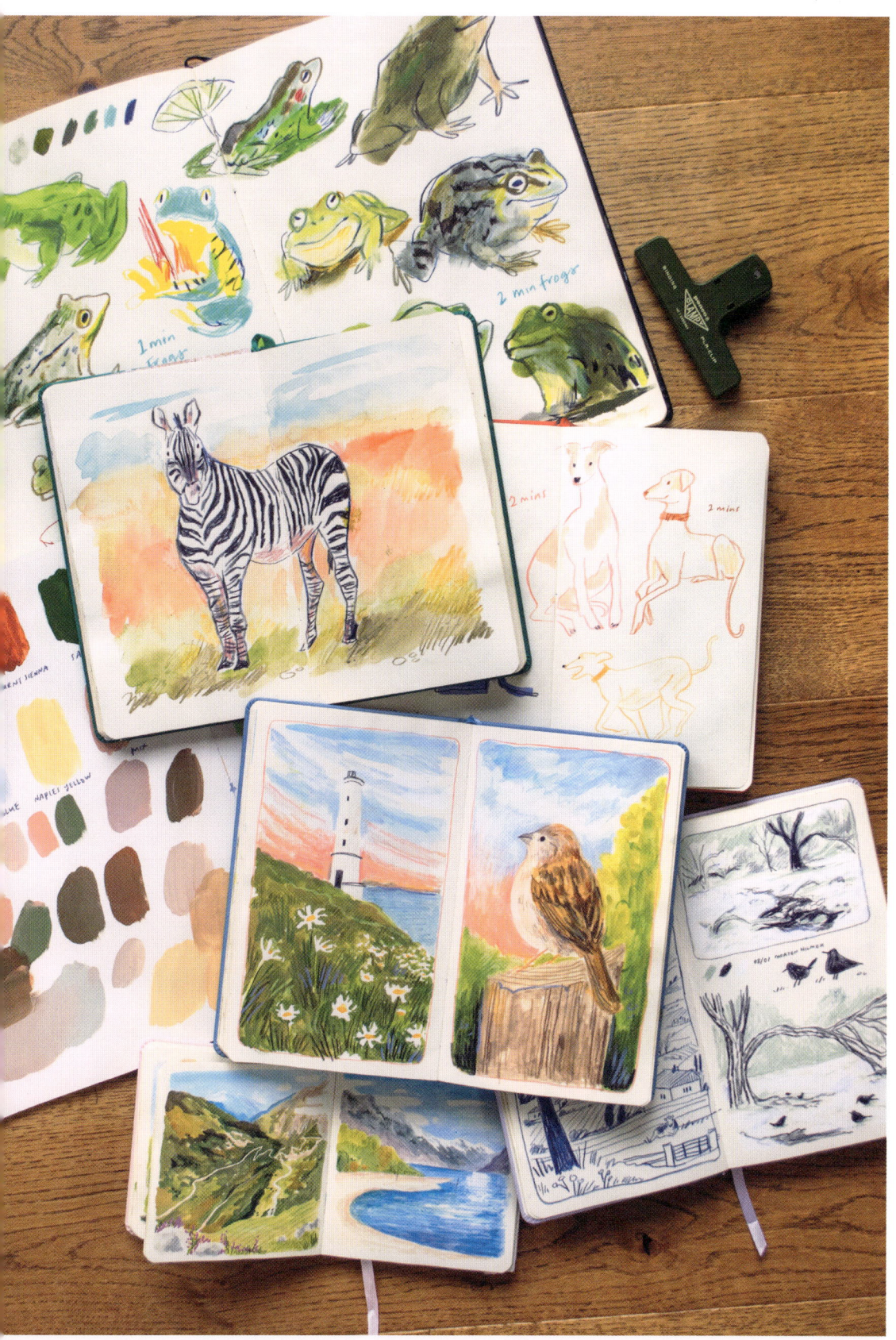

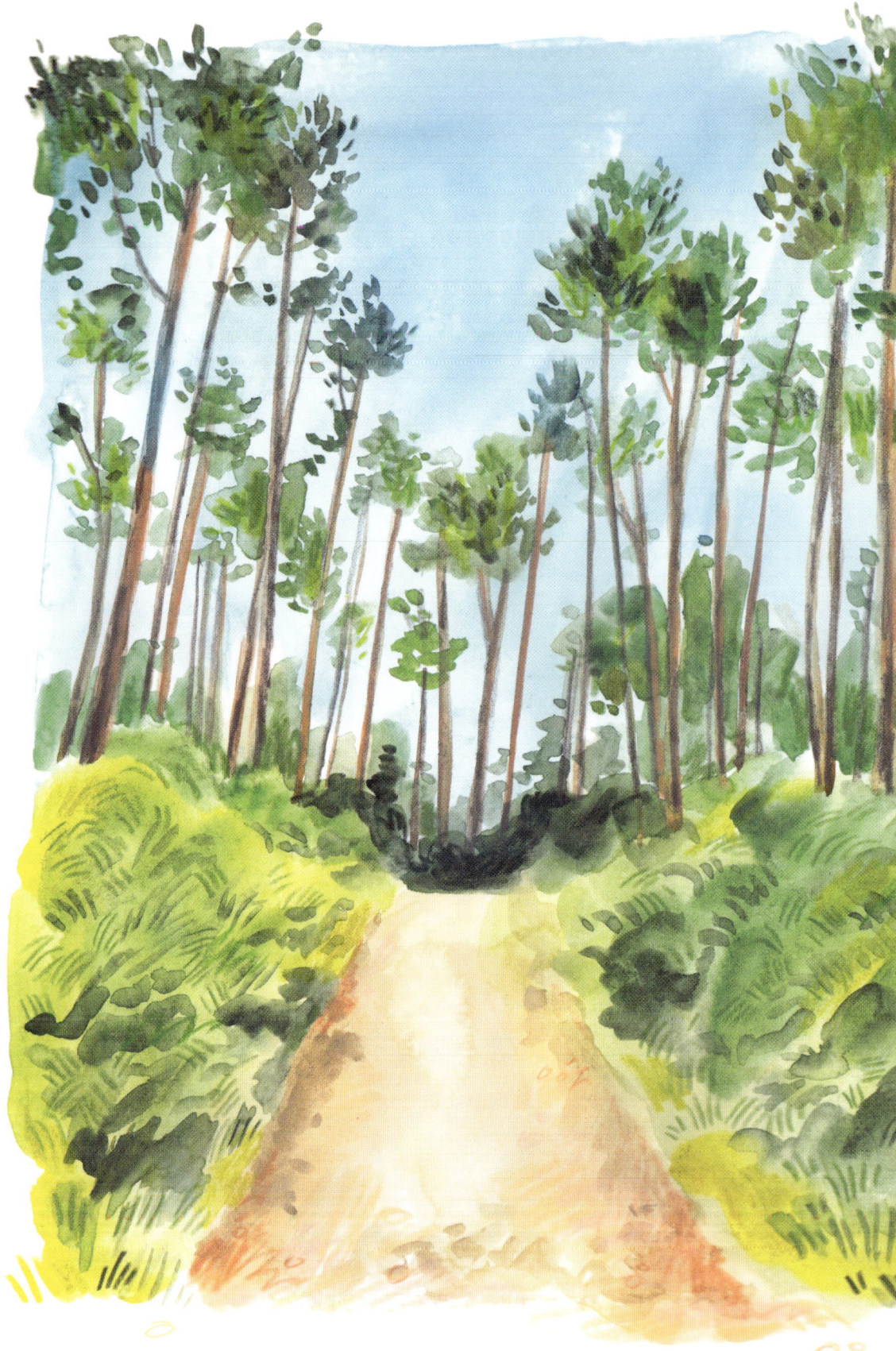

Finding inspiration

This is the topic that crops up the most among artists!

I want to caveat this by saying that it's totally normal to not feel inspired all the time – even if social media makes you believe otherwise. Sometimes you just need time, but you can also boost your inspiration in other ways. Here are just a few ideas that I find helpful when I need some inspiration.

Head outside. Getting some fresh air really helps to clear my thoughts. I usually snap photos while I'm out on walks (urban or rural) and paint what I see.

Visit an art gallery (or look online) and take inspiration from artists whose style is totally different to yours. It can be a good idea to branch outside of the usual art you're drawn to and really notice elements from other styles. You don't have to love it, but you might find you discover a new colour combination or topic that you'd like to explore in your own sketchbook.

Looking at your favourite artist's work is also a great way to feel inspired. You can find inspiration by looking through books that feature their work, or watching YouTube videos they've made and browsing their Instagram page to spark your own creativity.

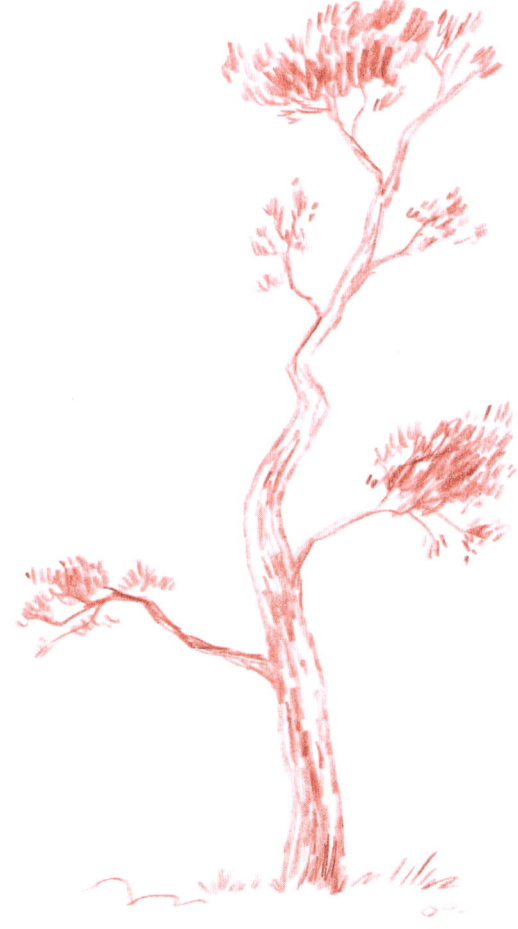

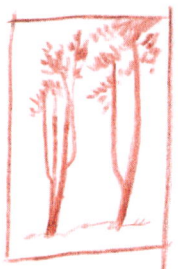
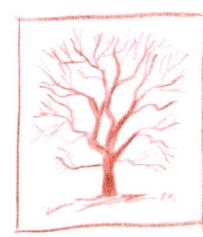

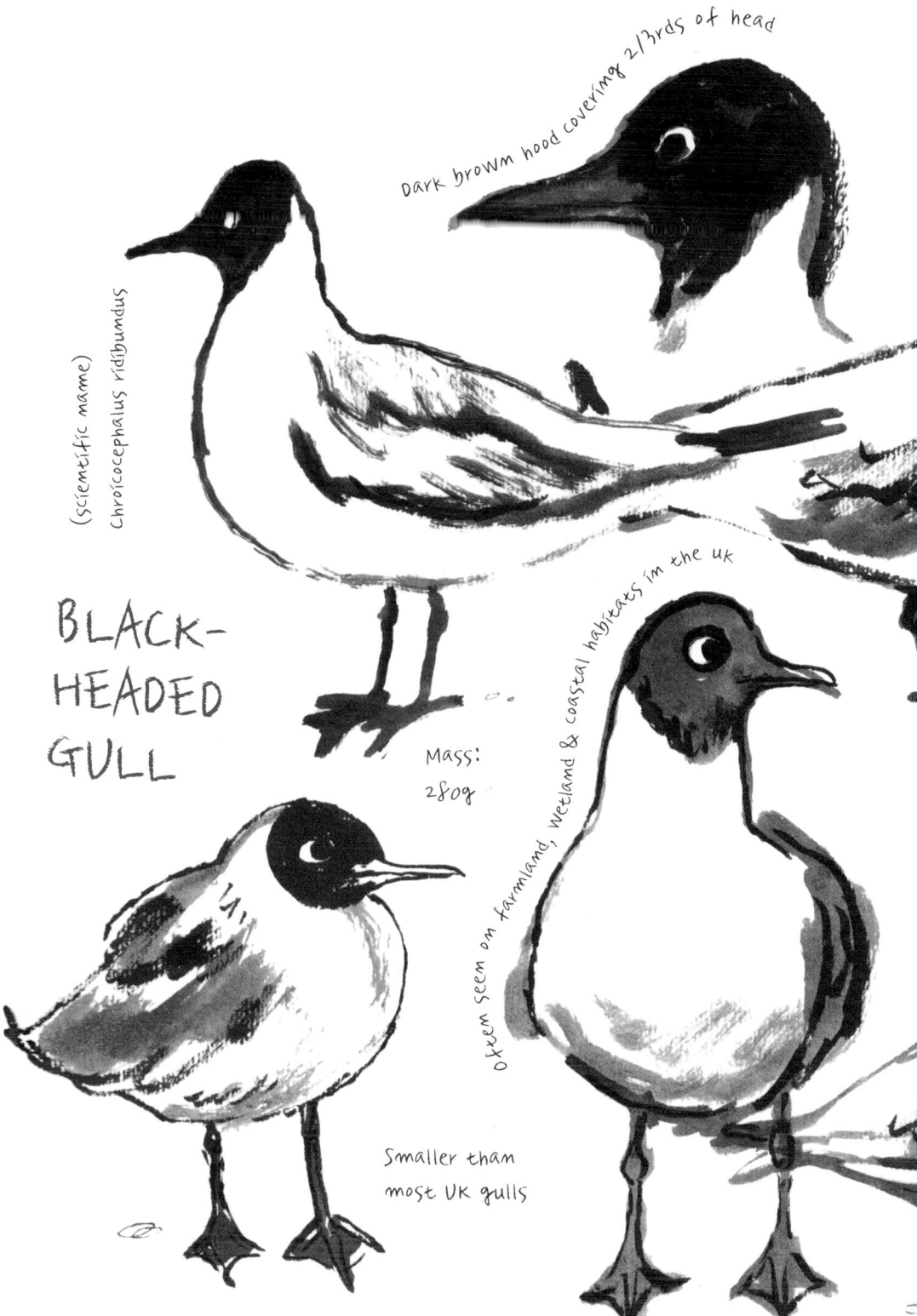

Dark brown hood covering 2/3rds of head

(scientific name)
Chroicocephalus ridibundus

BLACK-HEADED GULL

Mass: 280g

Often seen on farmland, wetland & coastal habitats in the uk

Smaller than most UK gulls

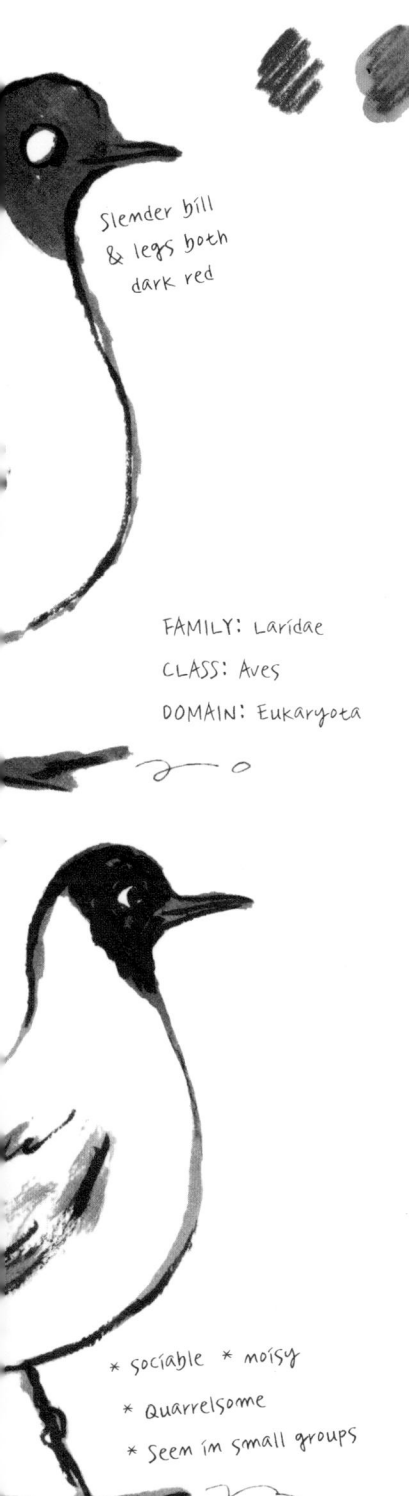

Slender bill
& legs both
dark red

FAMILY: Laridae
CLASS: Aves
DOMAIN: Eukaryota

* sociable   * noisy
* Quarrelsome
* Seen in small groups

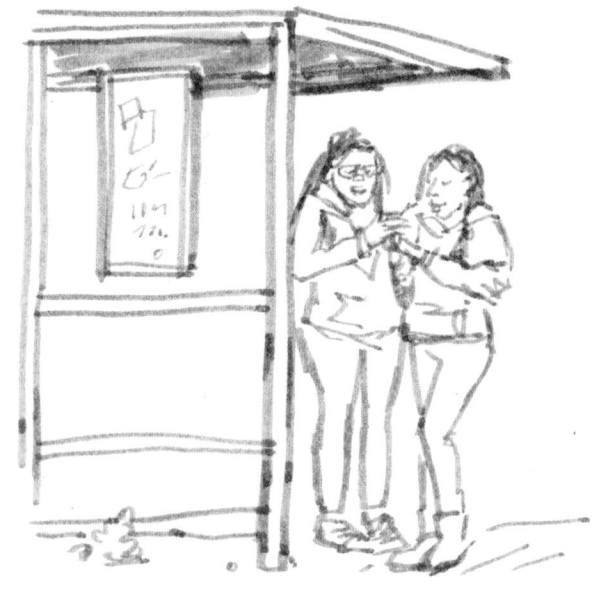

Taking a look at previous work you've created in your sketchbooks is another lovely way to find inspiration from your own art. There may be a piece you absolutely adore, and you can use that to inspire future work. What is it you like about it? How can you recreate that or explore it further?

You can also find inspiration in the most random of places: a pattern on a cushion while you're out shopping, the way a person is standing on the bus that makes you suddenly want to capture their pose, a colour combination of a friend's wall paired with their brightly-coloured sofa, or a little bird that hops in front of you on a walk. Inspiration can be found everywhere!

Need some more ideas? I've listed more prompts on page 148.

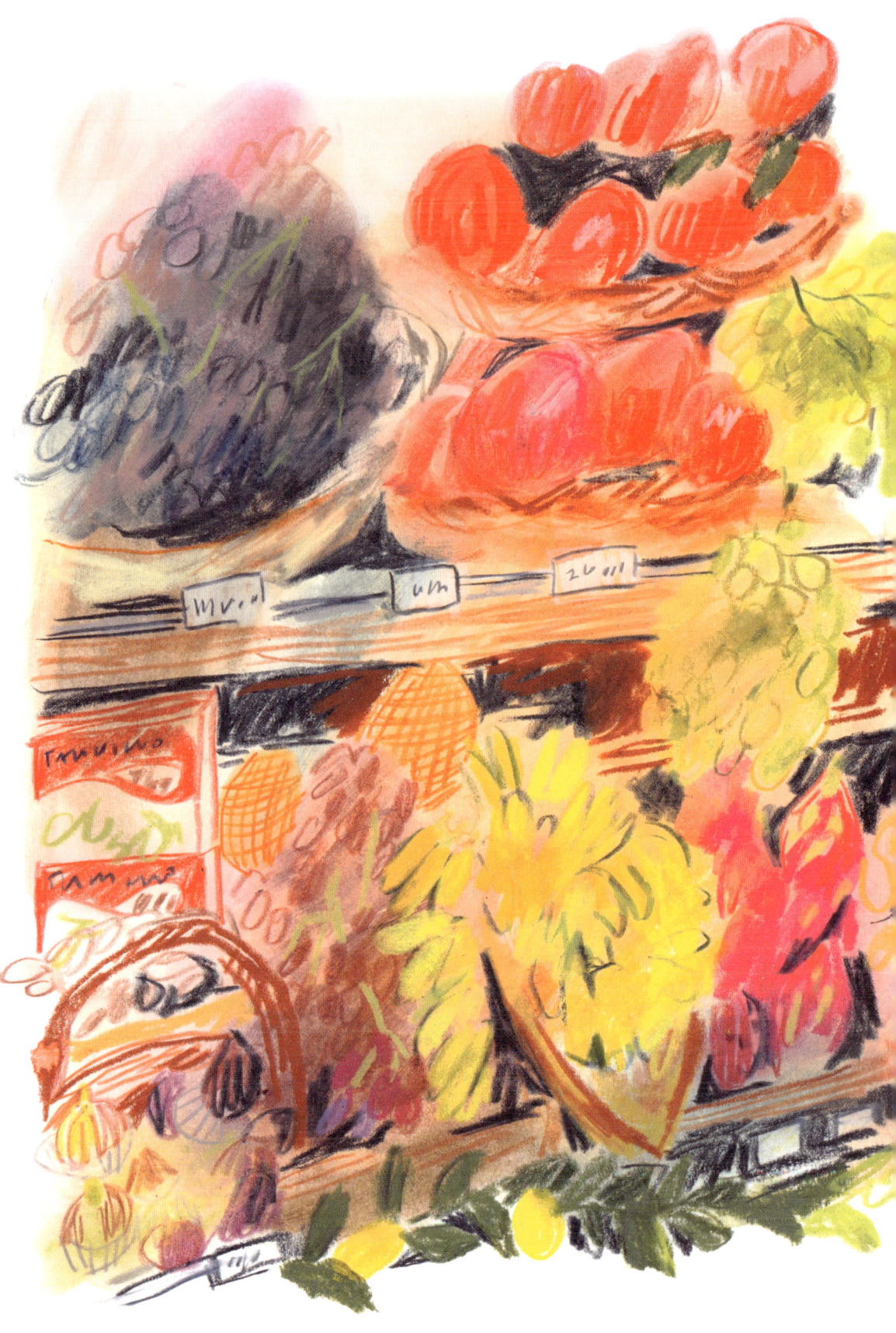

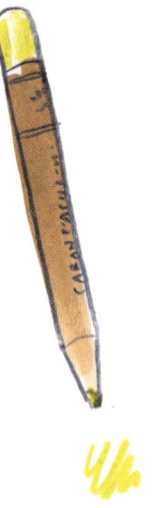

Tools and mediums

I'm a big believer in the idea that you don't need fancy, expensive or even a lot of art supplies to create with. I've seen amazing art from a cheap ballpoint pen, and even sketchbooks filled with drawings made using a twig dipped in ink!

That said, I do want to share some common tools and mediums that may inspire you with new ways to create. Changing your art supplies is a great way to boost your creativity as you explore more methods and techniques.

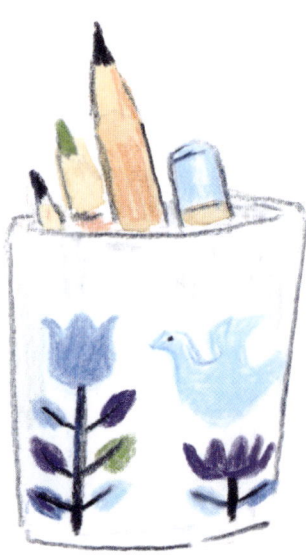

Types of sketchbook

There are many sketchbooks on the market, and it can be good to have multiple, rather than sticking to just one size or format. I love the variety and options available to me of working in lots of sketchbooks, and you'll find some work best with specific mediums.

SIZE

Firstly, let's pick a size. They range from tiny to gigantic, but if you're a beginner I'd recommend veering towards the smaller end of the scale. It can be a bit daunting filling a huge A2 spread, so A5 is a good place to start.

I tend to pick my sketchbooks based on how I'm feeling – do I want to go small because I only have ten minutes and want to keep it manageable? Or do I want to fill a spread with big, gestural marks that need a bit more room? Your sketchbook size can determine these things.

STOCK

The chosen stock (or paper) of your sketchbook often depends on your medium. Some sketchbooks contain good middle-of-the-road paper that works with most mediums, usually labelled as mixed media paper. Some are specialist and made for a specific art supply, such as markers or watercolours.

The tone of paper also varies. Some have pure white paper, while others are ivory-toned or off-white. You can also get paper that is brown or grey, which works well for tonal studies.

PAPER TYPES

Rough = Very textured
Cold-pressed = Slightly textured
Hot-pressed = Smooth

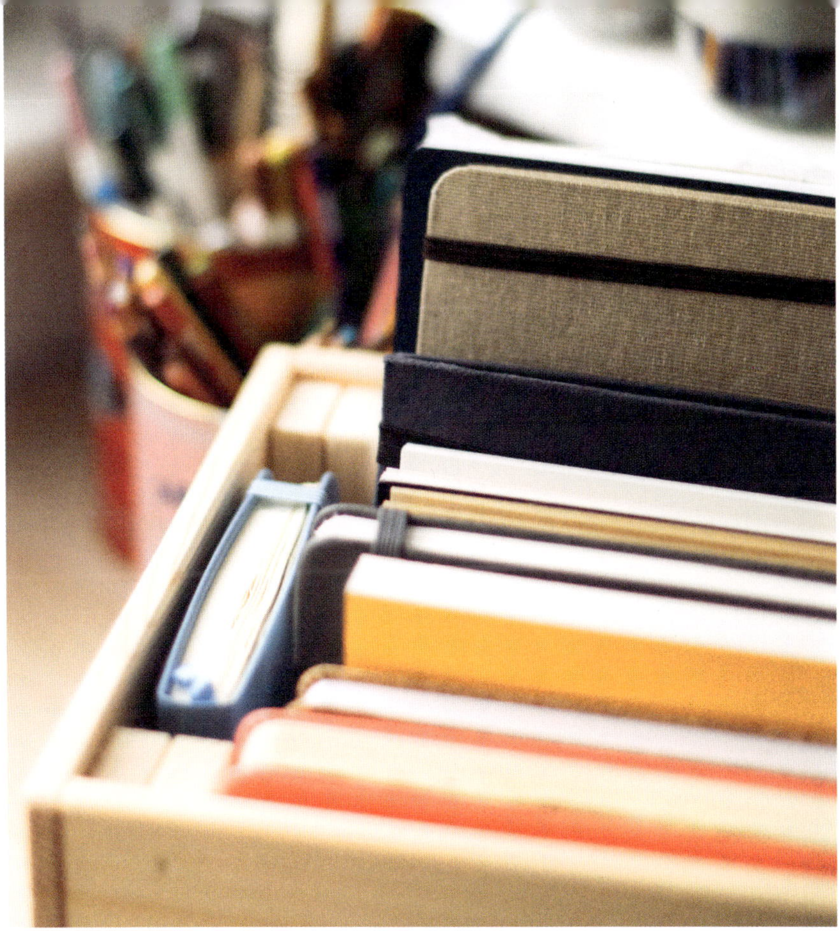

BINDINGS AND COVERS

There are also several different binding and cover options for sketchbooks. They may be spiral bound, which means the pages are held together by a wire coil and have perforated holes so individual pages can be removed easily. Casebound sketchbooks use sheets of paper that are often sewn down the centre, providing full spreads of paper on which to create. If you prefer to paint easily over the centre of a spread for a larger surface area, look for a layflat sketchbook.

A hardcover sketchbook is hard-wearing but heavier, so often not preferable if you like to take your sketchbook on location or out and about with you. Softcover sketchbooks use lightweight covers, so are much easier to transport but provide less support (though this is not an issue when working on a hard surface). It's personal preference as to what type of sketchbook you like to work in!

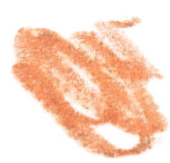

Dry and wet materials

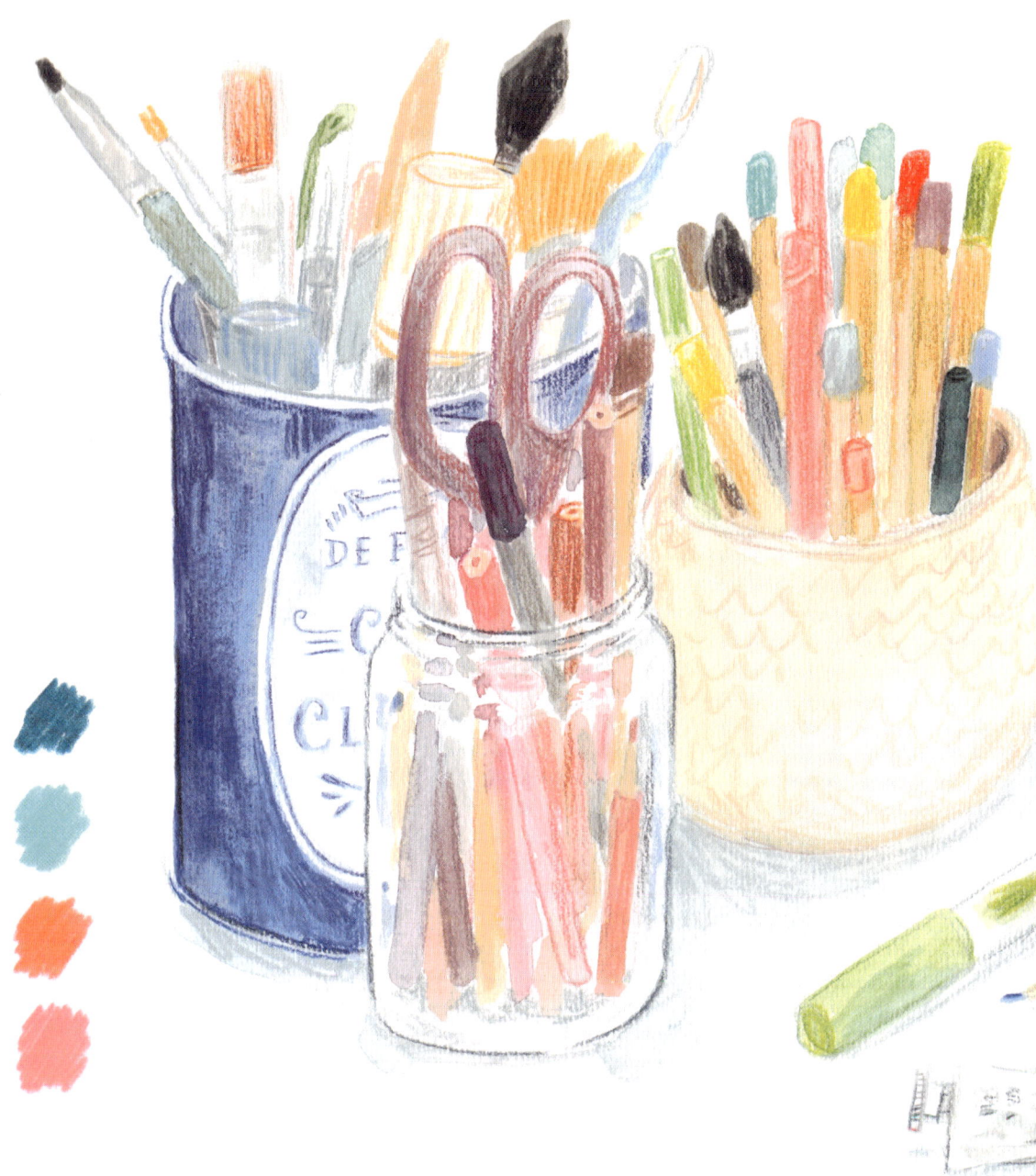

Dry materials are generally items that you don't need another tool to use. They include things like pencils, pens, markers, pastels, graphite and charcoal. Wet mediums include materials like paint or ink, which are often applied with a tool such as a paintbrush.

There are many books and tutorials available on using these mediums that go into a lot of depth on technique – or you may prefer to explore, experiment and play without knowing the 'rules'!

I do recommend swatching and playing around with any new art supplies you get. Try out new colours and see what the consistency is like, apply them to your sketchbook and see how the paper handles them. What mediums can you layer on top? Are they something you'd use as a base or for final touches?

Experiment with various ways to layer your dry and wet materials and find what works best. Usually a wet layer goes down first, but an oil pastel going down before wet materials can create a great wax resist, so there are many ways to experiment. Some pencils may work best over gouache compared to acrylic, or you can test out other materials on top like brush pens or other inks.

Play around and enjoy the process!

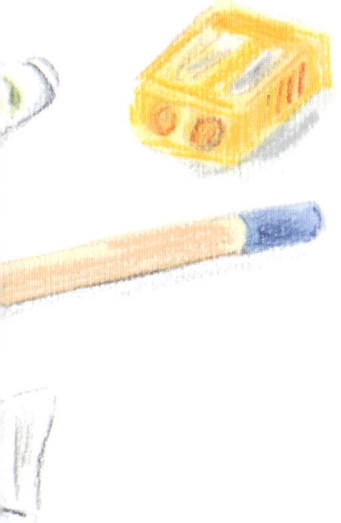

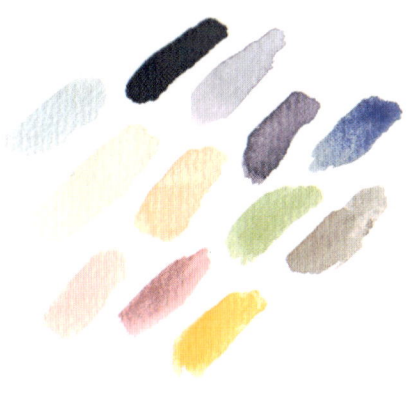

Brushes

Not all types of brush are listed here, but these are some common ones. Each type of brush comes in various sizes, with different bristle materials and lengths. Depending on the type of marks you'd like to lay down with your brush, the shape will help determine the details you can achieve.

ROUND

Round brushes are very versatile, and are the brushes I use the most. They have a tapered tip that can be used for detail, but when pushing down on the brush and using the whole length of the bristles, you can place a large amount of colour and be looser with your application.

FLAT

Flat brushes are another versatile type of brush: you can create wide strokes by using the full square shape, or sharp, straight lines when using the edge of the brush.

MOP

Mop brushes hold a large amount of water so can be a little trickier to use. They're perfect for watercolour and great for washes of colour, but can also be used for smaller details and lines when gently applying the tapered tip.

FAN

Fan brushes are great for blending and creating texture. Soft textures are easy to create with this brush when blending and feathering paint, but you can also use it for harsher textures. I love using these with a dry brush technique to create interesting marks.

DETAIL

Detail brushes are very small and often used for small details and linework. The bristles are slightly shorter, and this brush is great for control and precision work.

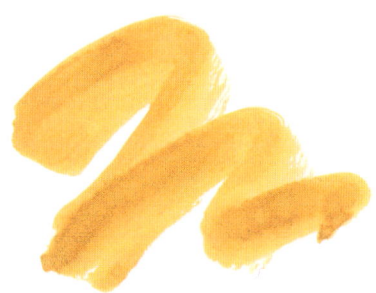

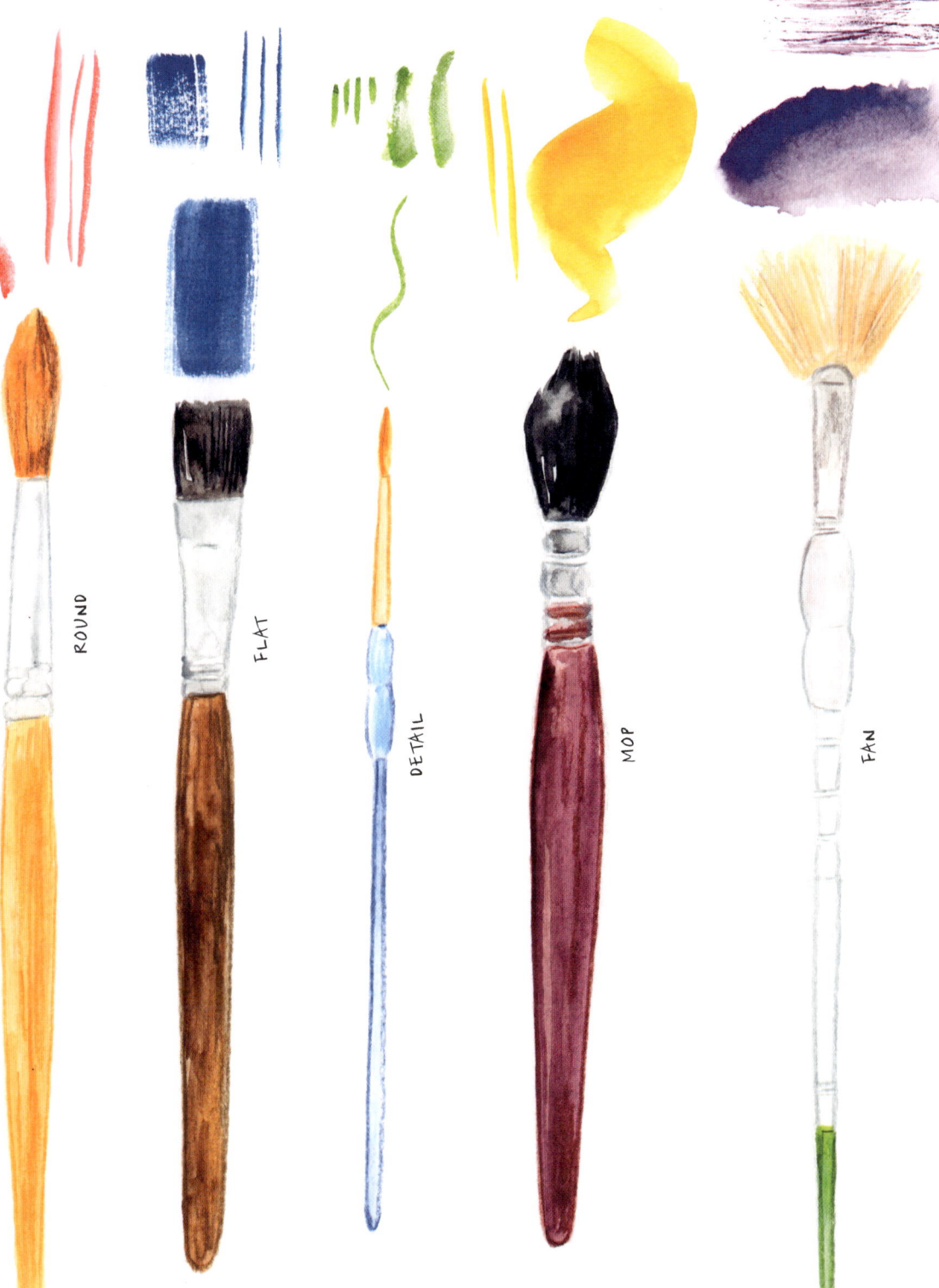

ROUND

FLAT

DETAIL

MOP

FAN

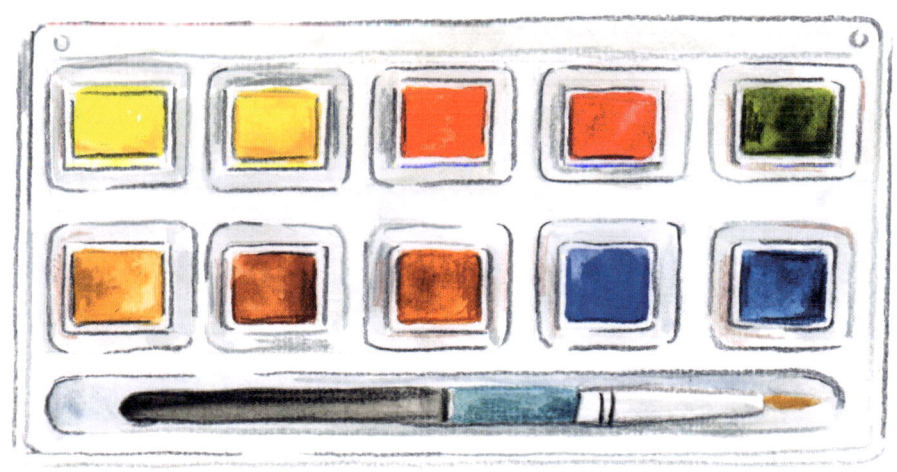

WATERCOLOUR

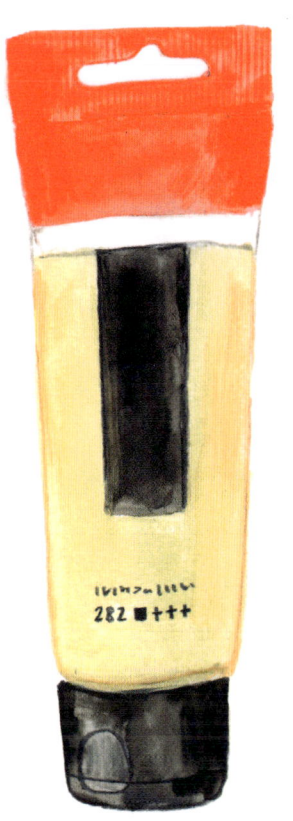

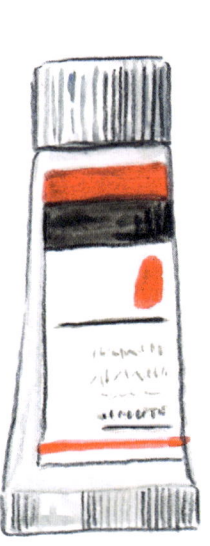

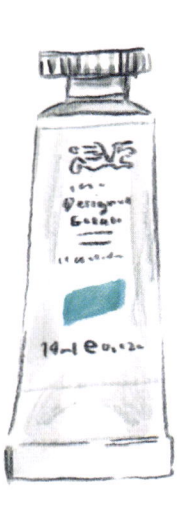

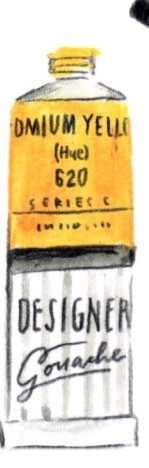

ACRYLIC

GOUACHE

paint

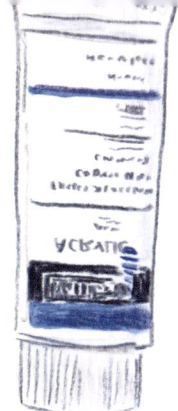

There are many different types of paint, such as acrylic, gouache, watercolour and oil. You won't want to use oil in your sketchbook as it takes a long time to dry, but the other paints are very common to use when sketchbooking.

WATERCOLOUR

A lot of artists start with watercolour, which can be bought in pans or tubes. Watercolour palettes contain multiple pans, which are little blocks of pigment that are activated with a wet brush. Watercolour works brilliantly on its own and is applied in layers to build up the pigment, and many dry mediums such as coloured pencils and pastels can also be layered over the top. Due to the amount of water used in its applications, it's generally best to use a sketchbook that has watercolour paper.

ACRYLIC

Acrylic paint is bought in tubes or pots, and is usually the most affordable of all the paints. It's easy to mix and readily found, with various types including medium or heavy body (which determines the thickness of the paint). You can get student grade and professional acrylics, with the former sometimes being lower in pigment (though still great for sketchbook practice and experiments).

It's fast drying and can be applied thickly to your page (an impasto technique) or applied thinly when watered down.

Unlike watercolour or gouache, however, it cannot be reactivated. If you squeeze too much onto your palette, be sure to use it up, as you won't be able to reuse the paint once it's dried. It's great for layering, but if using non-matte acrylic, and depending on the thickness applied, some dry mediums won't lay on top.

GOUACHE

Traditional gouache, like watercolour, is water-based and can be used in a variety of ways. It can be reactivated with water so palettes can be reused, or paintings can be rewet. Various dry mediums can be layered on top because it dries matte.

Gouache is opaque and creates vibrant, pigmented colour. It's a very versatile paint that can be used thickly for flat colour but also can be watered down and used like a wash.

Acrylic gouache has the intensity and richness of traditional gouache, but it cannot be reactivated once dried. Unlike acrylic paint, it generally has a matte finish.

Other mediums

There are a lot of mediums in the art world and you might find that you prefer one over another. You don't need to invest in everything, but if you're a mixed media artist, you may find your collection is quick to grow compared to an artist who sticks with one medium.

It would be impossible to list every medium in this book, so instead I've listed some of the supplies that are my personal favourites, and which you may like to try out:

* Coloured pencils
* Watersoluble wax pastels
* Acrylic ink
* Watercolour ink
* Brush pens
* Pan pastels
* Oil pastels
* Inktense blocks
* Acrylic markers

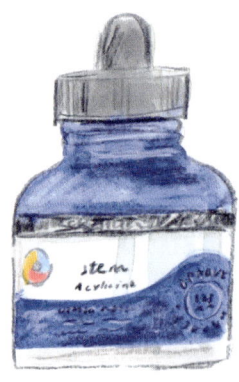
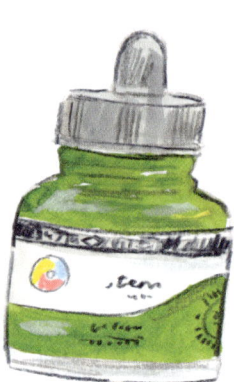

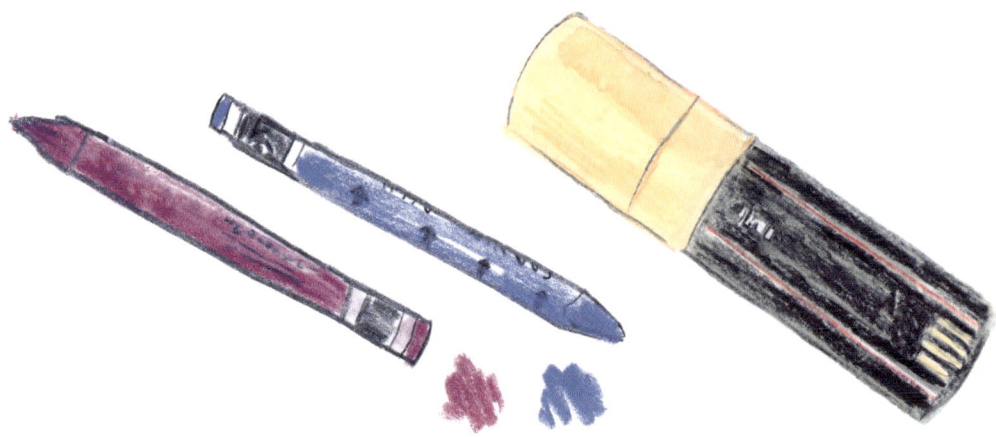

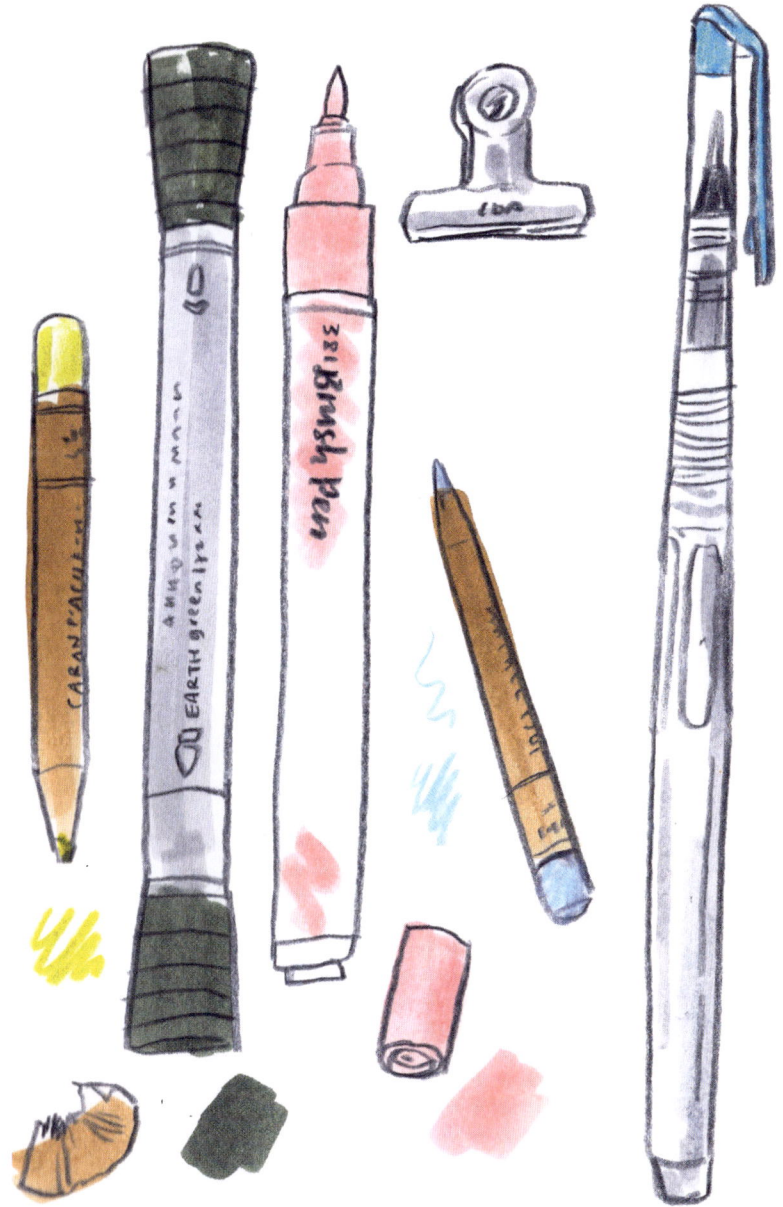

OTHER USEFUL ITEMS:

* Tear-off palette
* Clips
* Sharpener
* Pencil roll
* Eraser

In the techniques section (see page 71), I share ways you can use some of these materials and how to apply them into your sketchbooks.

Tools for drawing on location.

I find that when you're drawing outside, you need a different set of tools to those you'd use at home. There is generally more to think about when you don't have all your usual art materials to hand, and so there are certain tools that make your life a lot easier when filling your sketchbook on location.

Firstly, think about the size of your sketchbook. Bigger sketchbooks may be hard to carry with you, or difficult to balance if you don't have a hard surface. You may prefer to use hardback rather than softback sketchbooks (see page 54), or use smaller ones that are easy to transport in bags or pockets.

Water brushes are great for drawing on location. I used to take brushes and a water cup with me (you can

get collapsible ones if this is still your preference), but water brushes really changed the game for me. They come in various different shapes and sizes, but have a hollow barrel instead of a handle that you can fill with water. You simply squeeze the water through the bristles to wet the brush, rather than dipping it in a separate vessel. I like to take several of these brushes with me and keep similar tones to specific brushes to avoid dirtying the colours in my sketchbook.

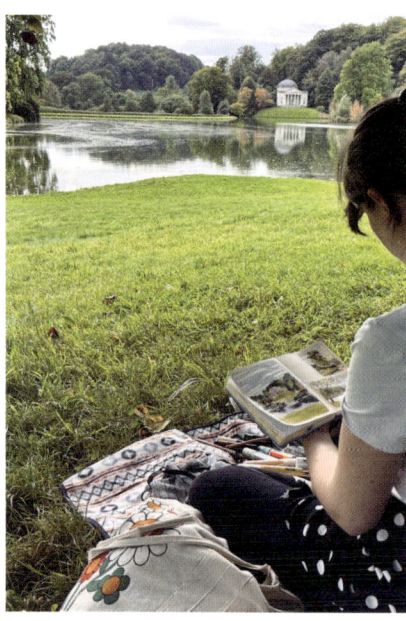

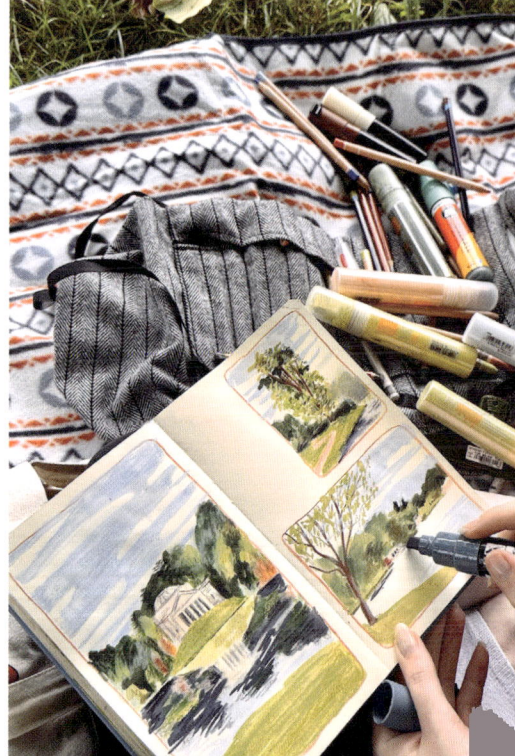

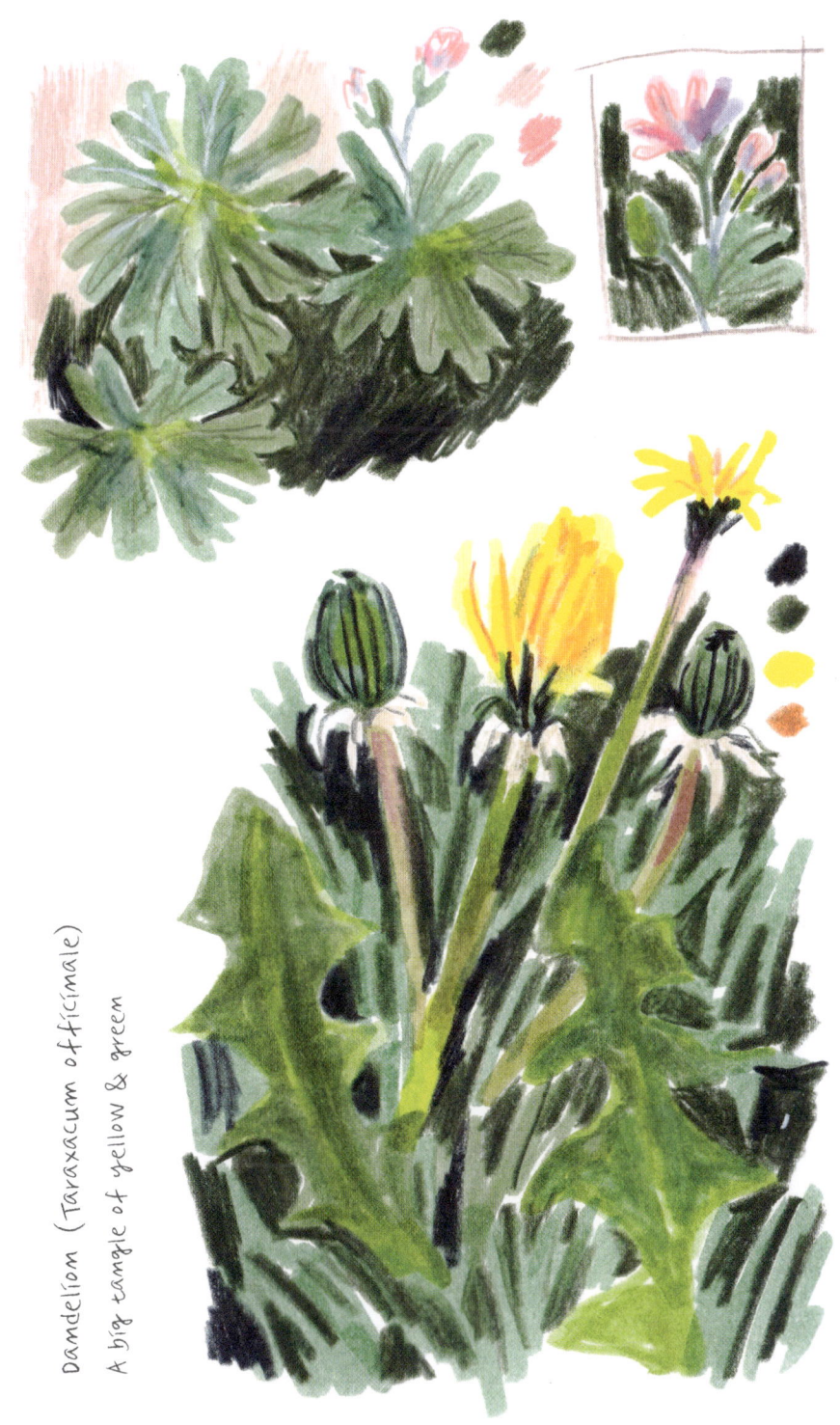

Damdelion (Taraxacum officinale)
A big tangle of yellow & green

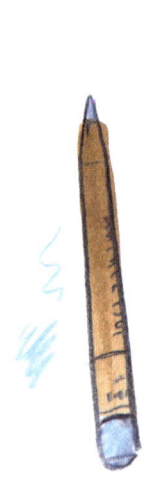

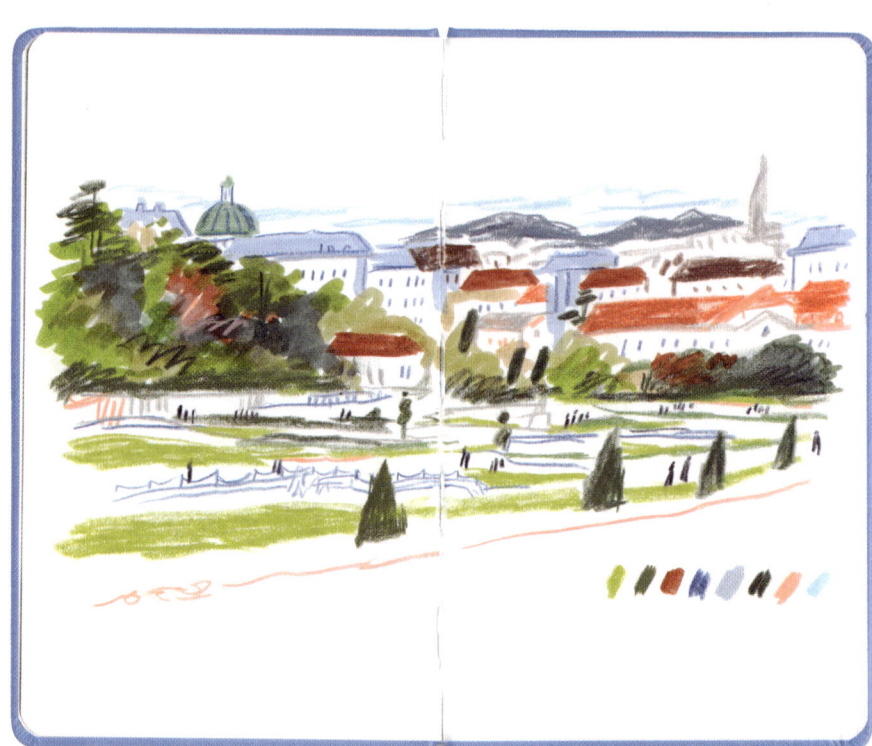

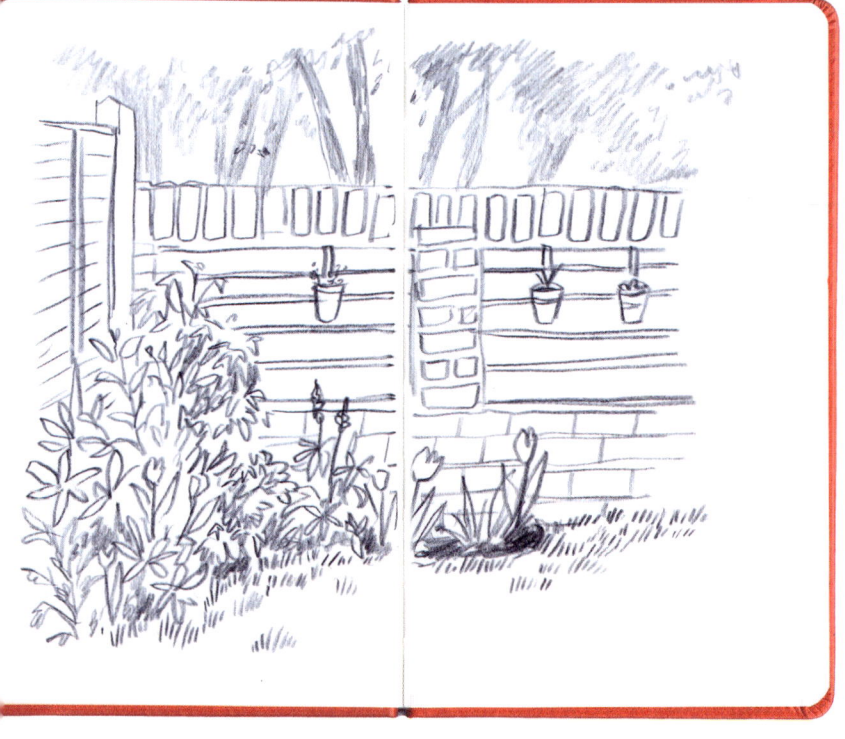

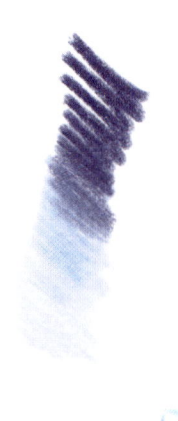

Folding stools are really helpful when drawing on location if there are no benches or other suitable places to sit. Drawing while standing is a great challenge but not always an option, or a blanket is another possibility depending on the terrain.

I often like to use dry materials when filling my sketchbook on location, but if you'd prefer paint, you can invest in a travel palette. Instead of taking many tubes of paints with you, you can dispense them into a compartmented palette, or even buy a palette that's already filled. Using your own palette is generally only good for water-based paints like traditional gouache or watercolour, as acrylics would render the palette useless once they hardened.

Acrylic markers are another great option that are really easy to use and very fast drying.

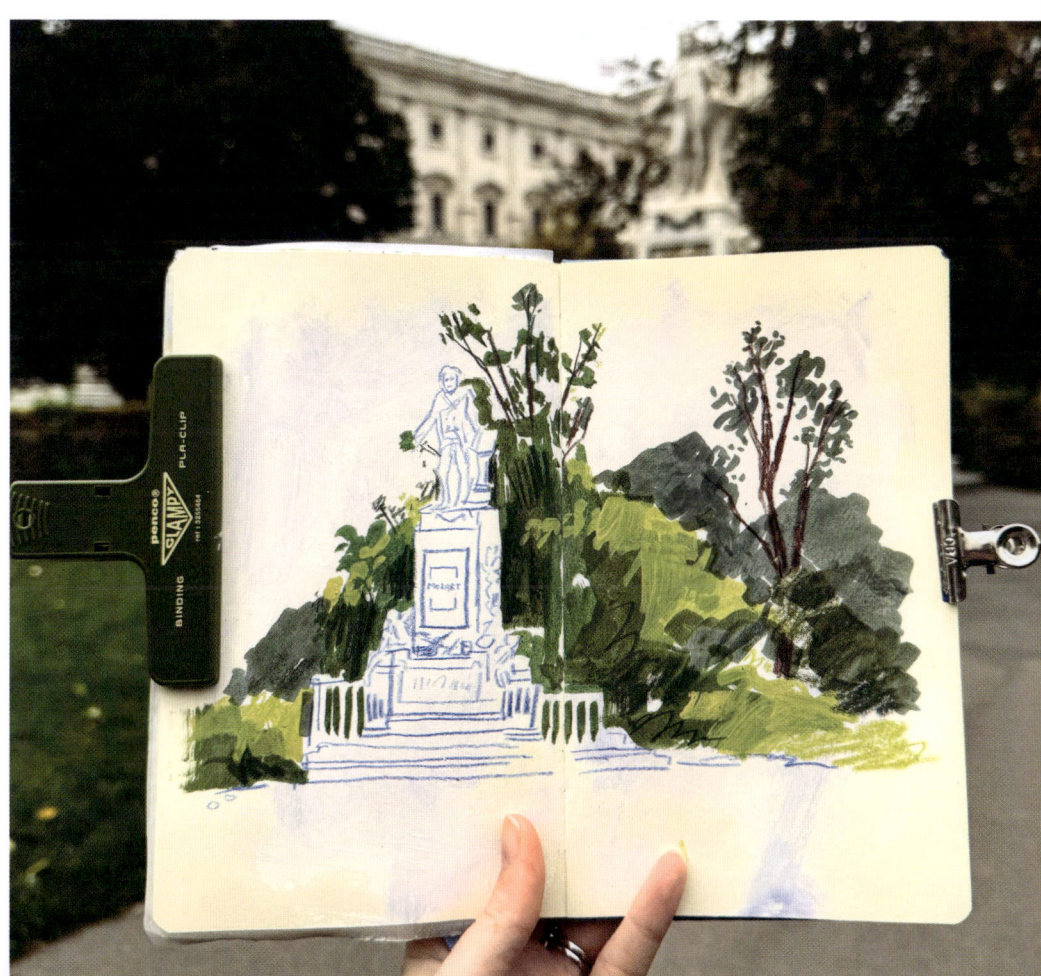

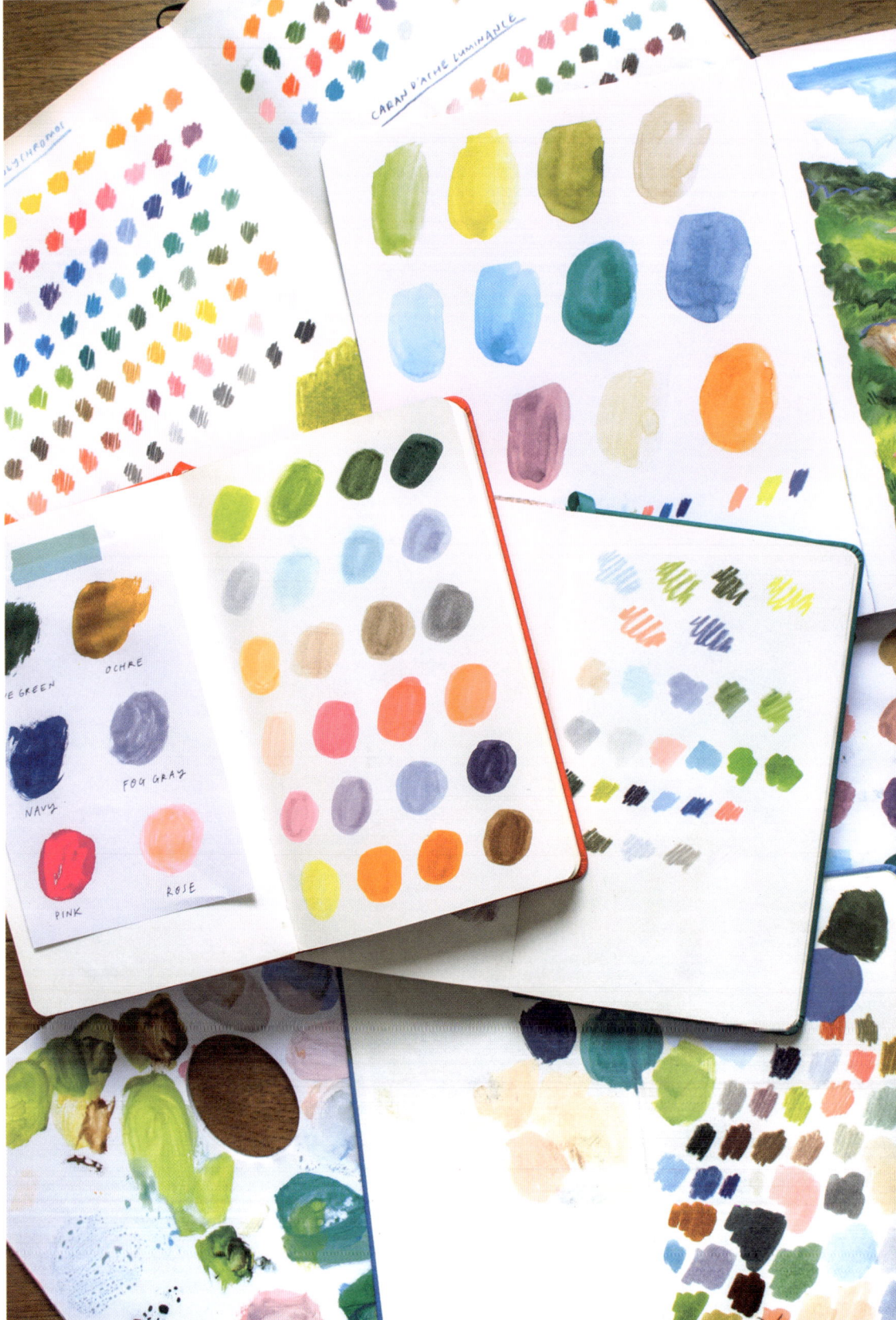

Colour

Colour is such a fundamental element within art, and a great topic to explore on your pages. It can make a huge difference to the atmosphere and mood of a sketchbook spread: it tells a story, creates a theme and can be explored throughout your sketchbook.

You don't need any formal training when it comes to colour, but a basic understanding of colour theory makes a world of difference. Just knowing a few key facts can change the feel of your work, prevent any frustrations when mixing colours and help you to understand why your art may not have turned out as expected.

As you continue to create, you'll probably find that there are some colours you use more than others, and it's in this way that you will create your own personal colour palette. For the moment, whether you know which colours you like or not – explore, experiment and play!

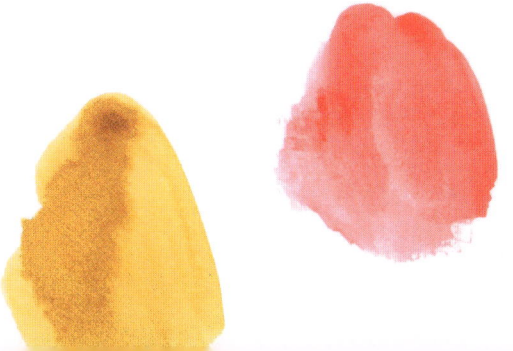

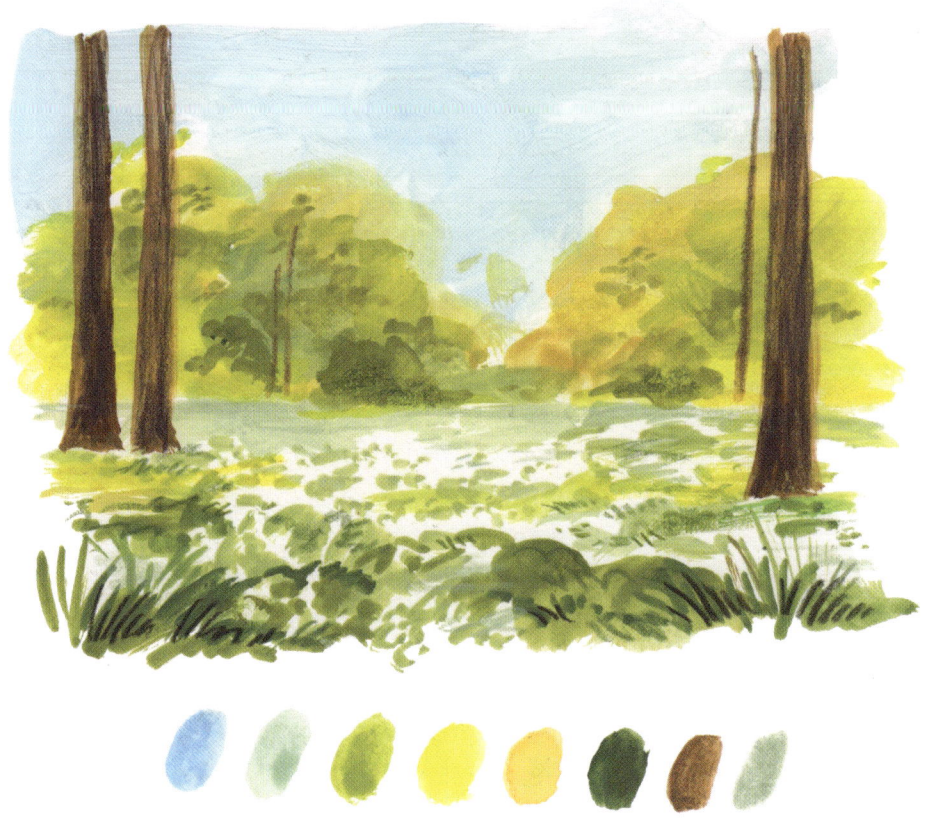

The importance of colour

Colour influences the overall mood of your sketchbook spreads, conveying emotions and stories. It's well known that specific colours affect our feelings and create associations, which is why companies spend so long picking colours for their brand, and why certain industries use specific colours.

Colour is often representational and, especially in realistic styles, it describes to the viewer exactly what you see. But it also doesn't have to be true to life, and that's why colour can be so fun to play with!

A landscape painted in greens, neutrals and earthy tones can be traditional and realistic. Swapping those colours for neons or other completely unrealistic tones, like purple, pink and red, creates a whole new atmosphere, even if you use the exact same marks and techniques.

Colour can also affect the way a viewer reads your art. If you want an element to stand out, you can use brighter, saturated colours so it's the first thing they see. Alternatively, you could tone down the other elements or your background by changing their saturation or value, so it 'pushes' your main element to the fore.

COMMON TERMS

* Colour = A general term used to describe the light reflected by an object, and can be further described using some of the words below.
* Tint = The lightness of a colour
* Shade = The darkness of a colour (but also used generally when describing different hues)
* Hue = The dominant colour
* Saturation = The intensity of colour

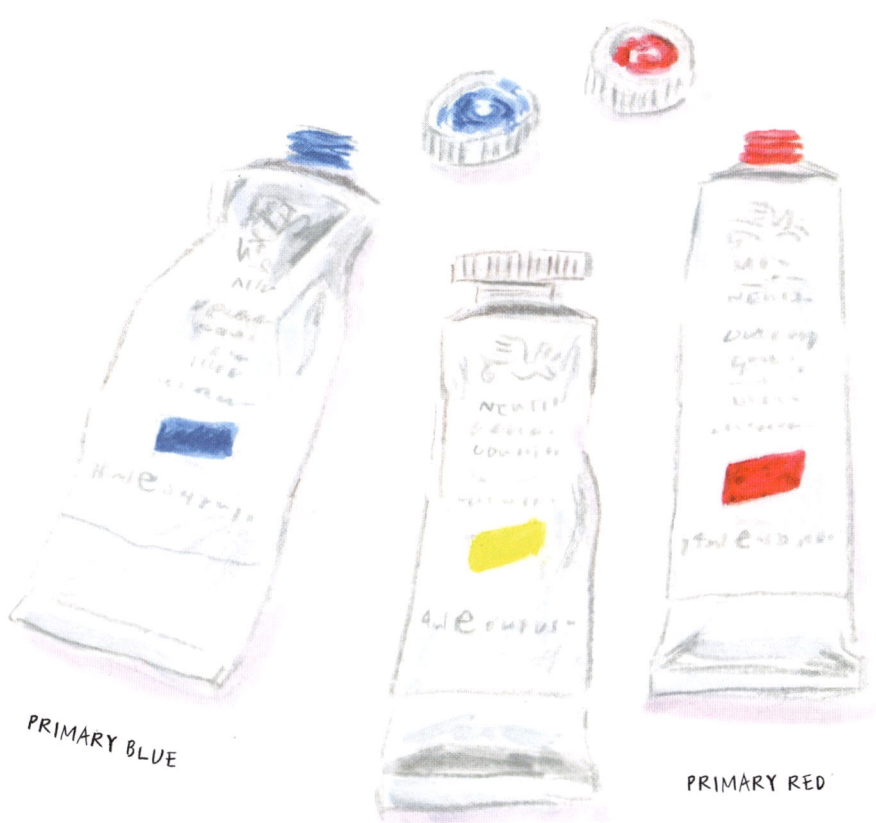

PRIMARY BLUE

PRIMARY RED

PRIMARY YELLOW

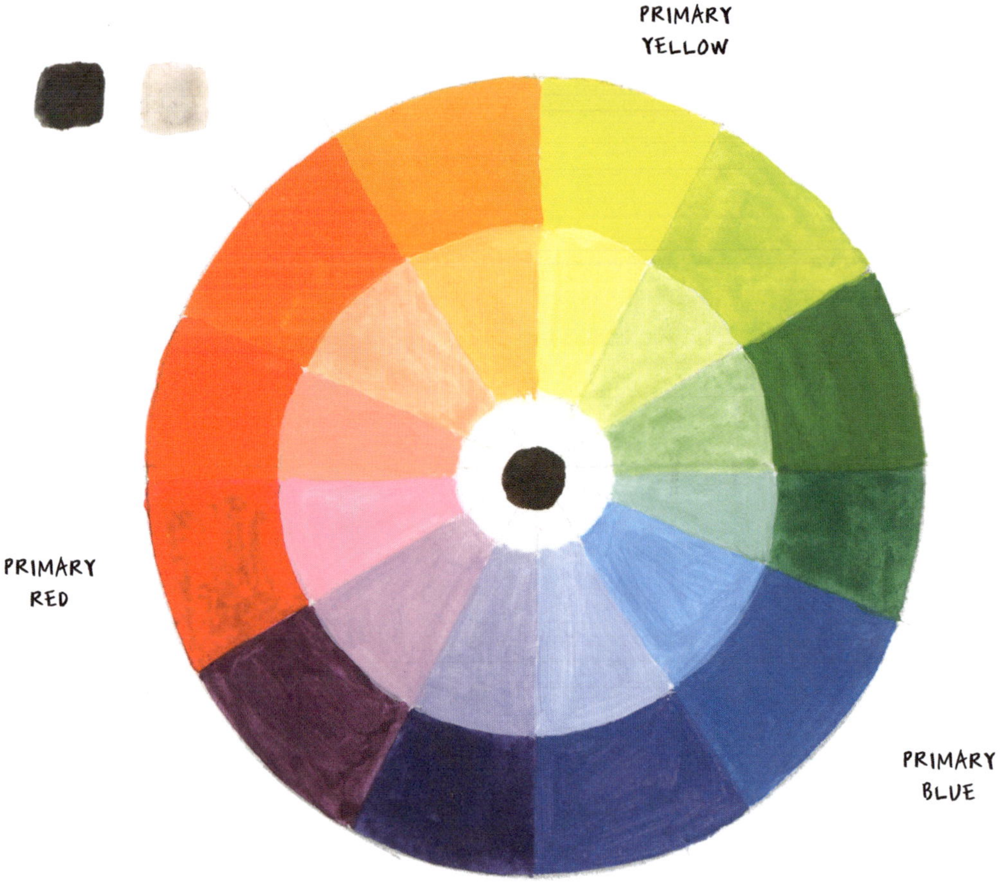

PRIMARY
YELLOW

PRIMARY
RED

PRIMARY
BLUE

Mixing colour

The colour wheel above features the three primary colours: blue, red and yellow. When you mix any two of these together, you create secondary colours, and these vary in hue depending on how much of each colour is used. Adding white and black to the mixes is also a great exercise, and will create different colour values.

The outer circle shows the primary colours, with the secondary colours between them. The inner circle shows the colours when mixed with white, while above the colour wheel are two swatches: the darker shade is the colour created when all three primaries are mixed together in equal proportions, and the lighter shade shows this colour mixed with white.

It's amazing how many shades you can mix from so few!

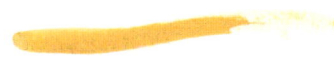

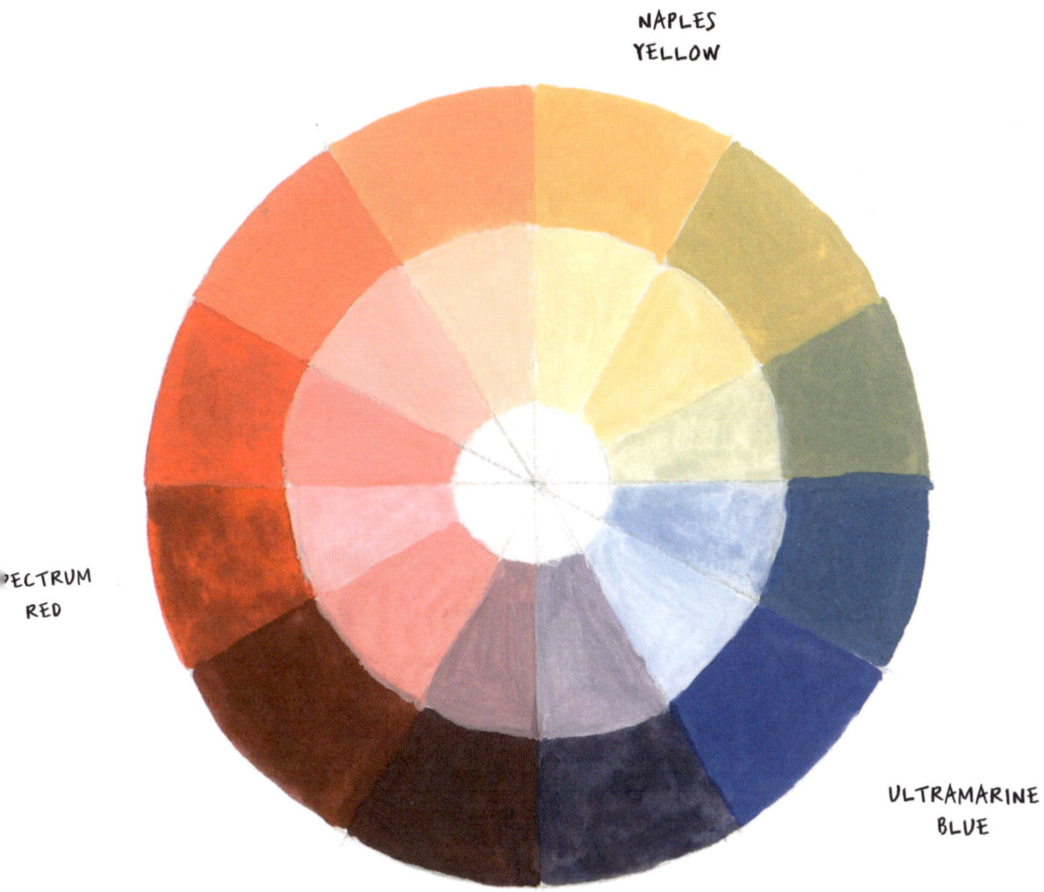

NAPLES
YELLOW

SPECTRUM
RED

ULTRAMARINE
BLUE

Often, when it comes to colour, you think of the bright primaries. Yet I find the fun and exploration comes when you start to alter the hues of these colours and apply them to your palette. On this colour wheel, you can see a yellow, but it is Naples Yellow rather than Primary Yellow. When mixed with Spectrum Red, rather than Primary Red, a soft peachy shade is created instead of a bright orange. An olive-type green is created when the Naples Yellow is mixed with Ultramarine Blue. The same rules apply as it did with the primary versions of these colours, but you get very different hues.

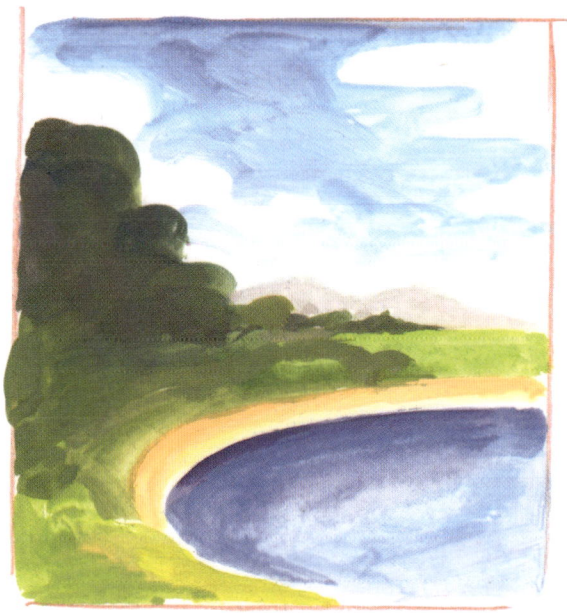

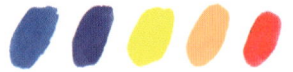

LANDSCAPE WITH PRIMARIES + WHITE
– NO BLACK

LANDSCAPE WITH PRIMARIES
+ WHITE AND BLACK

When mixing various colours, you will also want to create light and dark values. The standard response is to mix colours with white and black, but you can create a lot more tones by mixing with other colours. Sometimes mixing with white can create a chalky colour, while mixing with black can dull the shade. Black and white can still be used to mix colours for your paintings, but keep in mind there are plenty of other options at your disposal.

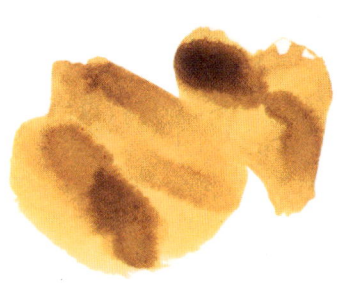
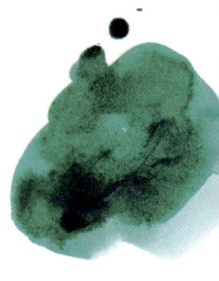

CREATING SHADES AND TINTS

Here are some ways to lighten and darken your paint swatches, showing the difference between them. Lighten with white, or a lighter colour within that hue. Darken using black, a complementary colour, or a darker colour within that hue.

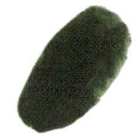
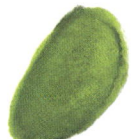
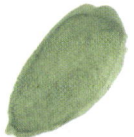

CHROMIUM OXIDE GREEN

LIGHTENED WITH LINDEN GREEN

LIGHTENED WITH WHITE

From left to right: Chromium Oxide Green, lightened with a lighter shade in the same hue (Linden Green) and with white (Permanent White). Mixing without white can create more vibrancy.

Below from left to right: Primary Blue, darkened with a darker shade in the same hue (Ultramarine Blue), with black (Ivory Black), and with a complementary colour (Spectrum Red). Mixing without black can create richer shadows.

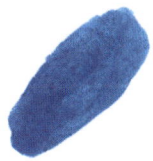
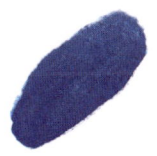
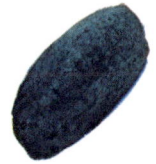
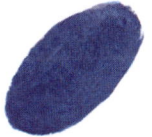

PRIMARY BLUE

DARKENED WITH ULTRAMARINE BLUE

DARKENED WITH BLACK

DARKENED WITH SPECTRUM RED

Once you've learnt about mixing colours, it's also helpful to understand how to pair them together to create colour palettes.

COMPLEMENTARY AND ANALOGOUS

Complementary colours are from opposite places on the colour wheel, so they really stand out when used in your work as they create a big contrast, for example a yellow and a purple. An analogous colour palette features colours from the same area of the colour wheel, that often sit next to each other, so they create a harmonious feel.

You can use this knowledge of complementary and analogous colours when mixing your own hues, too. If you want to tone down a colour, add the complementary colour to it – similar to the previous exercise where we darkened the blue. My favourite example of this is adding red to my green in nature, which makes it feel more natural and believable in a landscape.

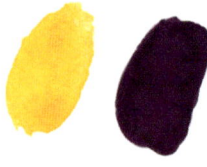

COMPLEMENTARY

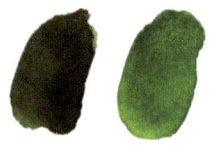

ANALOGOUS

COOL AND WARM COLOURS

You can also create colour palettes using cool and warm colours. Cool colours have undertones of blue, purple and green, while warmer colours have undertones of red, orange and yellow. These can have a big impact on the mood and atmosphere of your artwork.

You can use purely warm or cool colours in a painting, or a combination. When paired with each other, they can have a big impact and create a great contrast. For example, if you'd like an element to stand out, use a warm colour surrounded by cool colours.

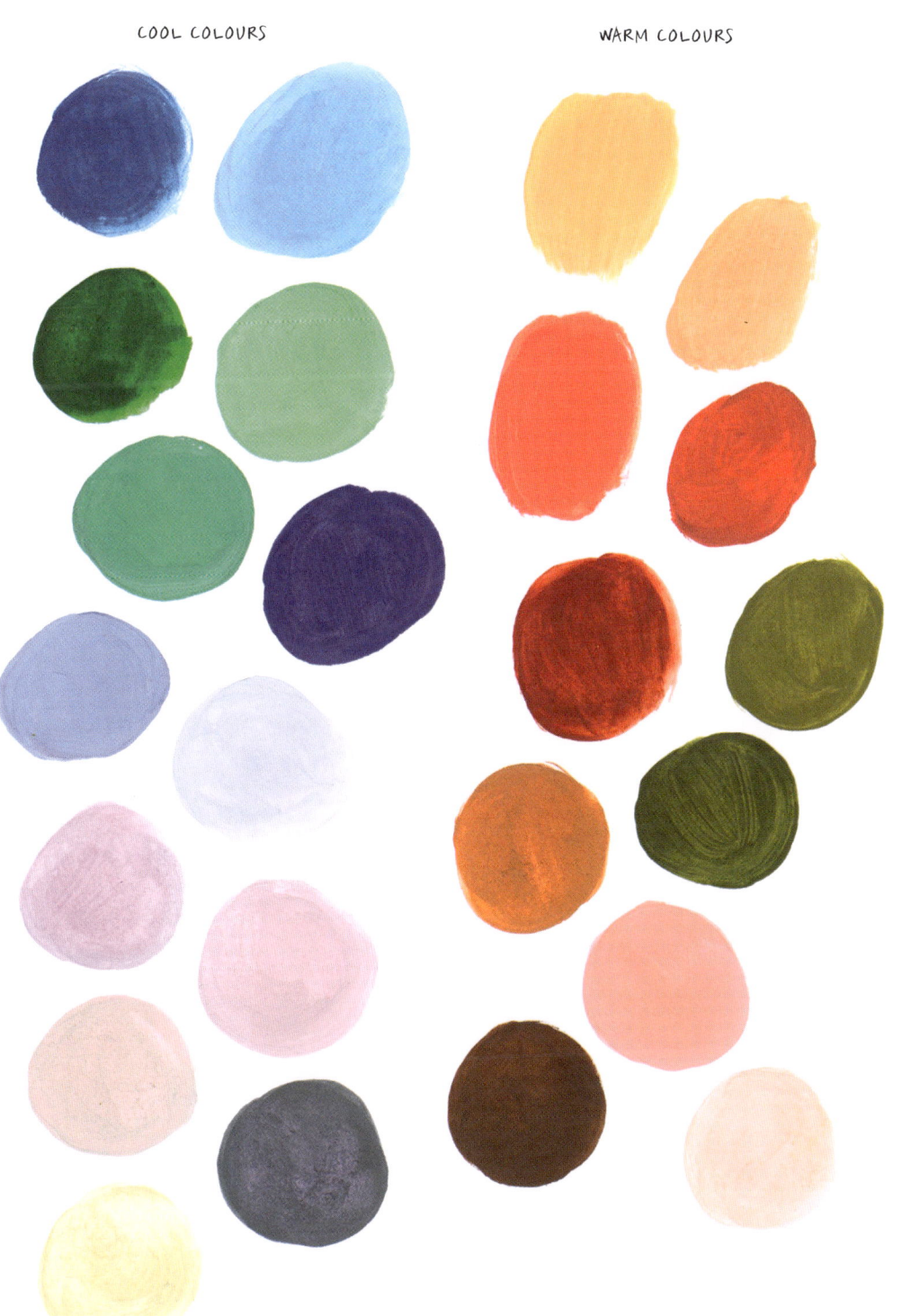

Starting palette

You don't need a million different colours to get started. It can be really overwhelming when picking paint tubes from the art store and there are hundreds of different colours in front of you to pick from!

Having your own 'go-to' colours can really help to limit overwhelm and also create your signature style. You may build your palette slowly and naturally over time, as you find yourself reaching for specific colours more often than others. You also might want to grab some random colours to experiment with, and add them into your palette if they work with what you have.

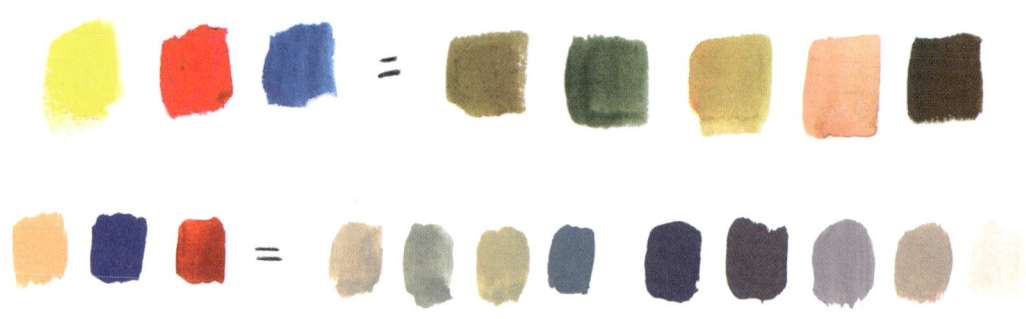

If you're building your colour palette from scratch, the primary colours are a great place to start. Most art supplies come in primary colour sets because so many colours can be mixed from them, and they often also contain black and white, which can be used for mixing your shades and tints (see page 65).

Once you've mixed some of these colours, pick a few at random and see how they look when you place them next to each other.

Grab a light, mid and dark tone in the same way and see if they work together. If you take a tint and a shade (see page 61) from analogous colours, they will probably sit well together, but what happens when you pair the two with a shade from a complementary colour? Do these colour combinations feel dark and moody, or light and airy when placed together? Maybe even happy or mysterious? Colour is so powerful!

For art supplies that can't be mixed, such as dry mediums like pastels, pencils and pens, I recommend choosing tones that relate to your favourite subject to draw, such as neutrals and skin tone for portraiture, and natural, earthy colours for landscapes.

Colour can be subjective, so go with your gut if you think certain hues look good together. You may like clashing colours, or prefer a more cohesive palette.

Have fun experimenting and see what feels best.

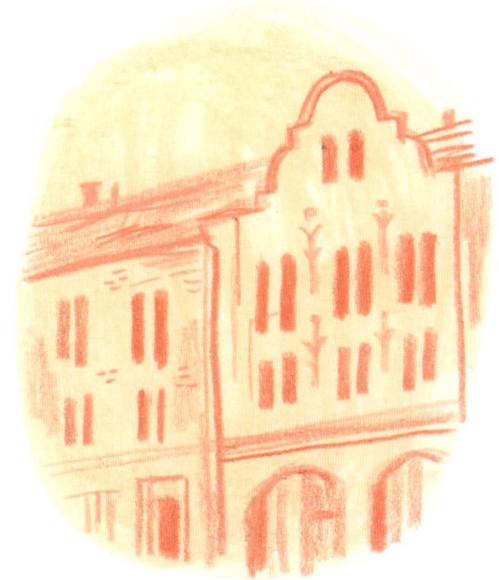

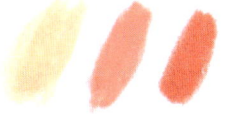

LIMITED COLOUR PALETTES

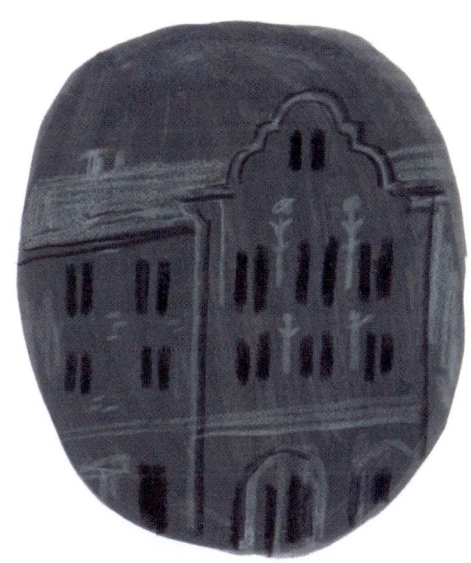

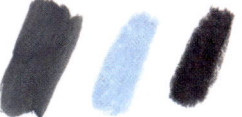

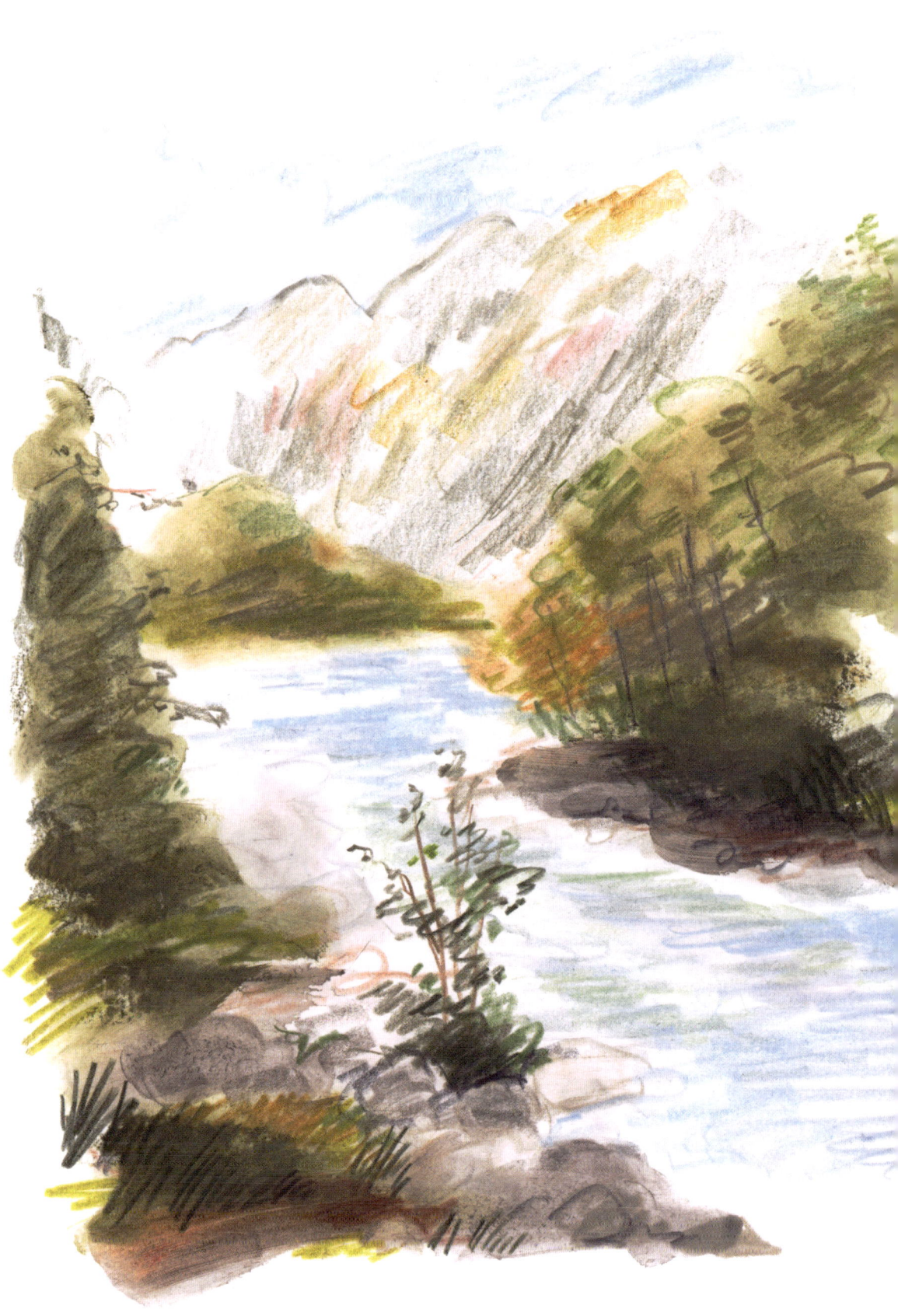

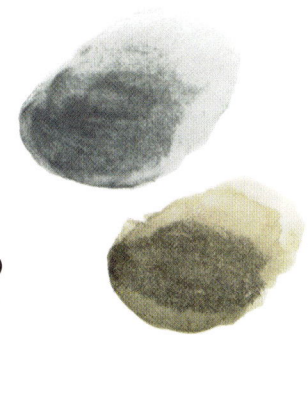

Techniques for mixed media

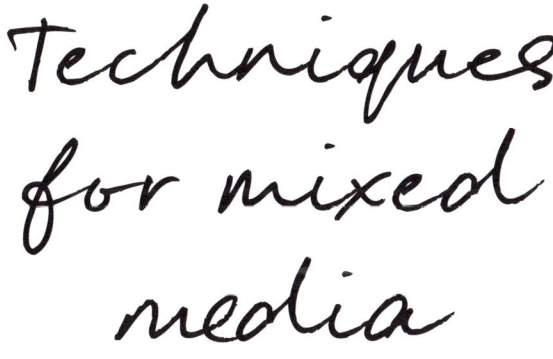

Some artists have a preferred medium that they work in and develop their skills with. There are books that focus on these specific specialisms in a lot more detail, whereas I tend to dabble in a number of them!

In this chapter, I'm sharing various techniques you can explore with your art materials, as well as how you can combine them. You can experiment with these in your sketchbook pages or apply them to the projects that I share on pages 95–141.

Whatever art supplies you use – even if not mentioned in this book – the techniques outlined in this chapter are a great way to get to know your materials, and I highly recommend just playing around and having fun. Explore their capabilities, add water, apply dry, or combine a few to see what happens. . . the opportunities are endless!

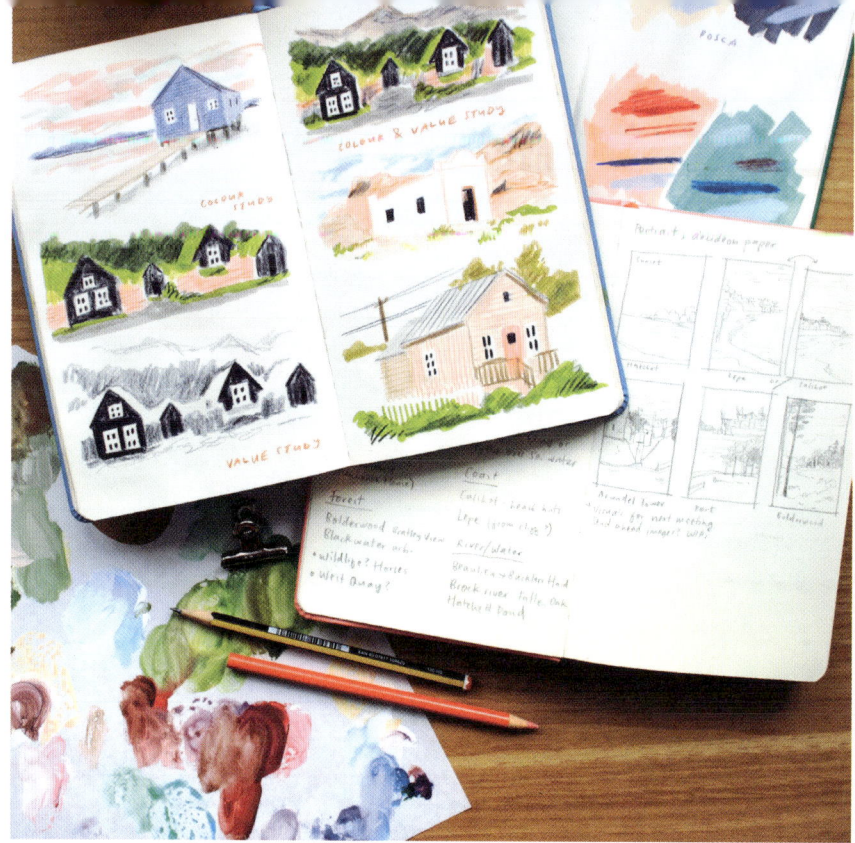

Using mixed media

I love using mixed media because it really enhances my playful side. I'm a huge believer that art should be fun and more about the process than the results. Mixed media combines multiple mediums to create a piece of art, and the combinations really are unlimited. It's also a good way to develop your skills and your practice, because you get to try out lots of things and really work out what makes your heart sing!

As I said earlier, there are no rules in art-making. Anything in this book can be adapted and changed depending on what you feel like doing. That said, I do want to share some common methods of layering and ordering your mixed media, which may help your creative journey in a sketchbook. If you start throwing everything at a page, it may result in a big brown sludge, so use the following tips as a guide before jumping into your own mixed media combinations.

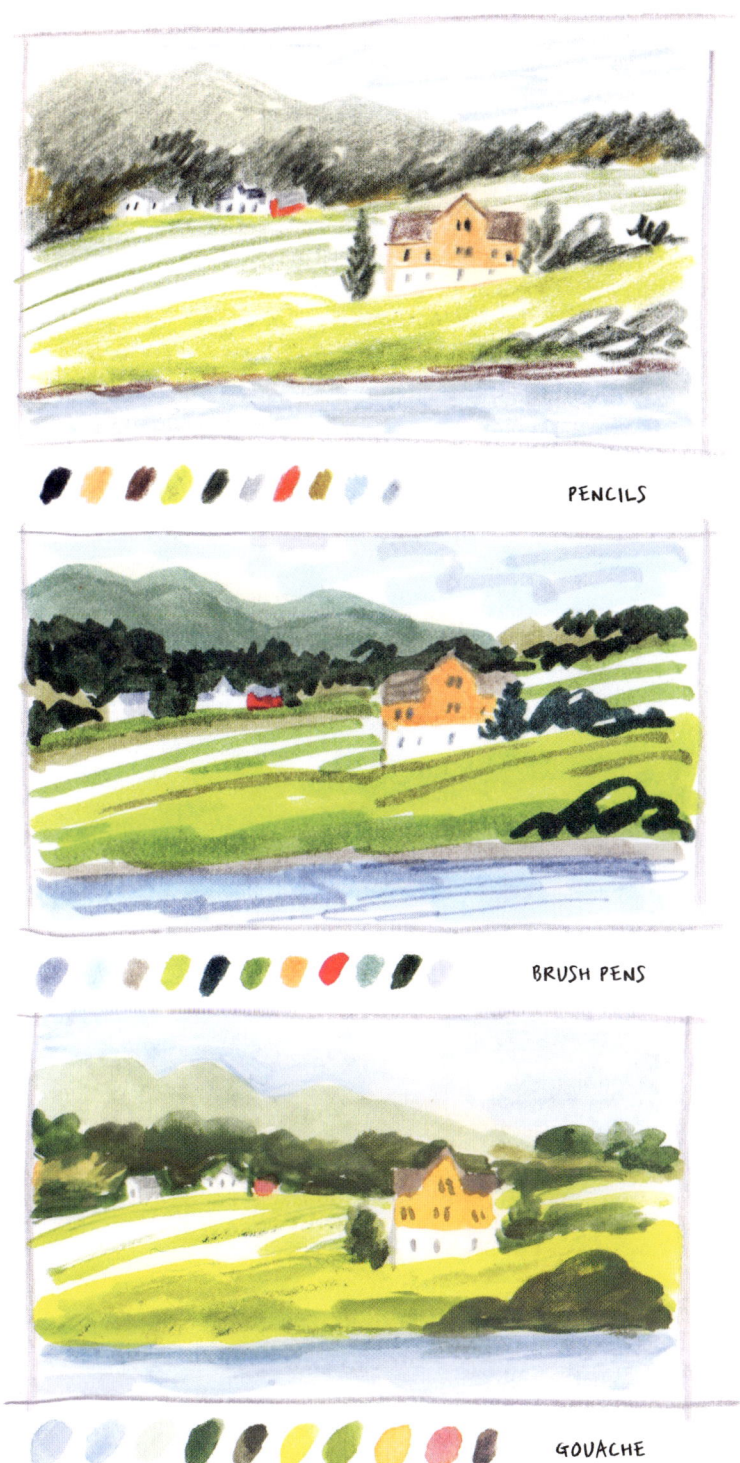

PENCILS

BRUSH PENS

GOUACHE

Usually when layering mixed media, you'll want to apply a base layer first. This can be paint, pastels, brush pens or even coloured pencils. Putting larger colour blocks and shapes down first is a good way to simplify and start creating.

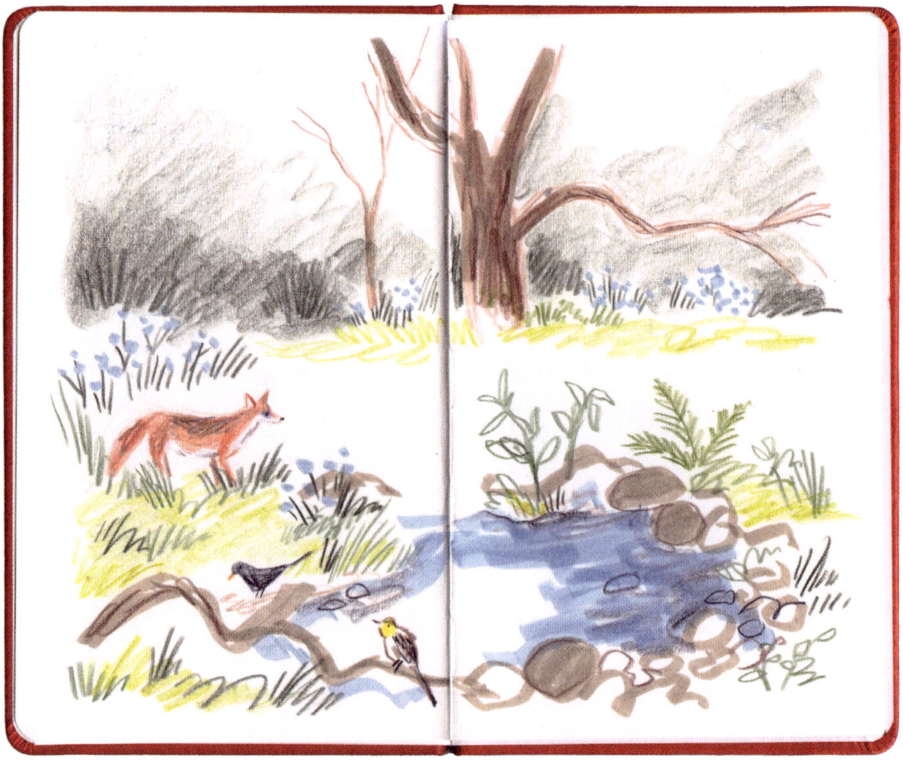

Then you can start adding on top. Go for medium or smaller shapes next and begin building your layers. You can add as many layers here as you need, incorporating patterns and building up different textures.

Your last step is details. This could be linework, smaller elements or final touches of colour. If using paint, apply it with a small brush, or use other mediums like pens, wax pastels or coloured pencils that give greater precision.

It's important to remember that some mediums can't be layered over others: wax- or oil-based mediums (like some pastels) will usually be applied last, unless you're using a resist technique (see page 92). I like using these mediums for final pops of colour and small elements of linework.

Often art needs trust and time before it looks 'good'. It can be tempting to give up when it's not going as you'd like it to, but I really encourage you to push through. It's amazing how much a piece of art can change throughout the process, so if in doubt – keep going! Adding layers and details can make a big impact on the final artwork.

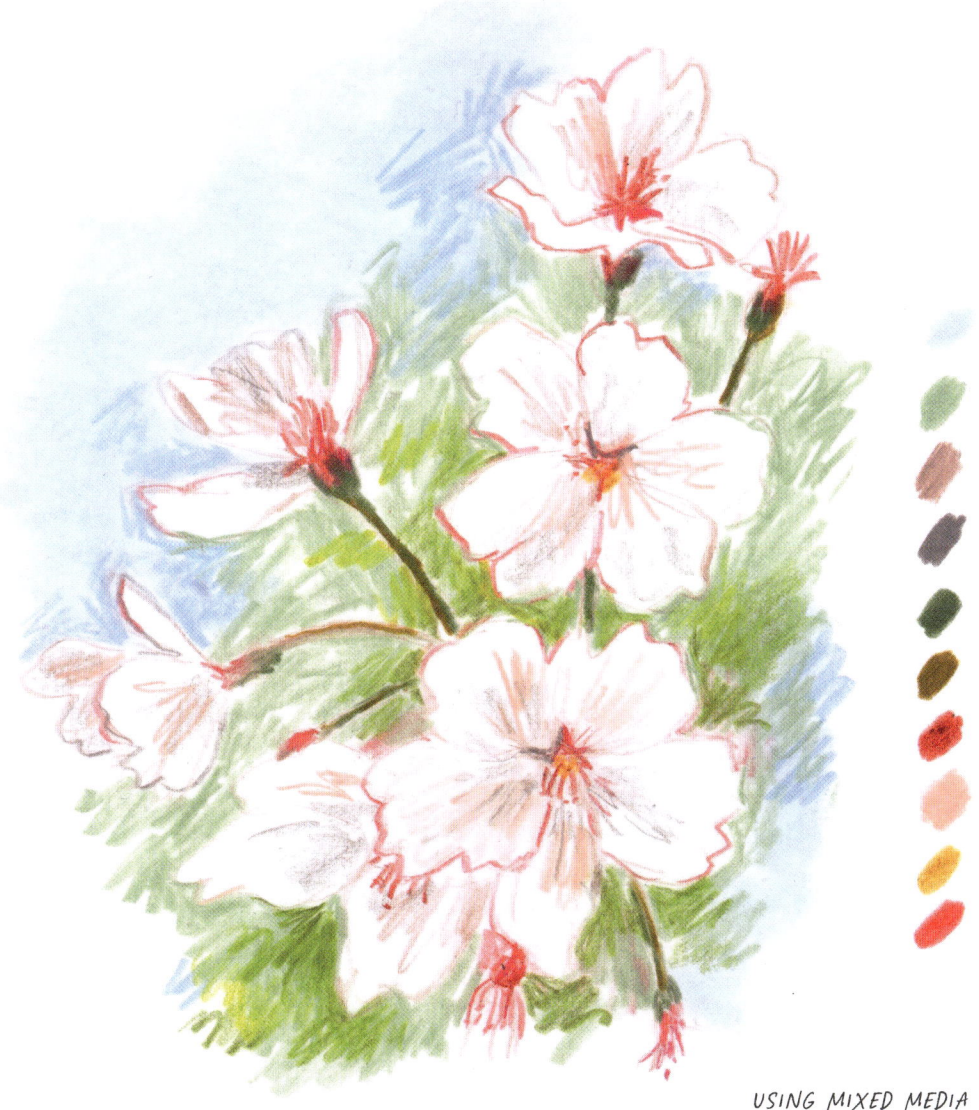

Techniques

GOUACHE

Gouache is a very versatile paint, it's water-based and can be reactivated. It's great for mixed media because it dries matte, so most dry mediums will layer on top without any issue.

There are generally two ways artists use gouache: either thickly applied in opaque, clear shapes, or with a lot of water and applied in washes.

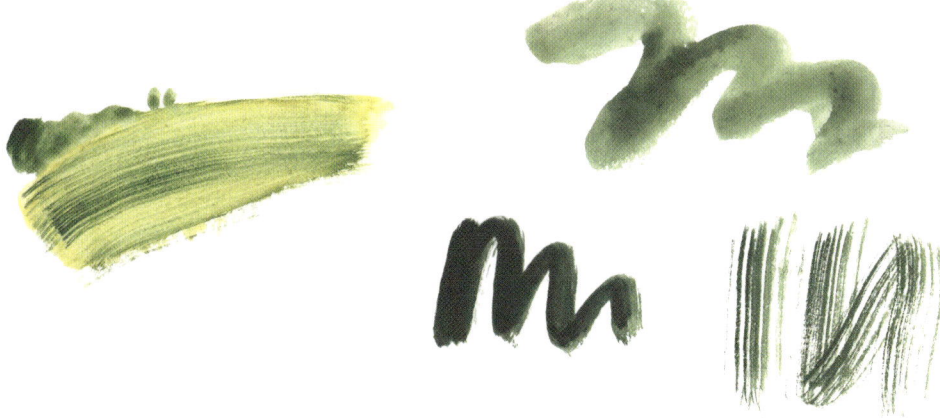

Using gouache for flat colour can create a wonderfully graphic style of painting that's a great base for art. You'll need water to spread out the gouache pigment but the more you add, the more your brushstrokes will show and the tint will change, so it can also be a tricky style to master.

Gouache often looks different when it's dried to how it looked when applied – usually darker tones dry lighter and lighter tones dry darker. It can therefore be tricky to recreate an exact shade when you're mixing your own colours.

The other way to use gouache is to water it down and apply it in a similar way to watercolour. You can change the consistency of gouache easily depending on how much water you add, and build it up in layers.

Because gouache can be reactivated, you'll need to be careful when working on top of it. As mentioned, dry mediums work well, however, if you're applying anything water-based, you'll find that it may reactivate the layer of gouache and pick up the colour underneath. It's possible when using thicker paint or less water, but something to keep in mind!

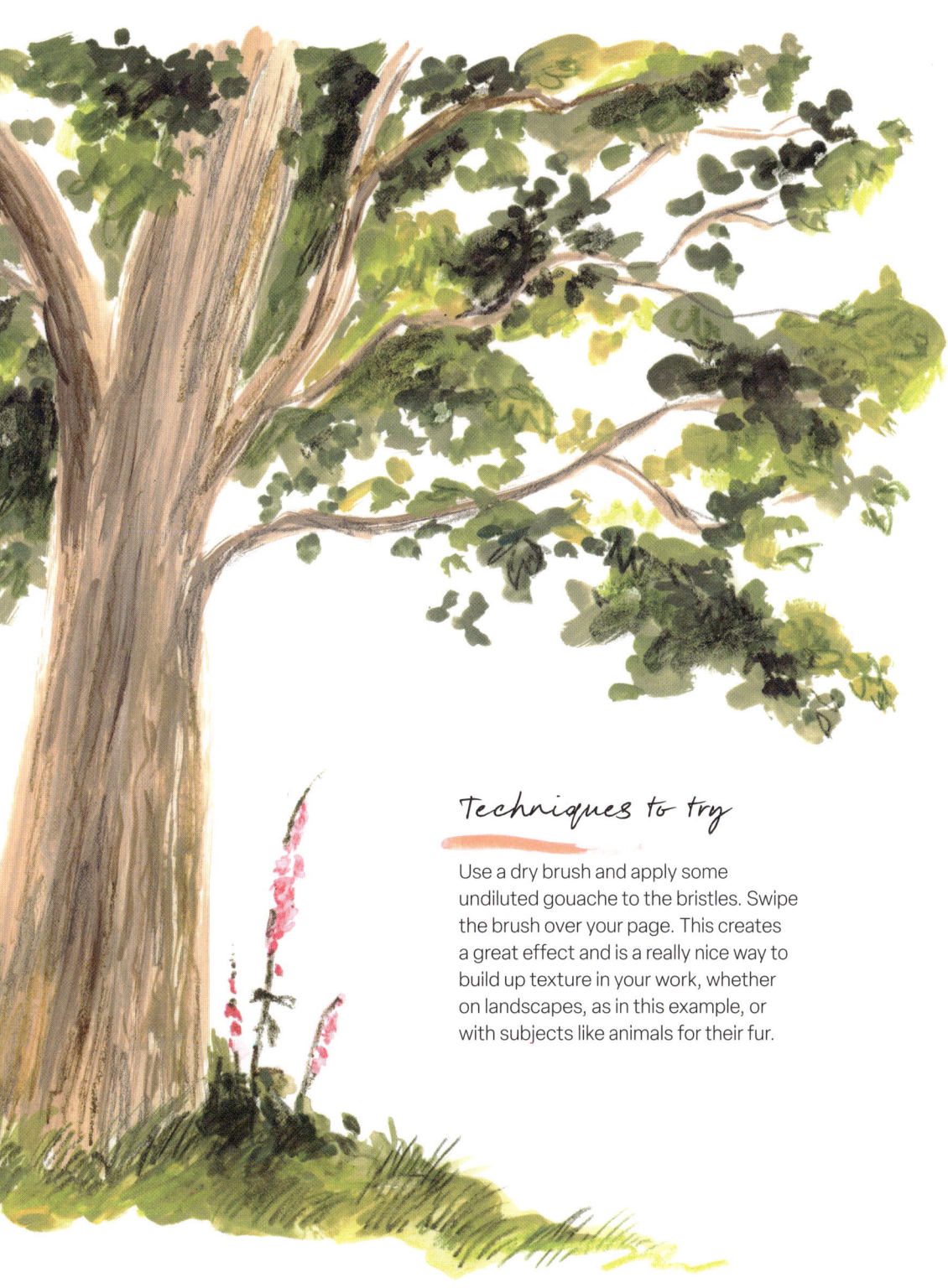

Techniques to try

Use a dry brush and apply some undiluted gouache to the bristles. Swipe the brush over your page. This creates a great effect and is a really nice way to build up texture in your work, whether on landscapes, as in this example, or with subjects like animals for their fur.

ACRYLIC PAINT

There are different types of acrylic paint, and just like any paint, the qualities of fluidity and thickness will depend on the grade and brand you buy. It is a great medium when working at a larger scale or creating thick layers of colour.

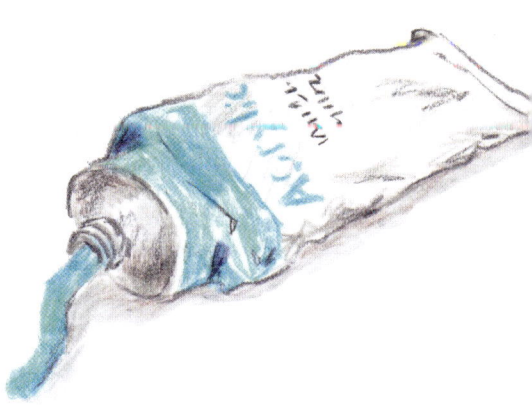

Acrylic is not reactivated by water, so once it's dry it's set for good! This means it works well as a base layer and is often used for large canvases. Some acrylic paints can dry slightly shiny, however, which makes other mediums harder to layer and sit on top.

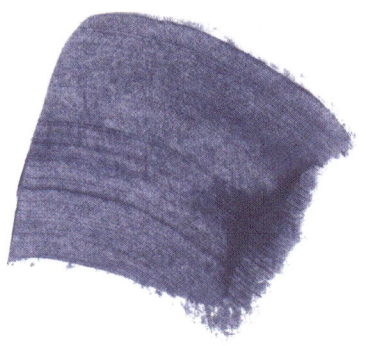

ACRYLIC APPLIED
WITH CARD

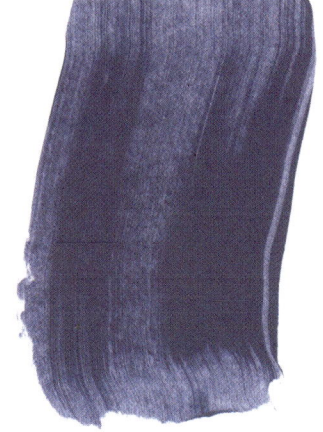

I also want to mention acrylic markers. They're well known in the graffiti world for applying smaller details, allowing more control than spray paints, but they're also great for sketchbook artists. You can buy ready-made colours with various-sized nibs, or mix up your own shades to create your own colour palette. They are easy to transport and throw in your bag for drawing on location, and great for accessibility as there's no need for brushes or water – just apply it like you would a pen.

Techniques to try

A great way to apply acrylic paint is with a thick piece of card. Put some paint on the edge and swipe it over your page to create a block of colour with no brushstrokes to be seen – a great way to add texture to a piece of art.

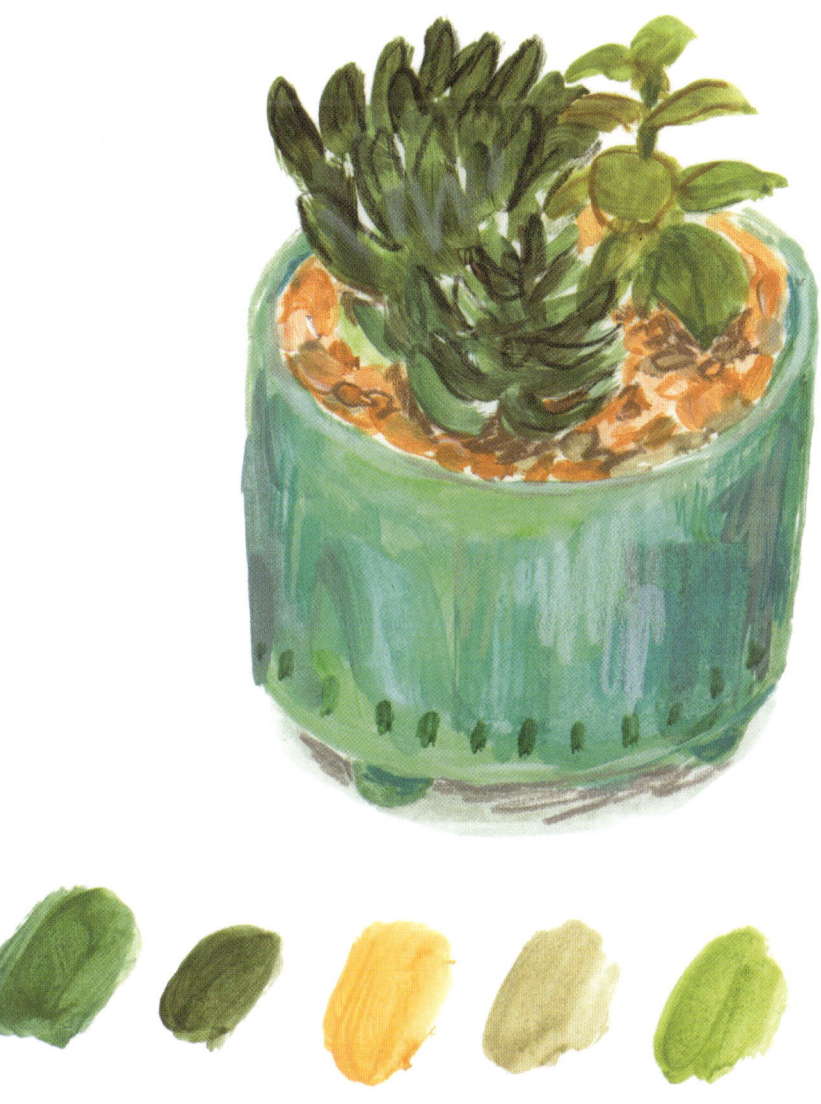

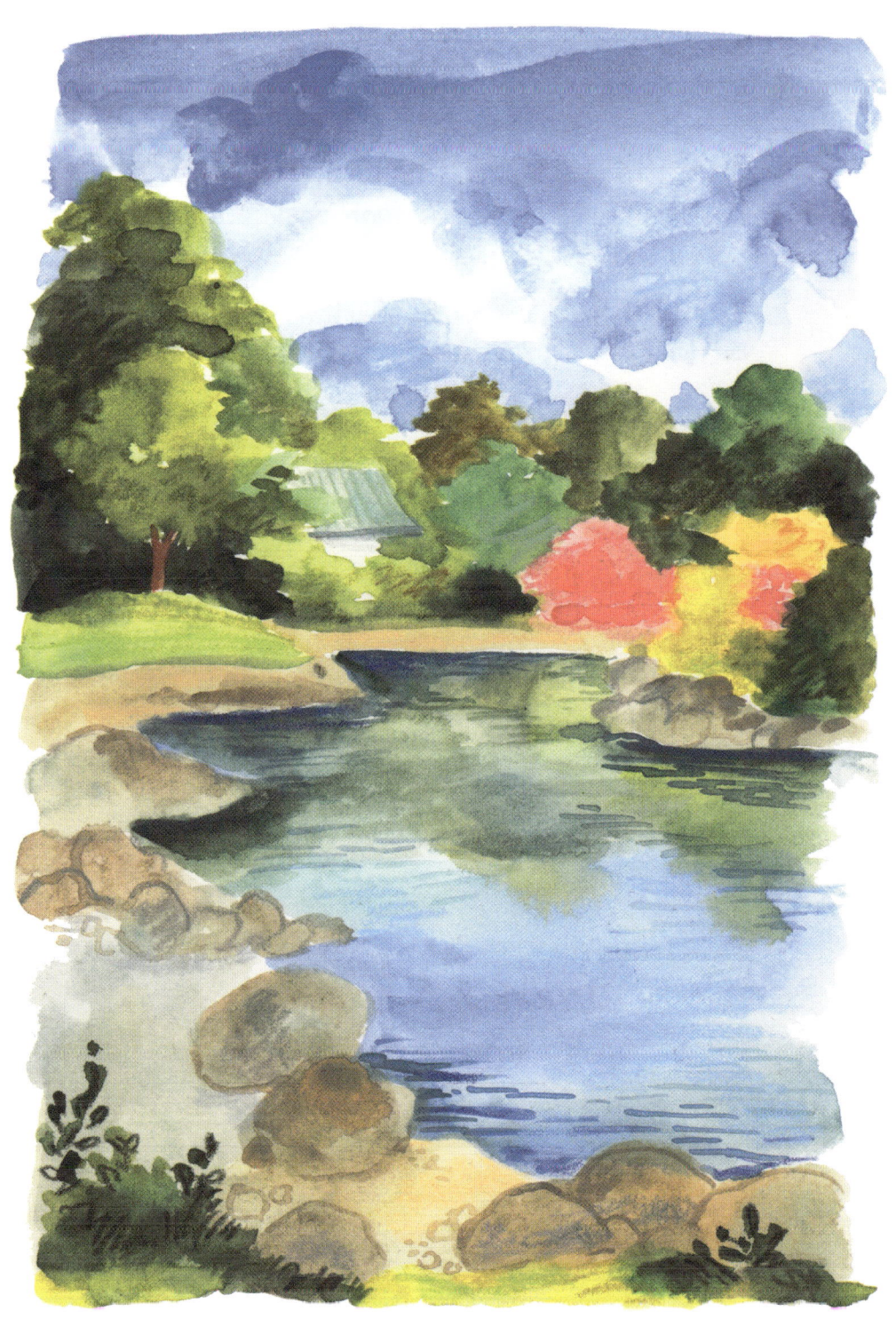

WATERCOLOUR

Watercolour is the medium a lot of artists start with. Again, the quality of paint differs between brand and type, but student-grade watercolours are a great place to begin if you've never used them before.

Watercolour palettes, which hold multiple blocks of watercolour pigment, work really well for painting on location. You can also buy watercolours in tubes, and this generally gives you more control when mixing colours, as well as a higher intensity of colour as it's squeezed from the tube before being diluted with water. One thing to note is that watercolour takes longer to dry than other paints, which may affect the layers on top depending on how fast you work.

Watercolour can be applied and built up in multiple layers once each layer has dried. You can also apply it with a lot of water and add more paint before it's dried, which is a wet-on-wet technique that creates beautiful blending, though can be difficult to predict.

 1 LAYER

 2 LAYERS

 3 LAYERS

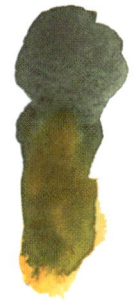
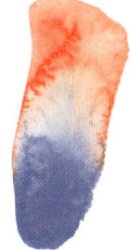
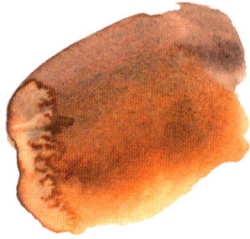

Techniques to try

While the watercolour is still wet, try dabbing off some pigment with a paper towel or tissue. This works wonderfully to create soft clouds and skies.

PENCILS

Pencils are probably the medium that everybody has at least one of, and they're extremely useful for artists. I generally use pencils in all my mixed media pieces as they're so versatile and can be used for base colours, or layered on top of most mediums for detail.

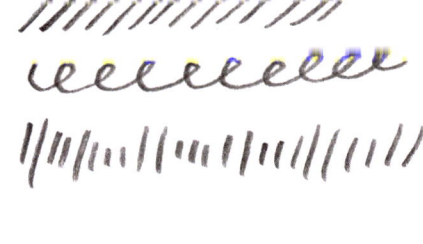

Pencils come in all shapes, sizes and a huge range of colours. As well as the standard graphite, you can also get water-soluble pencils and those with a pastel- or charcoal-based core.

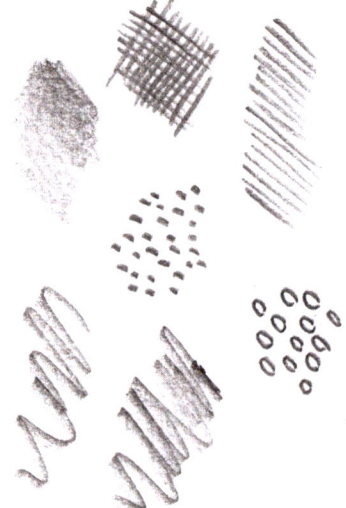

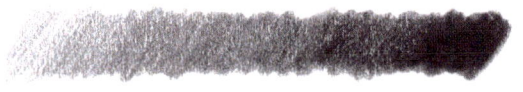

PENCIL PRESSURE

PENCIL BLENDING

The biggest difference between many brands of coloured pencils is the strength of the lead. The softer the lead, the easier it is to blend and build up colour slowly and in many layers. If the pencil has hard lead, it will need to be pressed harder to the paper to apply colour. Harder lead pencils hold their sharpened point for longer as the lead wears down much slower, making them great for finer details.

Pencils take a lot longer to lay down or cover an area, but can be used to create a wide range of textures and details. Applying pencil very lightly creates a soft effect, and this can be added to with the same colour to build saturation, or with other colours for blending.

You can also create various marks and lines with pencils, and alter the tone by applying less or more pressure.

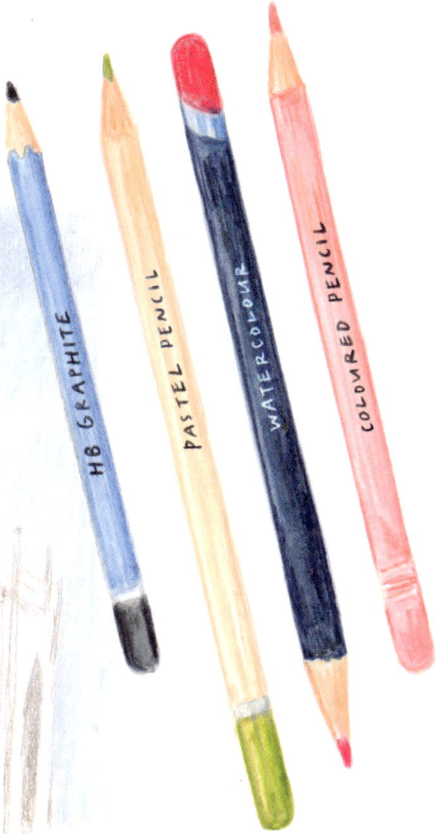

Pencil labels (left to right): HB GRAPHITE · PASTEL PENCIL · WATERCOLOUR · COLOURED PENCIL

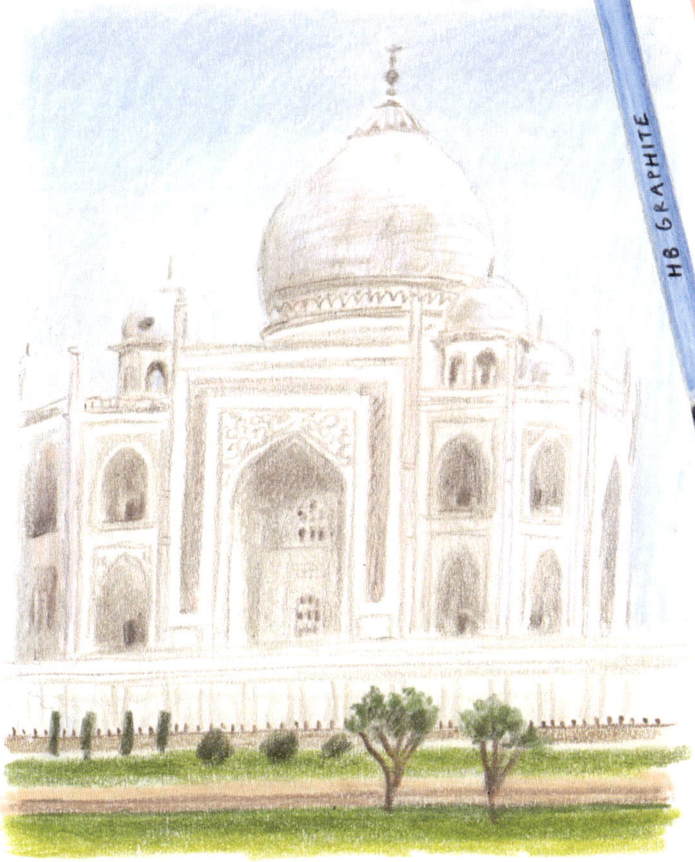

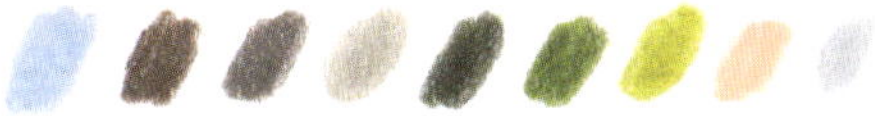

Techniques to try

Fill a page with marks from just one pencil. Use the pencil at various angles, build up pigment slowly, or drop the pencil on the page to create unpredictable marks. You can then apply the textures you create on future pages.

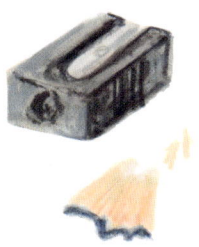

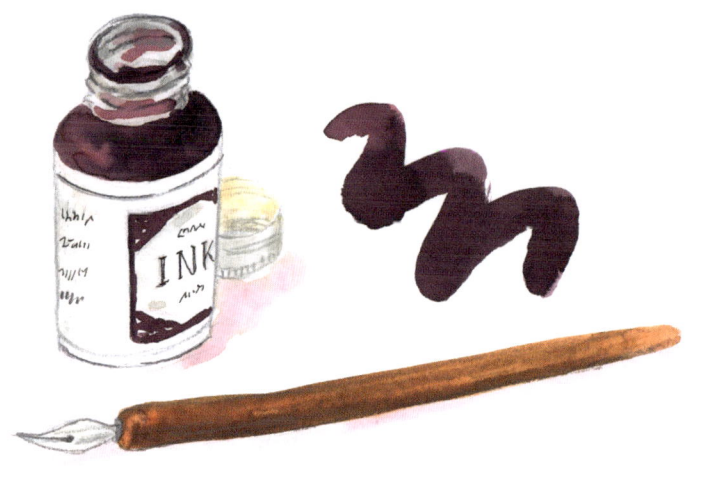

INKS

Inks are great for base layers and work really well with water. You can mix various amounts of ink with water to create a range of saturation, such as the different shades opposite made from 1 to 5 drops of ink.

Ink usually seeps into the paper so a thicker paper stock works best for this medium. Ink is often sucked up quickly by thirsty paper, which can reduce the vibrancy of the colour you see when first applied.

Ink is also perfect for detailed linework that's easy to control. Use it with dip pens or fountain pens – the line weight will vary depending on the pen used to apply it.

Techniques to try

Use a well palette to mix different shades of ink and water, and paint a value study. This is the application of one colour mixed into various shades to create a painting. Limiting the amount of colour you use and instead using just one, mixed in multiple values, can help to understand a composition. Use a photo or existing piece of art as your reference, and start by placing down the lightest tones first and working your way up to the darkest. This is a great way to practise tone in your art.

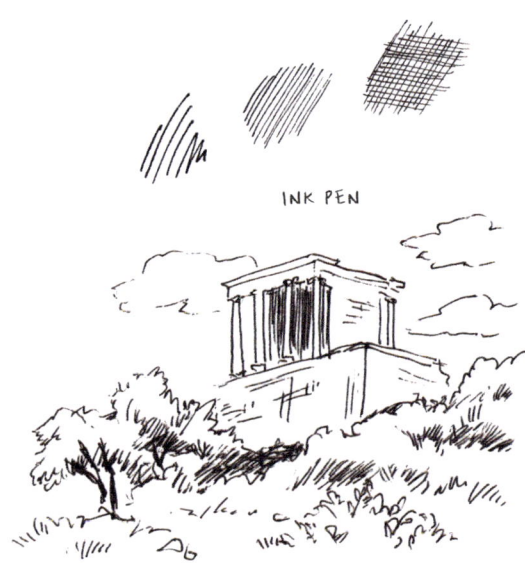

INK PEN

ACRYLIC INKS

Like acrylic paint, acrylic inks can't be reactivated with water, but they are much more fluid than their paint counterpart. They can be applied with a pipette or just with a brush, and are incredibly pigmented. You can water them down or use them straight from the bottle, depending on how opaque you'd like your painting.

Because of their low viscosity, they blend really nicely and it's easy to fill a spread. They dilute well with water, so you'll find a little can go a long way!

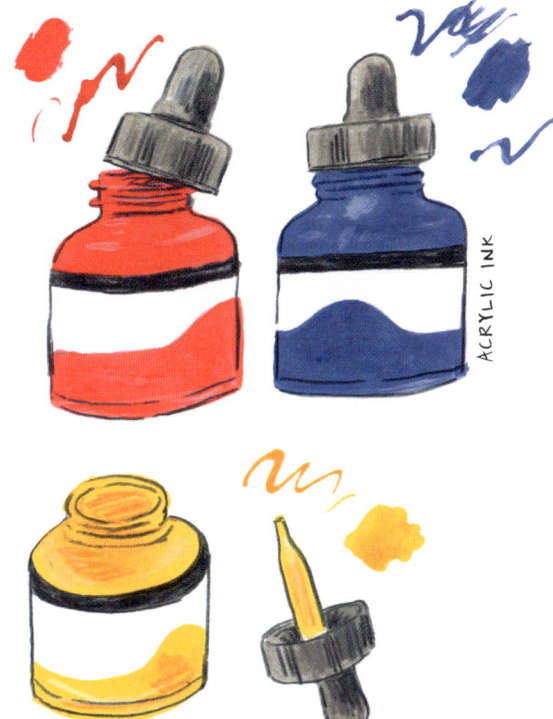

ACRYLIC INK

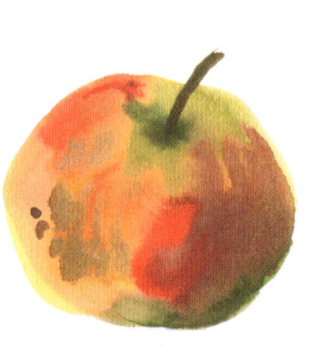

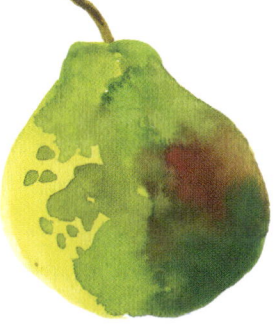

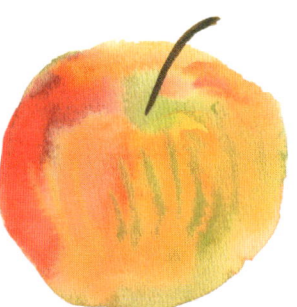

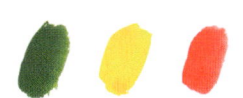

Techniques to try

Try a wet-on-wet technique when painting your subject. Apply a base colour, then add another colour on top before it's dried to see the ink mix and dilute with the colour below.

BRUSH PENS

Brush pens are a really versatile medium, great for linework or putting down blocks of colour. They're easy to carry with you and require no prep, so are perfect for quick sketches or drawing outside.

You may have seen them used for hand lettering, which is a great way to add personality and information to your sketchbook spreads, but they're also fantastic for creating art in their own right. There are many brands of brush pen, usually with varying nib sizes and ink flow, and they often have tapered 'brush' tips.

They are much firmer than paintbrushes and create lines of varying thickness, depending on how much pressure you apply them with. A heavy stroke creates thick lines, while light strokes give you thin lines – and you can easily alternate between the two.

Some artists get frustrated because they don't create a smooth colour, and instead highlight the marks used to apply it. This can vary depending on your paper stock, but I recommend leaning into the texture it creates and working with it. You can either build on top with other mediums or keep it as is and let the texture work with your art.

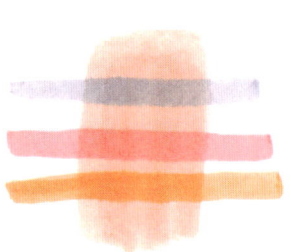

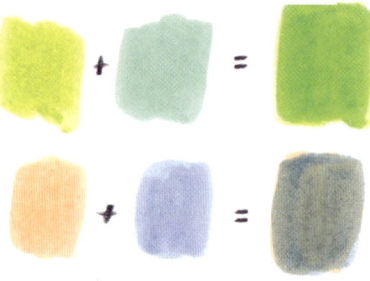

You can also buy blender pens that blend colours together, or for water-based pens you can use water to blend or smudge the colours. Scribbling some marks down on a palette as your 'paint' and then using a paintbrush on it softens the brightness and is a great way to mimic a watercolour effect.

You can overlay a base of brush pens with many mediums, such as pencils and pastels. You can also layer more brush pen on top, which builds the intensity of colour. If you're laying several colours, be sure to work from light to dark as light shades won't show up over dark.

Most brush pens are quite moist with ink, so it's best to work lightly rather than pushing hard. Depending on the type of paper in your sketchbook, it could also result in tearing or pilling (when the paper starts to disintegrate and pick up little specks of paper). This especially happens when adding lots of layers on thin paper.

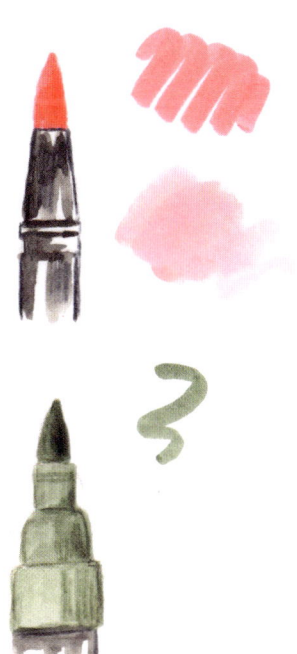

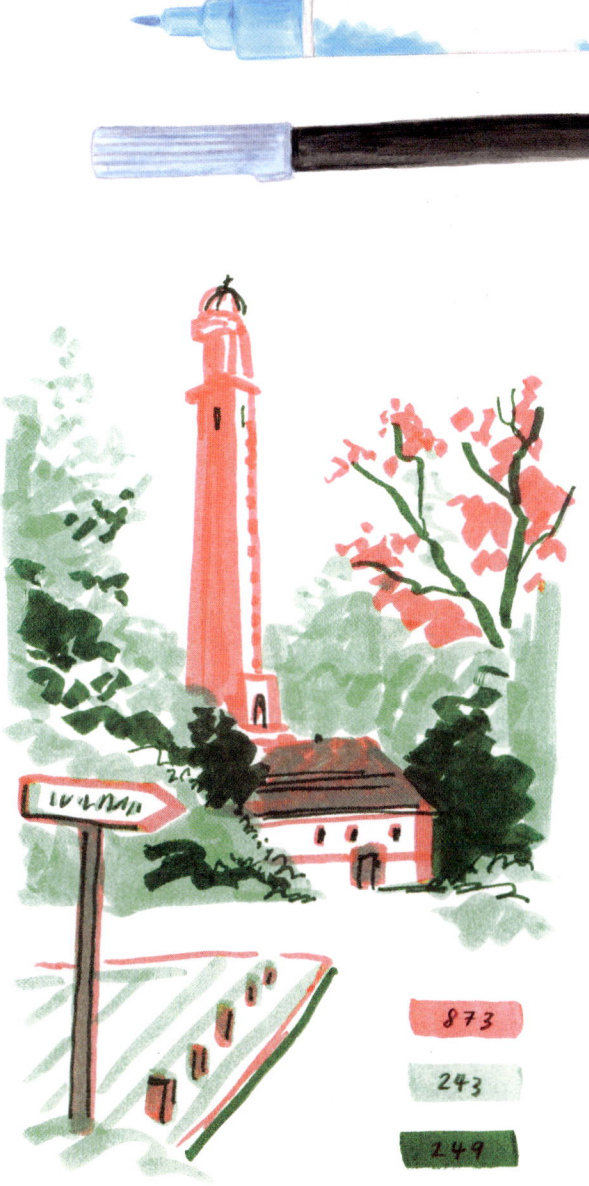

Techniques to try

Layering colours is a really interesting way to use brush pens, and you can create totally different hues! Test it out with a colour palette of three shades, and create a fourth by layering the colours.

873

243

249

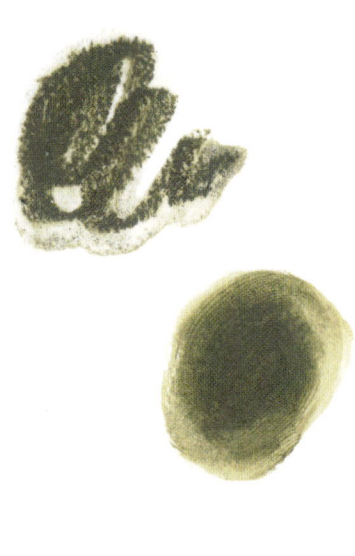

WAX PASTELS

Wax pastels may remind you of the classic crayons you used to create with as a child! While the latter are still a valid art medium, there are also wax pastels that have been created with 'grown-up' art in mind.

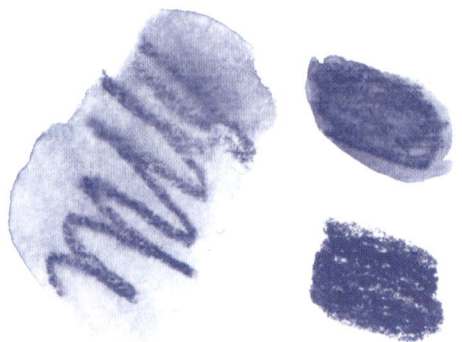

Wax pastels have a binder of wax and oil, compared to wax crayons which are just wax. It means they are softer and easier to blend because of the oil, and great for applying intense colour.

You can also find water-soluble pastels that can be used with or without water. These are more versatile than regular wax pastels, and are a fun way to play with texture. You can apply them as a base layer, scribbling wildly on your page, before transforming the marks with water and spreading out the colour.

I also find the water-soluble pastels useful for softening linework. When applied without water, it creates a harsh line, but this can be softened by applying water on top and smudging the edges. This can work well for feathers or softer textures found in nature.

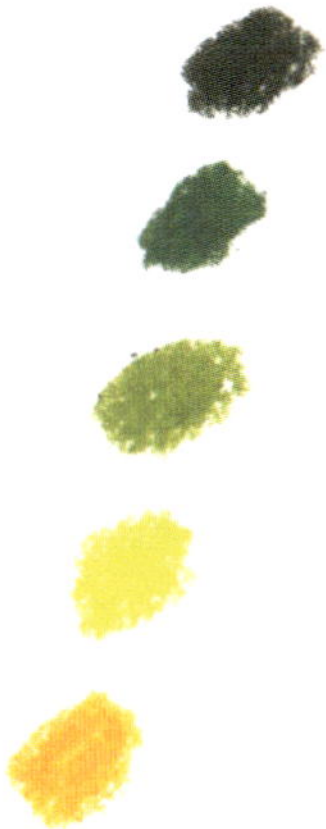

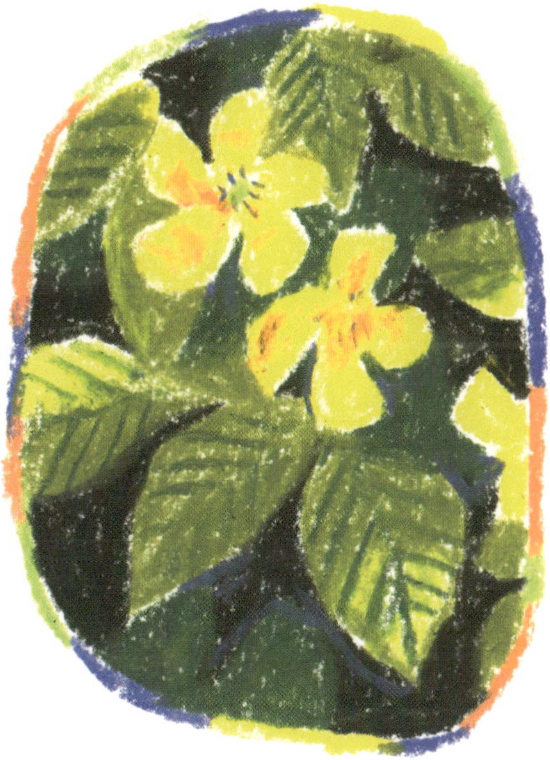

Techniques to try

Use a wet paintbrush to apply water straight into your sketchbook. Then use a water-soluble pastel on top before it dries and see how this softens your linework. This technique plays with the order of applying the water and creates a whole new effect.

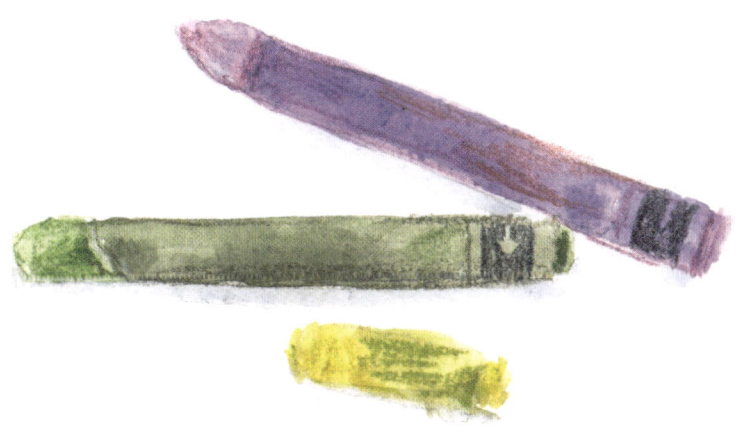

SOFT PASTELS

Soft pastels are a chalk-based medium and often found in stick form or shaped into pans. They are densely packed pigments that can give a great colour pay-off when applied to a spread.

You can use soft pastel sticks for linework or big blocks of colour by filling a page with lots of unpredictable texture. They work well for depicting rough elements like tree bark or stones.

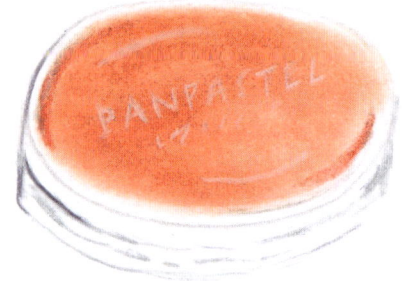

SOFT PASTELS

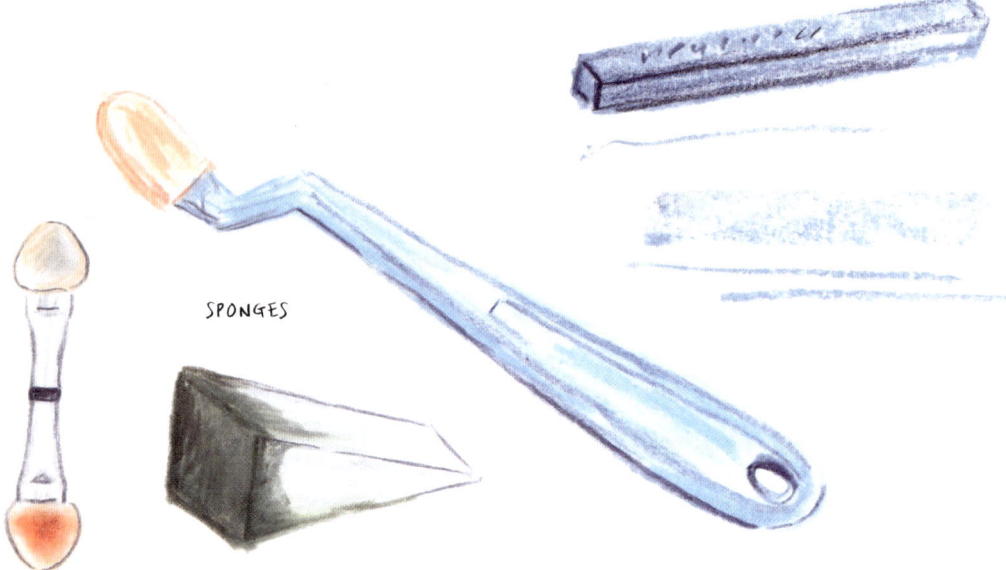

SPONGES

You can also apply pastels with your fingers or a sponge (pan pastels can only be applied in these ways). Make-up or art sponges are a good way to dust on layers of pigment, and these can be continually added to in order to build up colour. Some tools have removable sponges on the end, making application much easier to control and less messy. Often you'll find your hands covered in pastel dust, so these are a good way to keep yourself clean!

Pastels can be smudged and moved long after you've finished your art and closed your sketchbook, making the pigment less strong. You can apply a fixative spray to prevent this happening. Fixative spray is used to keep your marks and colour in place, and is usually applied in thin layers that need to dry between each one.

You can use dry mediums like pencil or wax pastel on top of soft pastels, but be careful with water-based mediums and brush pens, as you'll find the brush or nib will pick up the pastel pigment and could muddy your colours.

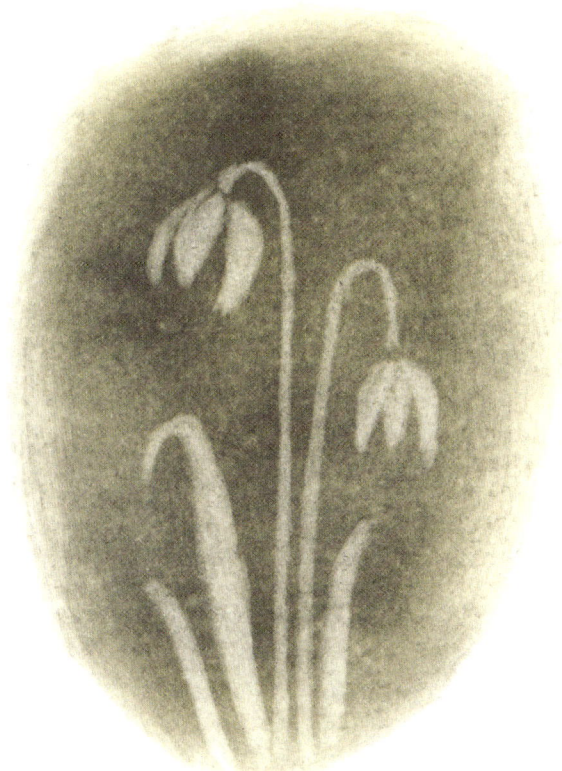

Techniques to try

Try rubbing out soft pastels with an eraser. Lay down a base of colour and then erase any areas you'd like to highlight, or make a motif using the negative space.

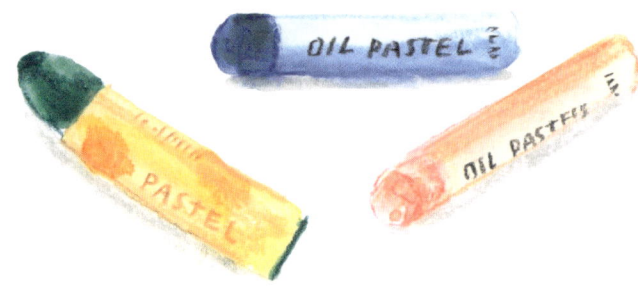

OIL PASTELS

Oil pastels are a unique medium that can create bold, vibrant colours and interesting textures. They are generally applied to the page quite thickly, and the softness of the oil pastel itself depends on the type and brand you use. Higher grade pastels are soft and buttery, and usually blend together and smudge very easily. Lower grade oil pastels are more affordable and rigid, requiring a bit more effort to blend.

They can be used in a variety of ways, such as applying them then scraping away, blending marks together, or applying in dabs for an impressionist technique. Or they can be combined with other mediums like watercolour to create a wax resist effect.

BLENDED   IMPASTO   WAX RESIST

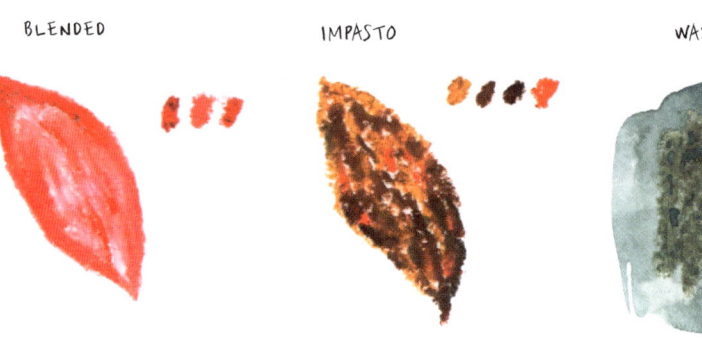

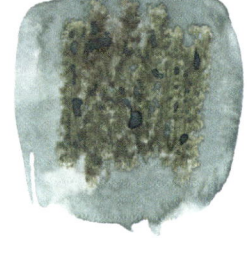

Techniques to try

Test out scratching away the oil pastel to reveal the layer underneath. Begin by applying a base layer using other mediums like paint or pencil, before adding oil pastel on top. Then scratch away the oil pastel to reveal the layer below. In this example, I used a cocktail stick to scratch away the pastel and draw small flower motifs.

SCRATCH AWAY

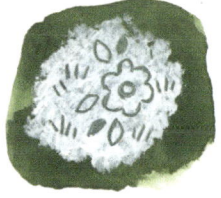

COLLAGE

Collage is a wonderful medium to try out in your sketchbook, and very easy to get started with. You can colour white printer paper with a medium of your choice to create your own coloured papers to cut from, or use recycled paper, envelopes and ephemera to get creating.

You can be more experimental with collage as it is very low risk. As you lay cut papers down, you can move things around and alter the order or add in more pieces. It's less permanent than any other mediums mentioned so far – at least until you stick it down!

It can also be used in conjunction with other mediums. For example, if you've created a painting but are unsure about a specific element, you can test out another idea with collage. This is a separate piece you can try adding on top of your painting, and is an excellent option for testing out multiple ideas before making a decision.

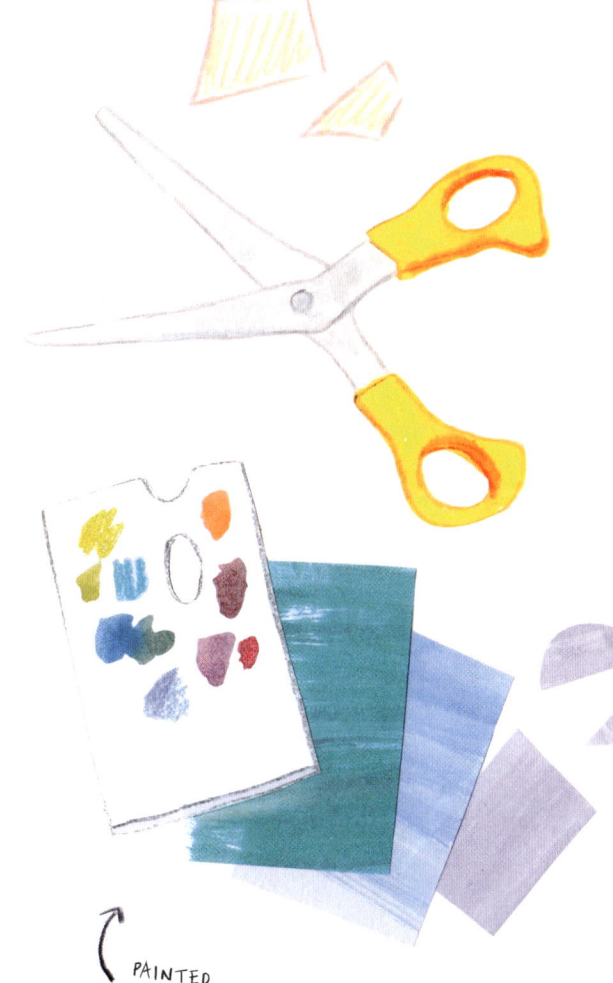

PAINTED PAPER

Techniques to try

Use your paint palette sheets as collage papers. This is a great way to use painted sheets that would otherwise be thrown away, and gives a really unique collage effect with plenty of texture.

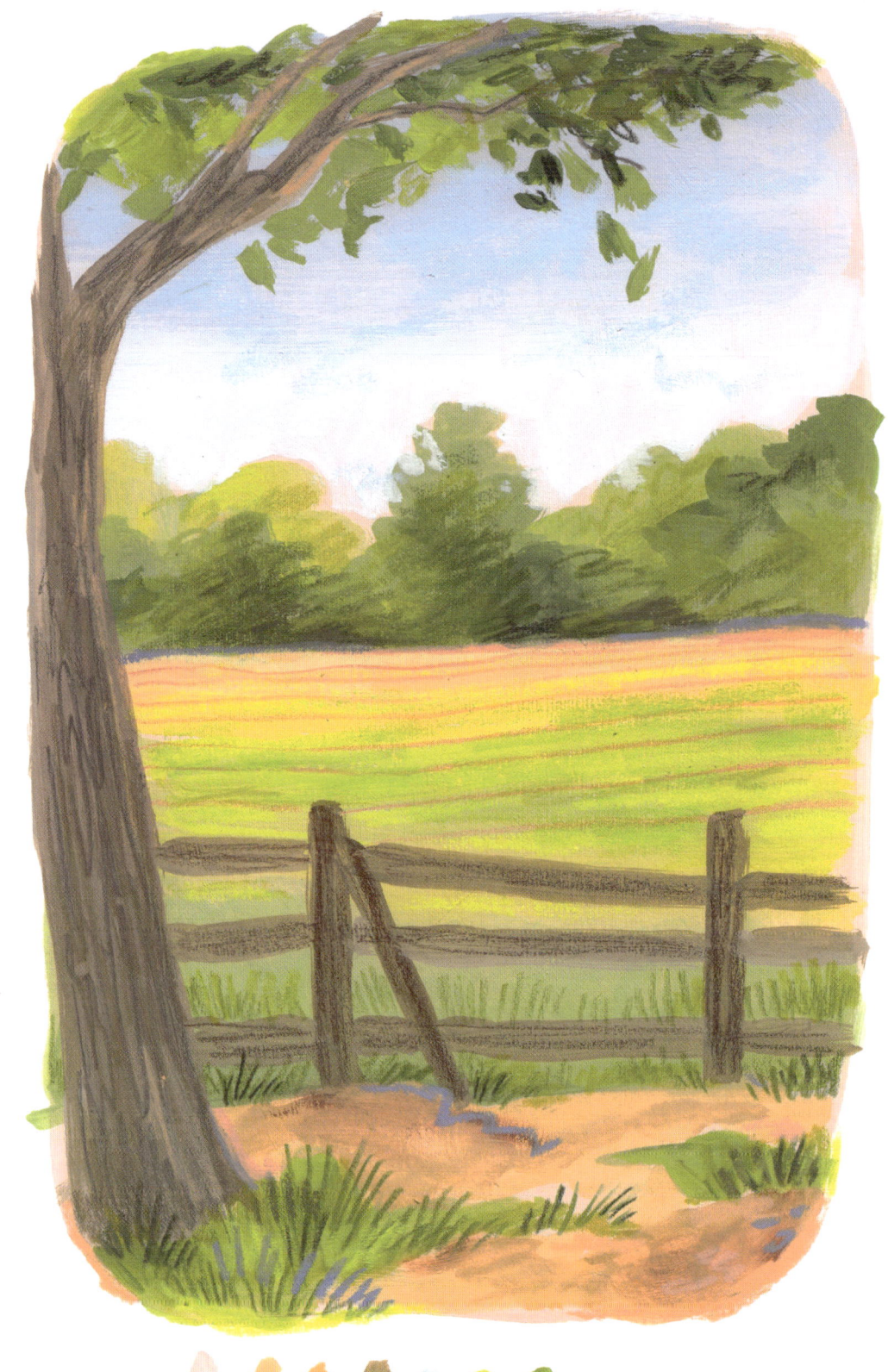

Projects

Now that I've covered the materials and techniques, it's time to see how you can apply them to create finished pieces in your sketchbook.

Each project contains a step-by-step guide but can also be created using different supplies and with different subjects, so you can repeat them time and time again. Feel free to go off-piste and use the mediums and ideas that feel good to you, or follow the step-by-step instructions precisely. Whatever approach you choose, I'm excited for you to create along with me!

Butterflies

Drawing a collection of a subject, whether it's animals, insects or flowers, is a really lovely way to fill a sketchbook spread. Using brush pens means you can lay colour down quickly and then work on top of the shapes, adding more and more detail.

I've chosen to focus on butterflies because they have such vibrant colours and multiple patterns, which creates variety on a spread. You can use reference photographs of butterflies, or simply use your imagination to create your own patterns and colour combinations.

MATERIALS: brush pens, coloured pencils, wax pastels (optional)

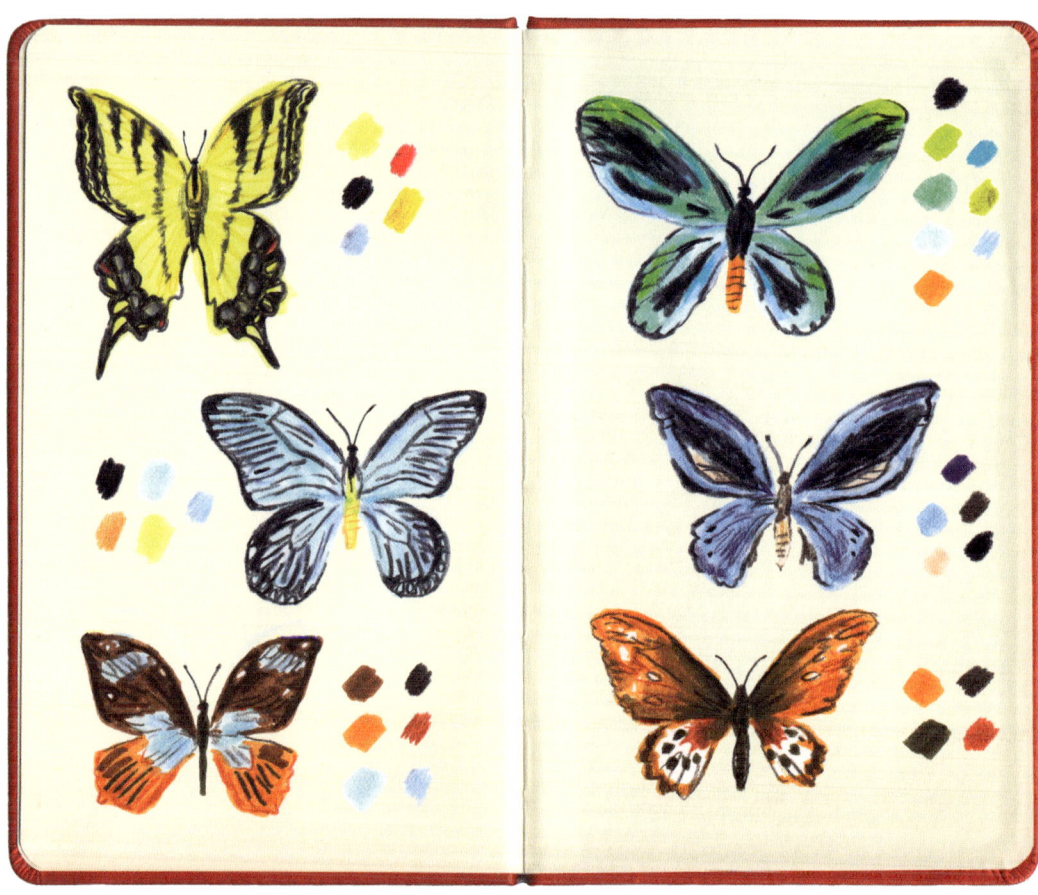

1. Start by drawing out the largest shapes, which are the butterfly wings and the body in the middle. Using brush pens, I started with the lightest colour for the base layer and then added other large sections of colour on top. Focus on the wing shape but don't worry about it being too accurate because you can use the next step to neaten things up.

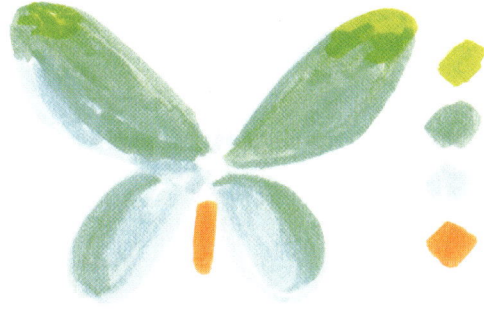

2. Take a dark tone coloured pencil and start laying down patterns on the butterfly. Use the shapes you've already placed to guide your lines, or if they're not quite accurate, draw new lines on top with your pencil. Keep things simple by just using one colour at this stage.

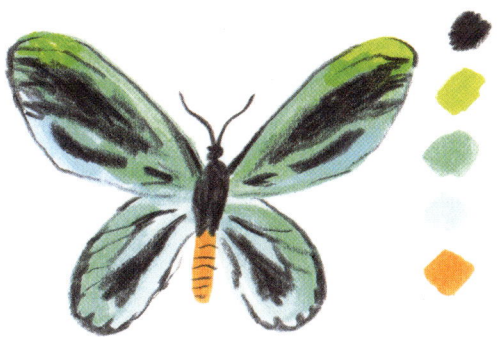

3. Lastly, it's time to add more patterns and details. Use various coloured pencils to add extra colour around the dark pencil you've already placed down. Apply various shades on top to mimic the multiple colours of butterfly wings and bring them to life. If you'd like them to be more vibrant, you could add wax pastels on top to highlight specific colours.

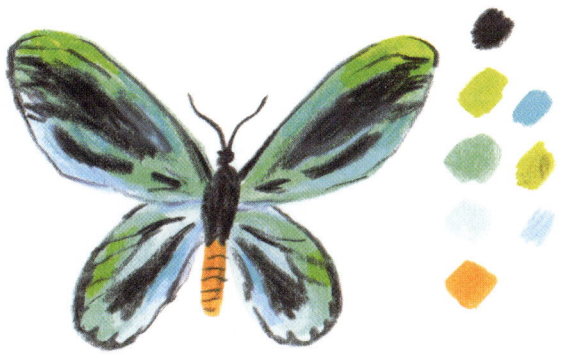

Travel sketchbook

A travel sketchbook is a wonderful way to document holidays and trips in your own unique way. It can be created while on holiday or afterwards by using photographs as your reference. It doesn't matter if it's a recent trip or one from years ago – it's a nice way to relive those memories!

You can use any materials you fancy for travel sketchbook pages and make them work with your style. I love to mix up my materials and sometimes really enjoy a minimal approach, so here's a technique for simplifying busy scenes by creating a fun and full spread.

MATERIALS: ink pen, pencil (optional)

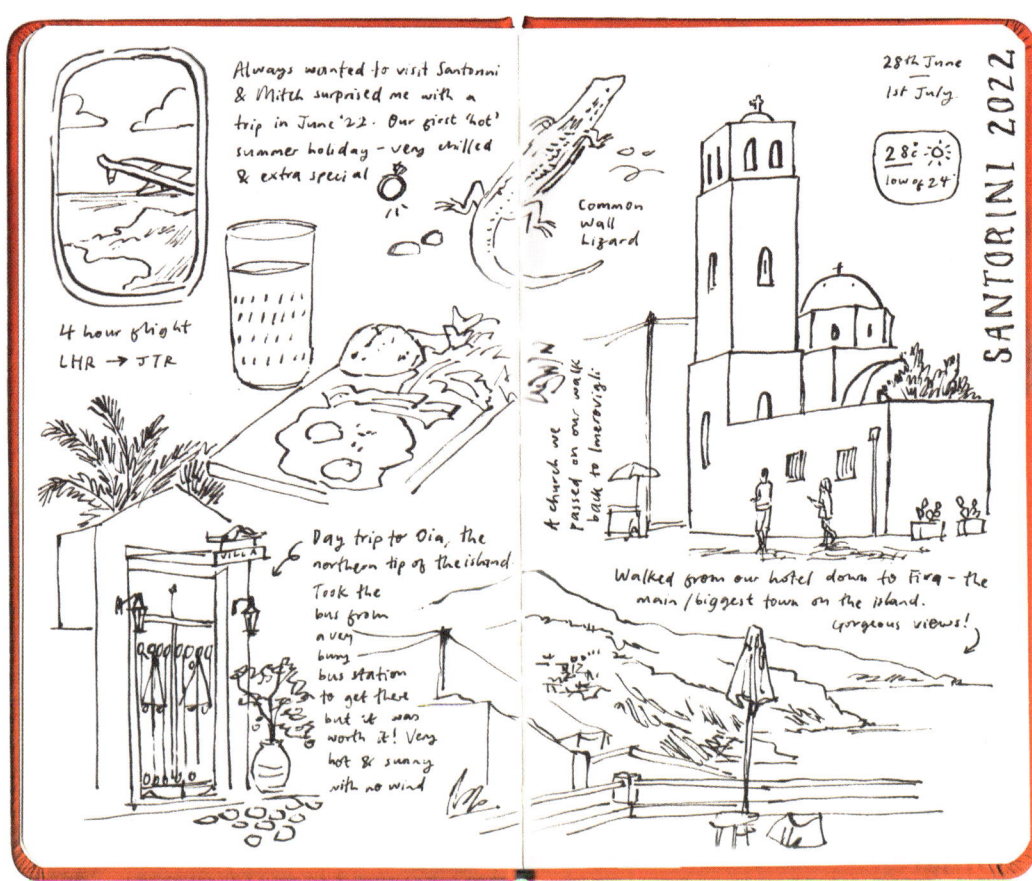

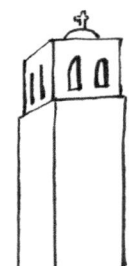

1. Start with the main or most important object you'd like to capture. For me, this is the largest element in the scene, which is the church. Use your ink pen and start drawing from one corner of the subject and work your way down from there. I'm going in without sketching first, but you can also use a pencil to lay down some lines before starting this step.

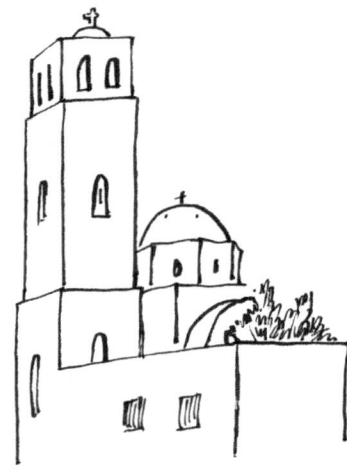

2. Keep things simple by just focusing on the main lines. This includes the outline of the shape and any larger details, like windows for buildings, or trunks and branches for trees. Don't worry if your lines are a little wobbly; it adds a lovely hand-drawn charm to sketches.

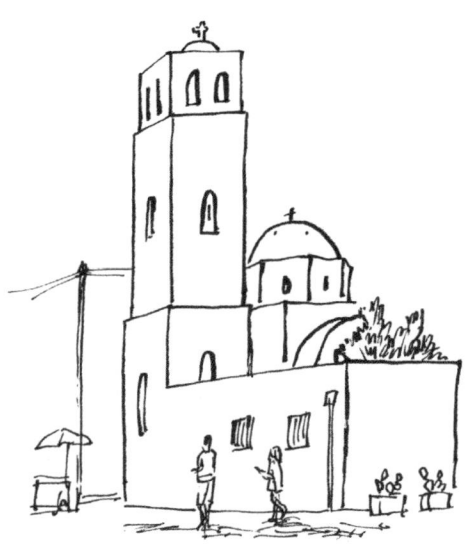

3. Now it's time to expand from the main object and add other elements around it. This helps to build a scene and add life to the sketch. I've included a telegraph pole, people walking down the street and smaller items like plant pots. Use small, scratchy lines for adding shadow or suggesting textured areas like the ground.

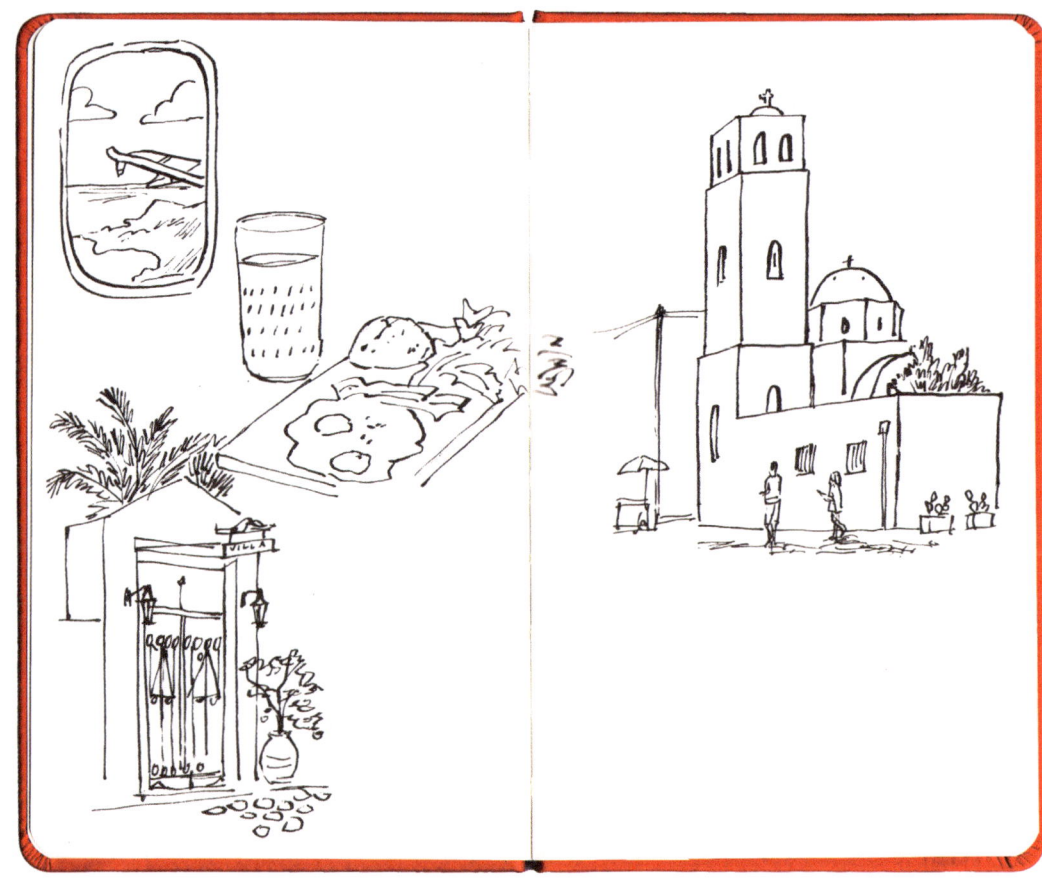

4. Fill other areas of your spread in the same way, with other elements from your trip, and don't worry about any gaps as you'll fill these with smaller drawings in the next step. Keeping things to the corners is a nice way to space them out, or you could even have them go over the central line of the two sketchbook pages if it's something that works in that orientation.

You could draw areas you've visited and loved, or just focus on activities from one day. If you don't have references for things you'd like to include, try using copyright-free image sites to find more generic references that would work, such as for the food you ate, or more popular tourist sites that have been photographed a lot.

5. Now it's time to step back and see how your page is looking. Are there any larger gaps you'd like to fill? Some suggestions for smaller items to draw are wildlife, local flora and snacks and drinks. Include things that make it personal for you, as well as the general scenery. Don't forget to leave some space for journalling, which we'll add next.

6. To finish, it's time to add some writing. This can be brief notes about what you've drawn or more personal anecdotes about things that may have happened on the trip. Write around the shapes of your drawings to create a more organic feel rather than a square block of text. You can also add a title and vary the orientation or style of your writing to make certain words stand out. Including the weather or the date is another way to add more detail to your travel sketchbook pages.

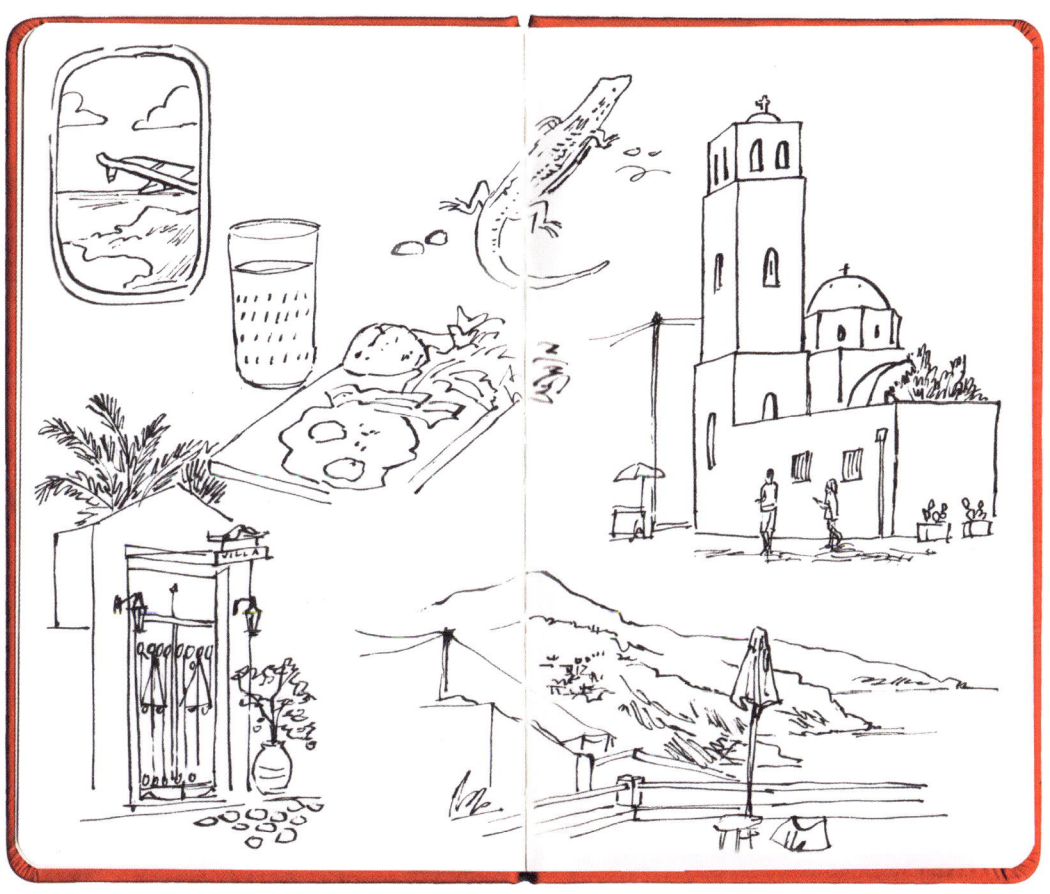

Limited colour scenes

Limiting your supplies and colours is a fun challenge that will push you creatively. It is very easy to grab every colour you have when sketching, but that can also lead to overwhelm, so pairing things right back is a really helpful exercise. These views are drawn from my imagination, but you can also use your own photographic references. If you're using references, a black and white photo will help with this exercise as it simplifies the colours for you!

This project will work with a range of mediums, as long as you have a light, medium and dark tone to work with (make sure the medium you're using for your darkest tone can go over the others, as this will be added last). Your colours don't have to match the original object or scene, so it's a fun way to play with colour palettes.

You will need three tones in total for each scene, and these can be a mix of brush pens or pencils (for example two brush pens and one pencil, or three pencils). The most important part here is to pick three different tones, a light, medium and dark.

MATERIALS: brush pens, coloured pencils

1. Place down a block of colour using your lightest tone. I've chosen oval panels and used brush pens and a coloured pencil to lay this down. Don't worry if there is texture here, such as the overlap of the brush pen – it just gives a base colour to work on top of.

2. Take your medium tone and start drawing in elements you'd like to include. Focus on the shape of the landscape and leave some areas blank so the base colour is showing. Block in only the basic shapes here rather than adding any detailed linework.

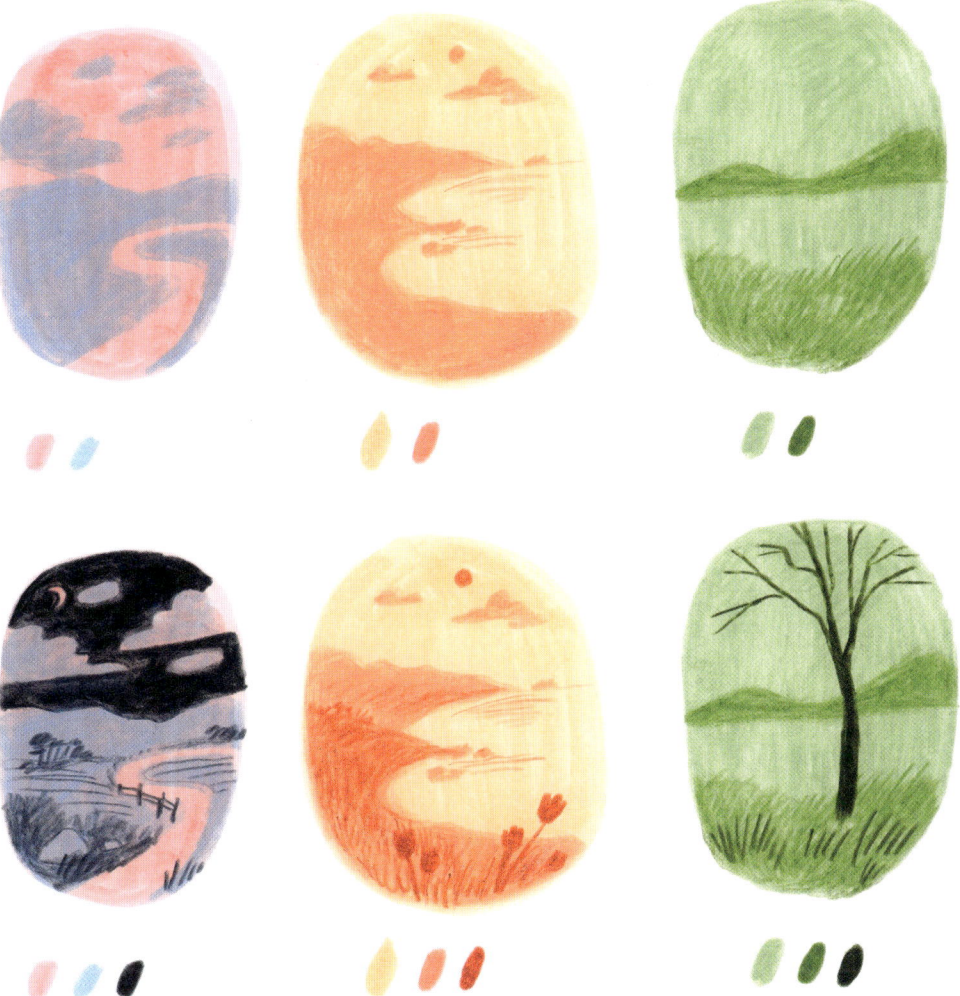

3. Now it's time to add the dark tone. You can use this sparingly, as in the orange scene, to go over areas already added with the medium tone to emphasize texture. You can also add completely new elements, such as the flowers in the foreground.

The pink and purple scene is the most detailed, and I've used the dark tone in a variety of ways. I've turned the sky into a night scene by drawing around elements like the moon and clouds so the lightest colour shows through. I've also drawn on top of the medium tone with smaller elements like fencing, trees and bushes.

In the green scene, I've added one main element with my dark tone, which is the tree, as well as a few lines underneath to give the suggestion of grass. This is a great way to add focus to your sketches. Play around with using just the three tones to highlight different elements in your scene.

Using Google Maps

This project uses a random pin drop on Google Maps to find a reference; in this case it took me to Croatia. Once you've dropped your pin, find a spot on Street View and rotate the camera to find different views to fill the spread. You can also do this project using any landscape reference and focusing on different areas of the image, as the page will be split into multiple panels.

MATERIALS: coloured pencils, acrylic marker

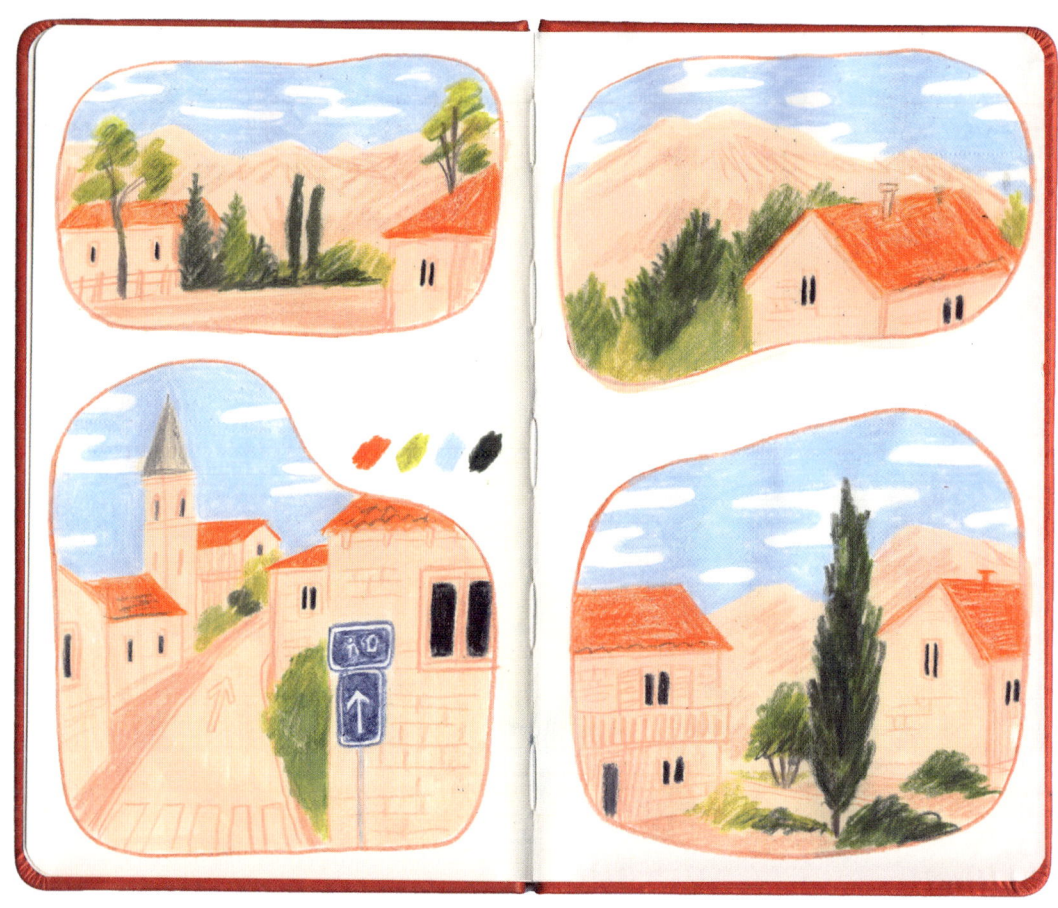

1. Using a coloured pencil, start drawing out the shapes that will work as your panels. Keep these organic-looking by rounding the corners and making uneven shapes.

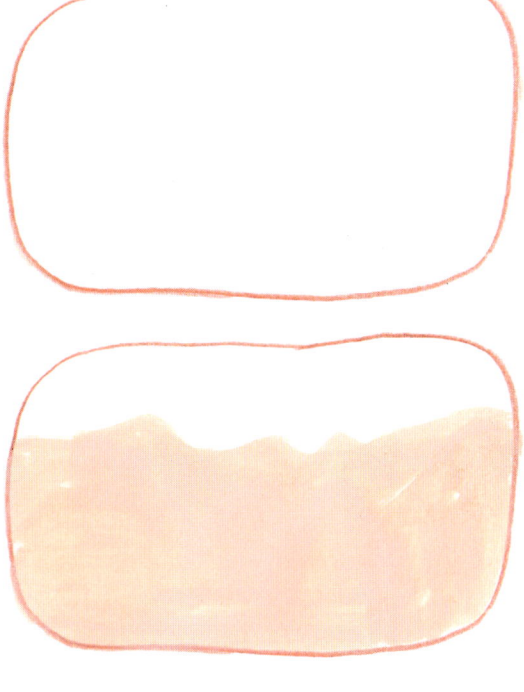

2. Take a light-toned acrylic marker and mark in the large shapes. Apply them to anywhere that isn't the sky – they can denote elements such as buildings, mountains or ground. If you want any areas to be white, such as signs, leave those blank.

3. Use coloured pencils to start blocking in the subjects in your landscape panels. Let the acrylic marker base show through for things like walls, buildings and the ground, and fill in areas like rooftops or foliage.

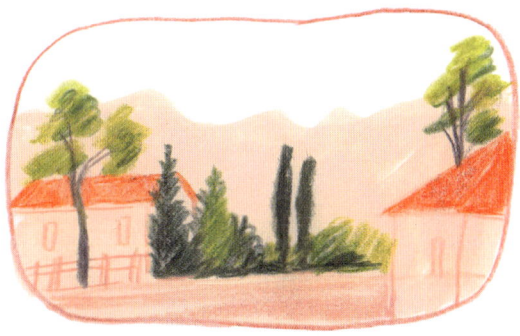

   Use a single colour for all of your linework to distinguish the various shapes, and add details to differentiate areas like brickwork, window frames and kerbs. By simplifying the colours in this way, it helps to create a cohesive, graphic style.

4. Time to add final details like intricate signs and window panes, and fill in the sky! Use a light blue pencil to colour in the area that you didn't fill with acrylic marker, leaving cloud shapes blank so the colour of the paper shows through. Use a dark pencil for windows and the single colour you used for linework to add scribbly shadows and textures to finish it off.

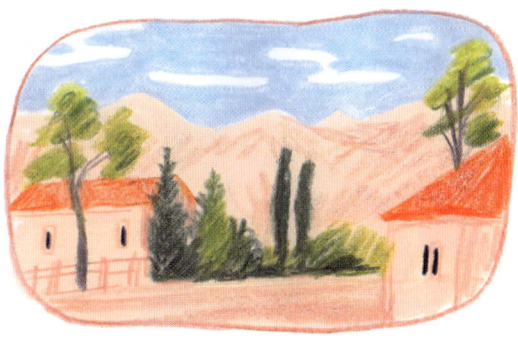

Ink floral

Flowers are a wonderful subject, with plenty of variety to fill your sketchbook spreads. We're using watercolours in this project, which are a great medium for building layers of colour. It works really well with subjects from nature, and it's easy to add other mediums on top for shading and detail.

MATERIALS: graphite pencil, pen with waterproof ink, eraser, round brush, watercolour, coloured pencils

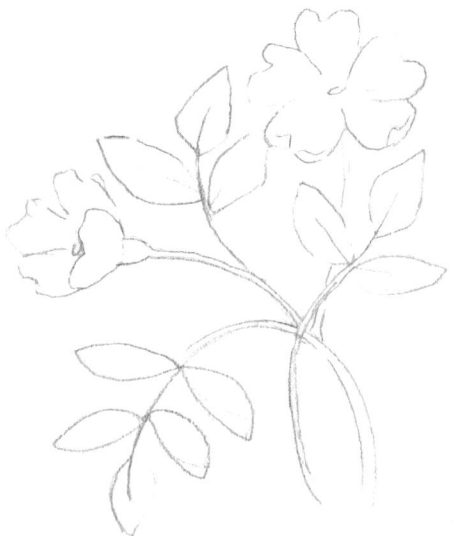
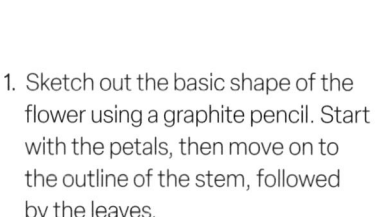

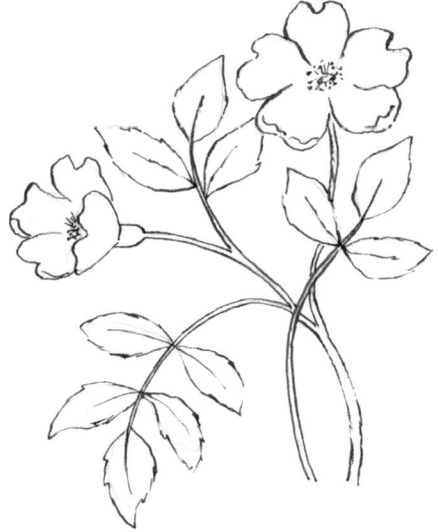

1. Sketch out the basic shape of the flower using a graphite pencil. Start with the petals, then move on to the outline of the stem, followed by the leaves.

2. Using an ink or fountain pen, go over your pencil lines. This doesn't have to be precise, so don't worry if you don't follow them completely. Hold your pen loosely to get more energetic lines rather than wobbly ones. When the pen lines have dried completely, use an eraser to rub out the initial pencil lines.

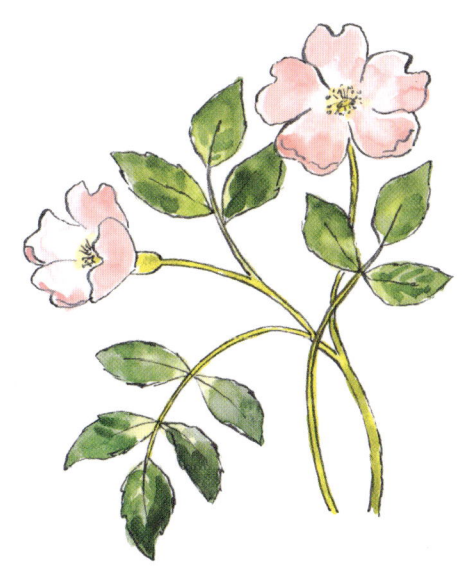

3. Now it's time to add colour. Use your round brush and watercolour to fill in your shapes. Start with the chosen colours of your flower before moving on to your greens, so the flower itself doesn't get muddy. I started with the pink petals and then added the yellow before moving on to the stem and leaves.

Mix up different shades of each colour in your palette to add variation and interest to your painting, rather than using just one flat colour. Adding darker tones of a colour on top of the original makes it feel much more natural and realistic.

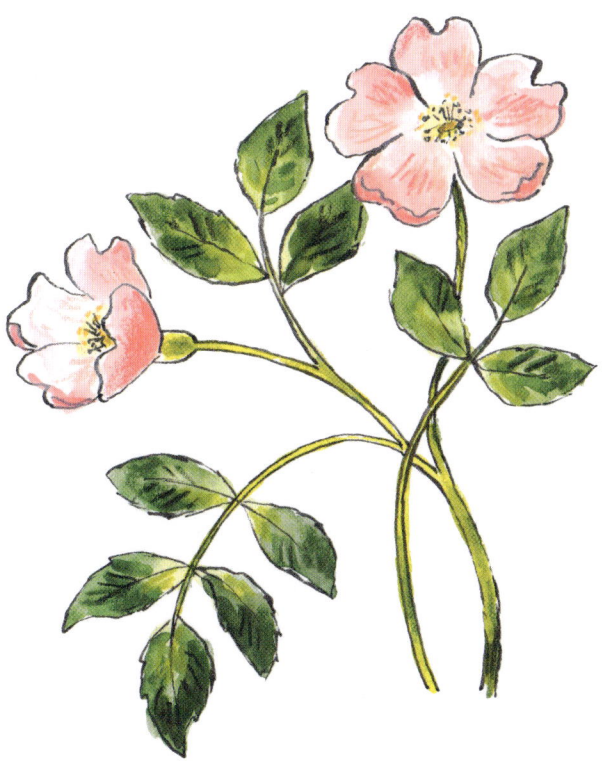

4. Let's bring this flower to life by adding some contrast. This step makes a big difference to the overall look as it helps the sketch to stand out on the page and highlights the details. Using coloured pencils, add smaller areas of colour and texture on top of the petals and leaves. Add linework using your coloured pencils for details like the veins or flower stamens. You can also go over your painted areas to add shading and depth to make the flower feel more realistic.

Visual journalling

Visual journalling is a great way to find connection in your sketchbook, and a good project for when you don't have much time to commit to art. A spread of visual journalling can be added to in small bursts over days or weeks by adding elements one at a time, rather than needing a larger chunk of time to complete a single artwork.

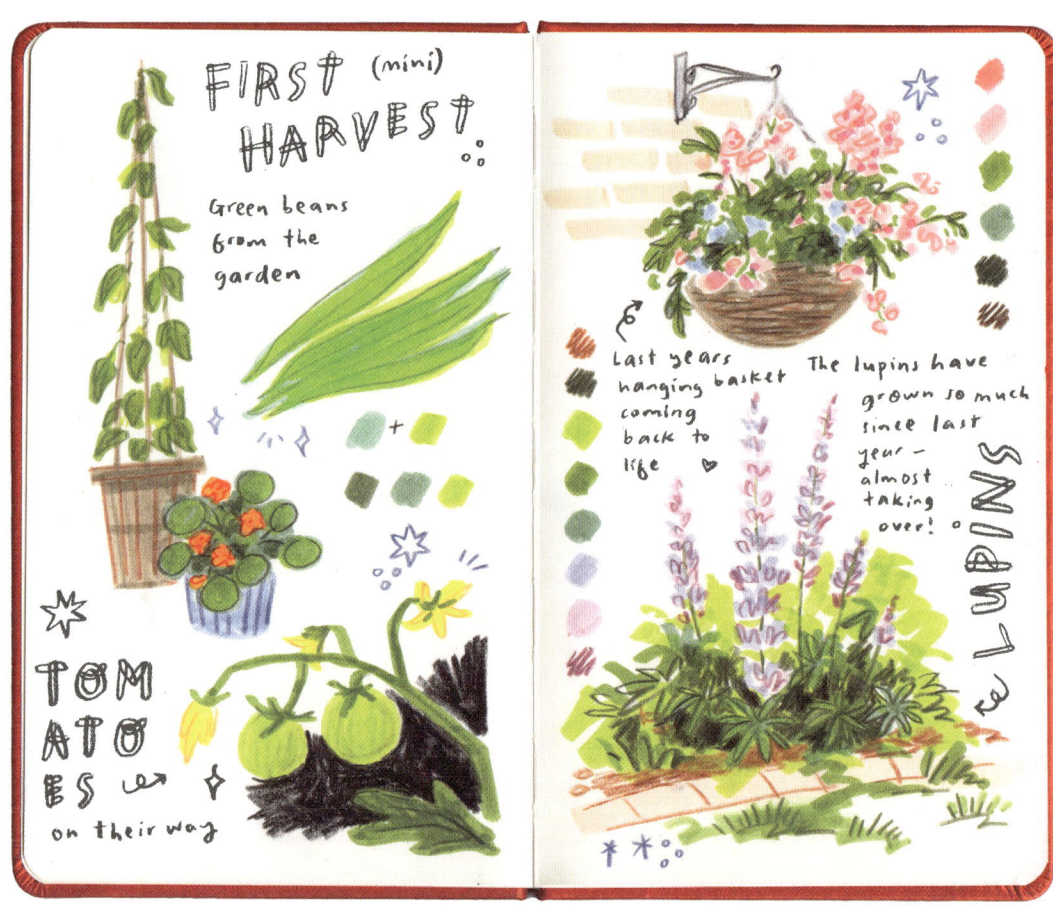

Visual journalling can be based on anything! It could be a diary of your daily life, or it could document a specific aspect, such as the supplies you packed for a trip or the clothes in your capsule wardrobe. The opportunities are endless, but for this project I'm sharing a peek into my garden.

MATERIALS: brush pens, coloured pencils

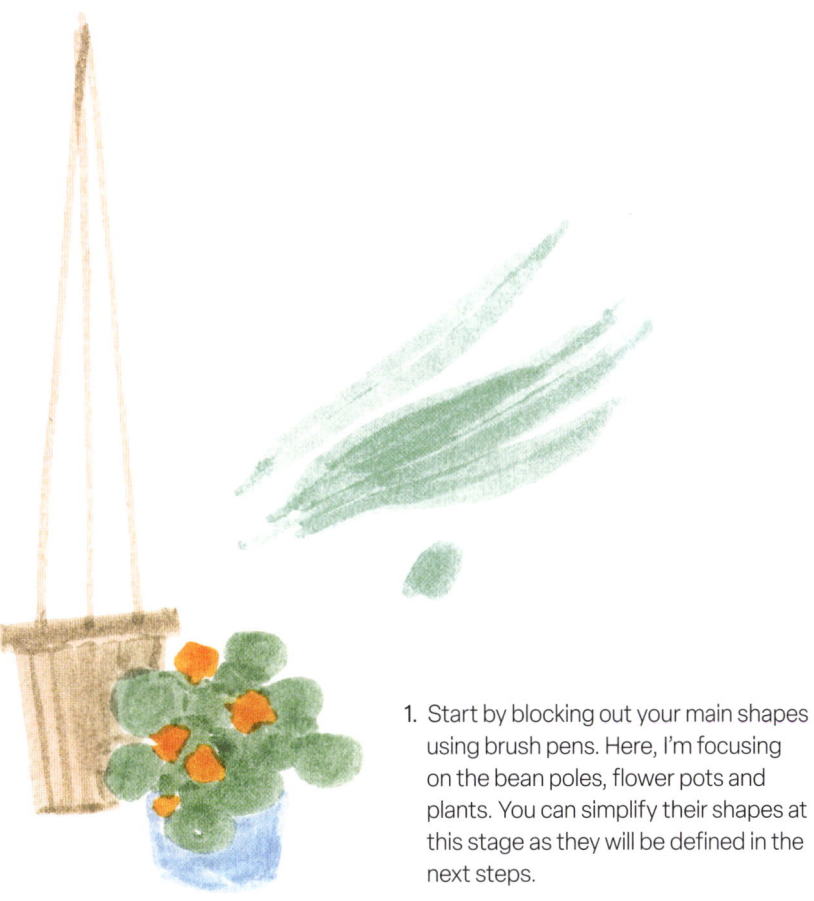

1. Start by blocking out your main shapes using brush pens. Here, I'm focusing on the bean poles, flower pots and plants. You can simplify their shapes at this stage as they will be defined in the next steps.

2. Layering brush pens to create new shades is a fun way to play with this medium. You can see here that I've created a totally new green shade by layering a brighter green on top of the shapes I'd already laid down. You can also use this technique to add shading, so I used a darker green to highlight some shadows in the leaves and a darker brown for the linework on one of the pots. Add any other smaller shapes you'd like to include, which can be layered on top of the shapes you laid in Step 1, or separately.

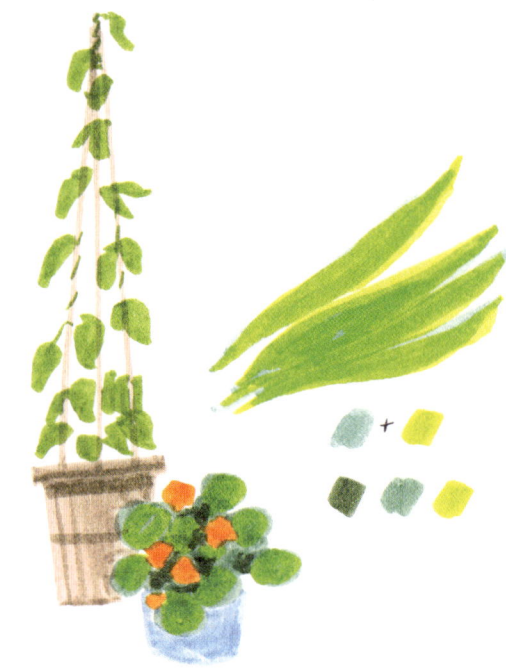

3. Use coloured pencils to neaten up your shapes by outlining them or drawing in extra elements that you couldn't achieve with the thicker brush-pen nib. I've outlined elements with a colour that is darker than the brush-pen colour underneath, but you could use just one dark tone for all of it if preferred.

You can see on the green beans where my lines don't match perfectly with the shape I laid down using the brush pens.

Having the colour outside of my lines adds extra character and creates a fun effect!

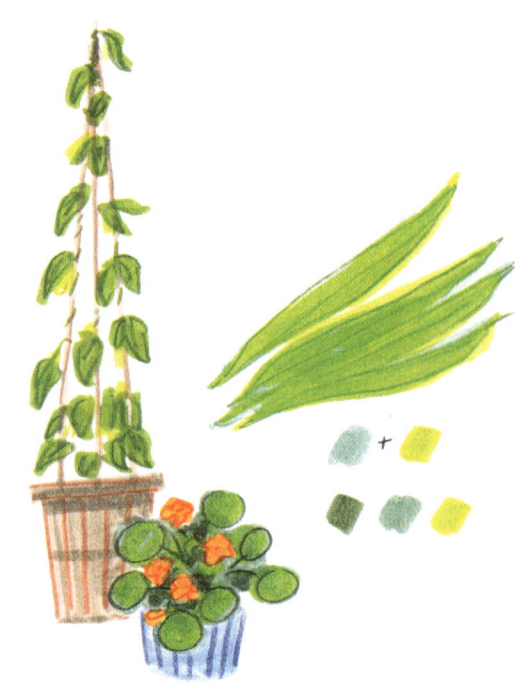

4. Finally, it's time to add the journalling element of your visual journal. In the same way as the travel sketchbook project on page 98, this can simply consist of labelling the things you've drawn, or more personal reflections and notes about your day. You can also add playful elements like doodles or different typographic styles.

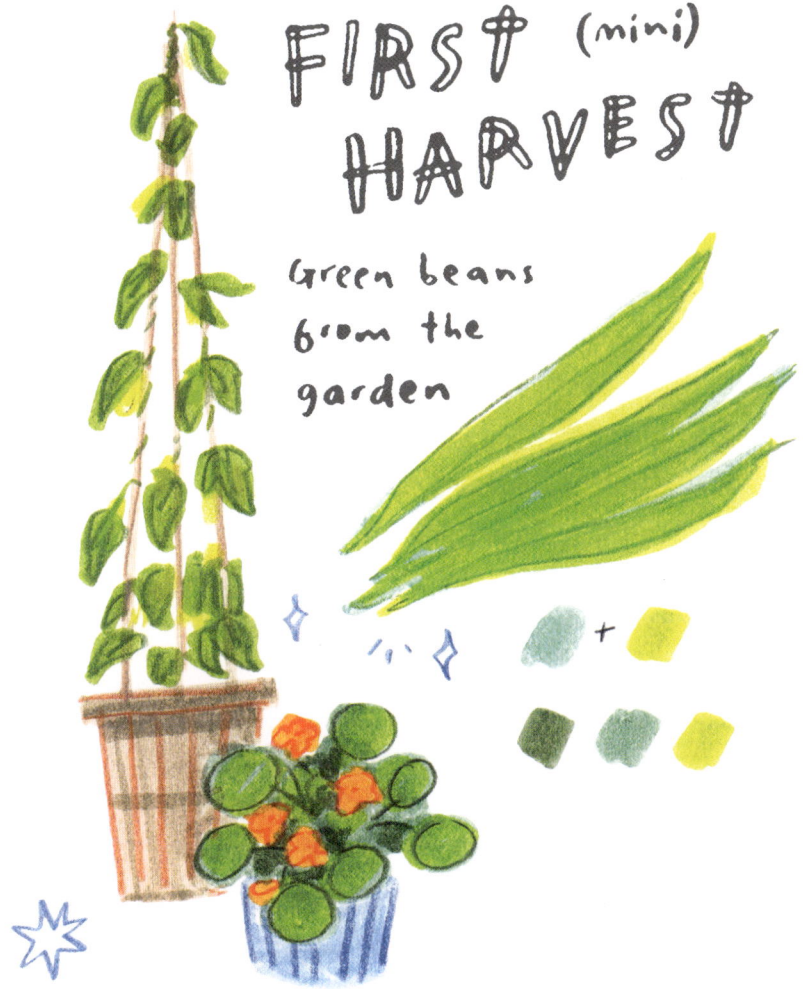

FIRST (mini) HARVEST

Green beans from the garden

Beach

Acrylic paint is a great medium for landscapes, creating an opaque layer to work on top of. I love painting beaches and coastal scenes with a summery colour palette, and the use of a block colour as a base layer adds richness. This project highlights how much this can affect the atmosphere of a painting – here, I've used a bold but warm colour that influences the overall colour and feel of the final piece.

You can do some quick thumbnail sketches to determine placement before you start painting your composition. My thumbnails here show a zoomed in and zoomed out option.

MATERIALS: acrylic paint, flat brush, small round brush, coloured pencils, wax pastels

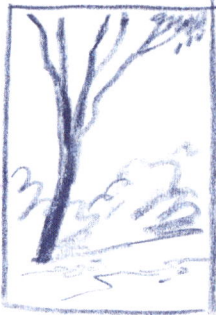
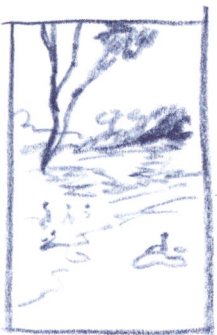

ZOOM IN   ZOOM OUT

1. Start by laying down a rounded rectangle with your main base colour using the acrylic paint and flat brush (see page 48). You can experiment by using both cool and warm colours to see how it alters the final painting, but here I'm using a warm, bold pink shade. If you'd like a more subtle effect, use a lighter base colour.

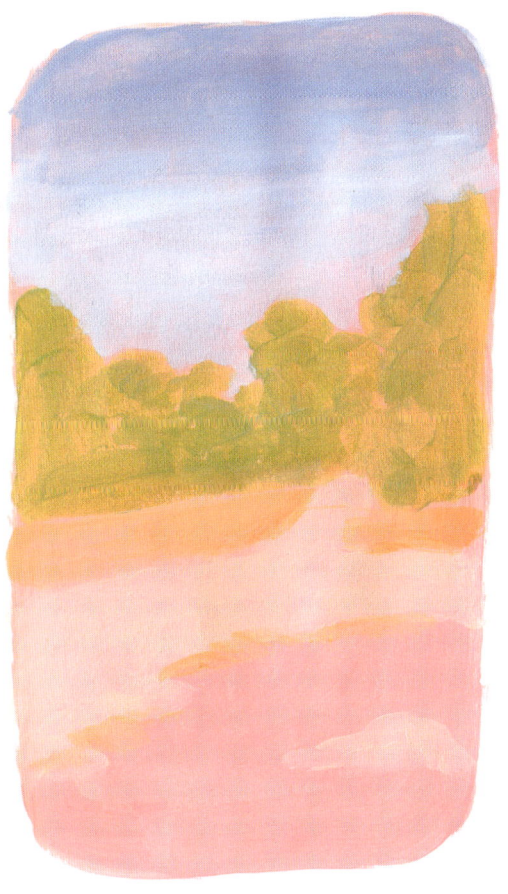

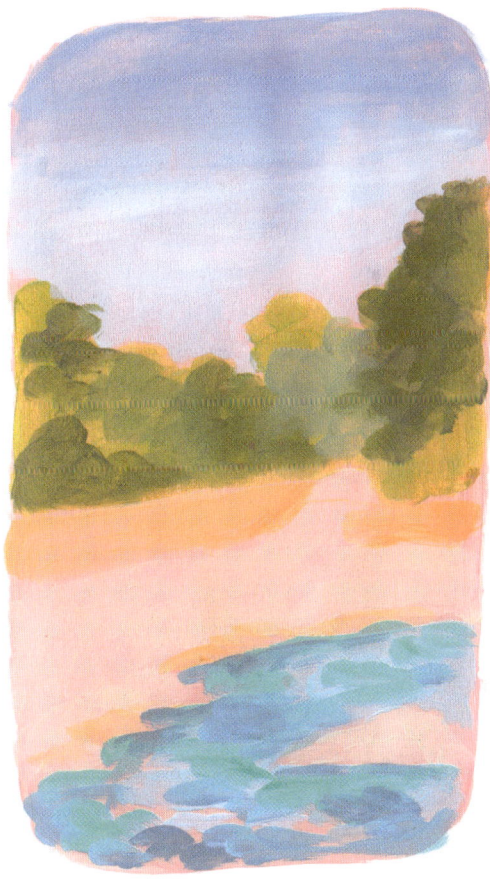

2. Once that's dry, start blocking in the main shapes with light colours. Don't worry about individual elements here, and merge similar colours together, such as simplifying the bushes and trees into one green shape. I've also added a subtle gradient to the sky. It's nice and clean because the acrylic paint underlayer is completely dry and can't be reactivated.

3. Now it's time to add in your mid-tones and your textures. Here you can start defining the individual elements on top of the layers placed down in Step 2. Vary your tones to pick out different trees and bushes, and add other colours you can see in the reference, like the turquoise of the water.

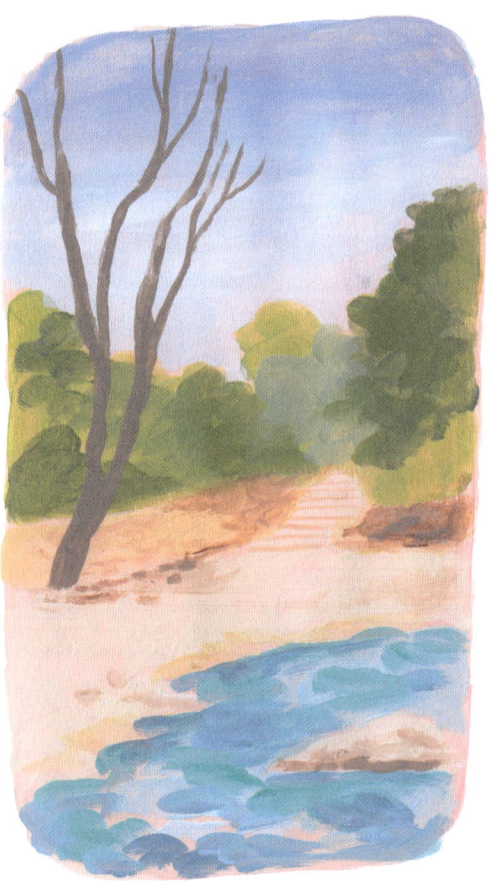 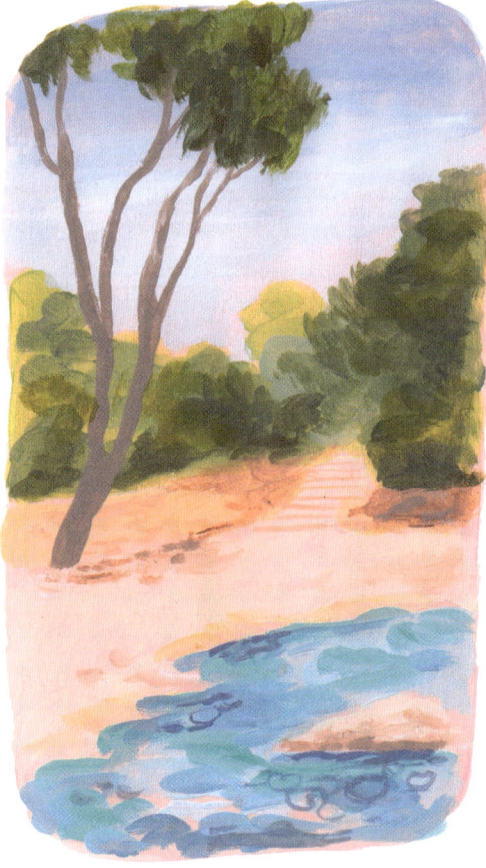

4. Using a small round brush, start adding smaller details such as shadows and textures, and bigger, more detailed elements such as trees.

5. Now onto dark tones. I find building up tones in this way, from light to dark, to be a good way to add richness and depth to a painting. Use this step to build up more of the textures, and to work on top of any elements you previously added, such as leaves to the main tree.

6. Once all your acrylic layers have completely dried, you can add coloured pencils on top, enabling you to add more defined details. Use scribbles and scratchy lines to add a bushy texture to trees and greenery, as well as adding elements like people and animals.

I've added a sunbather to this beach, which works well over the light colour of the sand. If you're working on top of a darker colour you may want to use a small brush and acrylic paint instead of pencil so the colour of the added element is more opaque and stands out.

7. Lastly, add a pop of colour with wax pastels. Use bright shades such as pink, violet or lime green to highlight areas around the painting. Use this sparingly with small strokes to enhance the piece rather than hide the texture and detail you've built up. This step finishes off paintings really nicely.

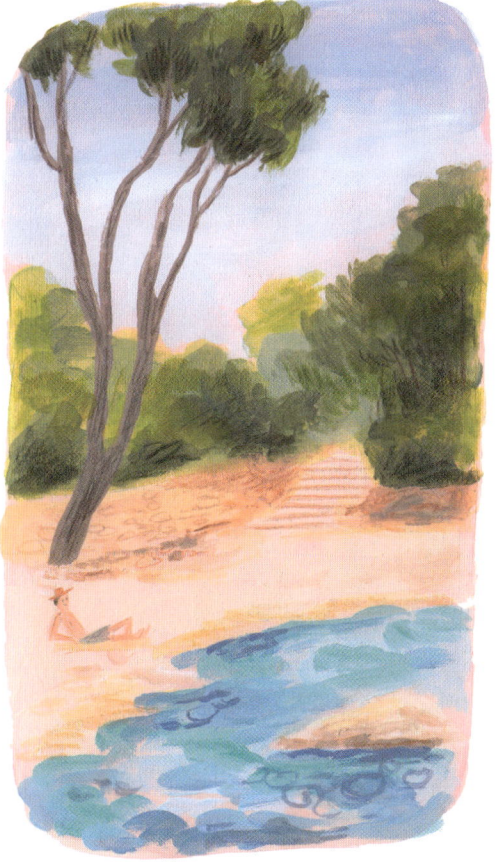
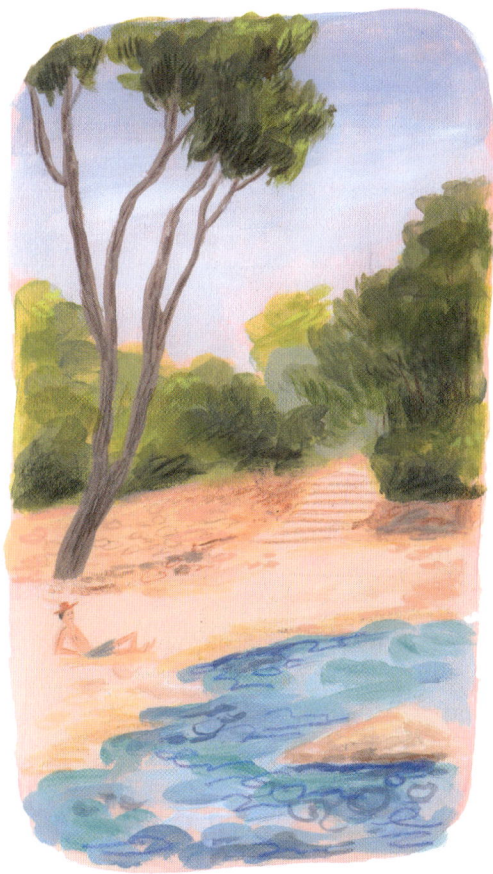

Observational Study

Observing from life, rather than using photographic references, is a great exercise requiring you to convert a 3D object into a 2D drawing in your sketchbook. It also gives you more control over angles, and you can make your sketchbook more personal by drawing things that mean something to you.

In this project we're focusing on mugs – a good subject for practising pencil control and curved lines, and you can also have fun with colours and patterns. Try out various mediums for this exercise; here, I'm using watercolours.

MATERIALS: graphite pencil, watercolour, round brush, coloured pencils

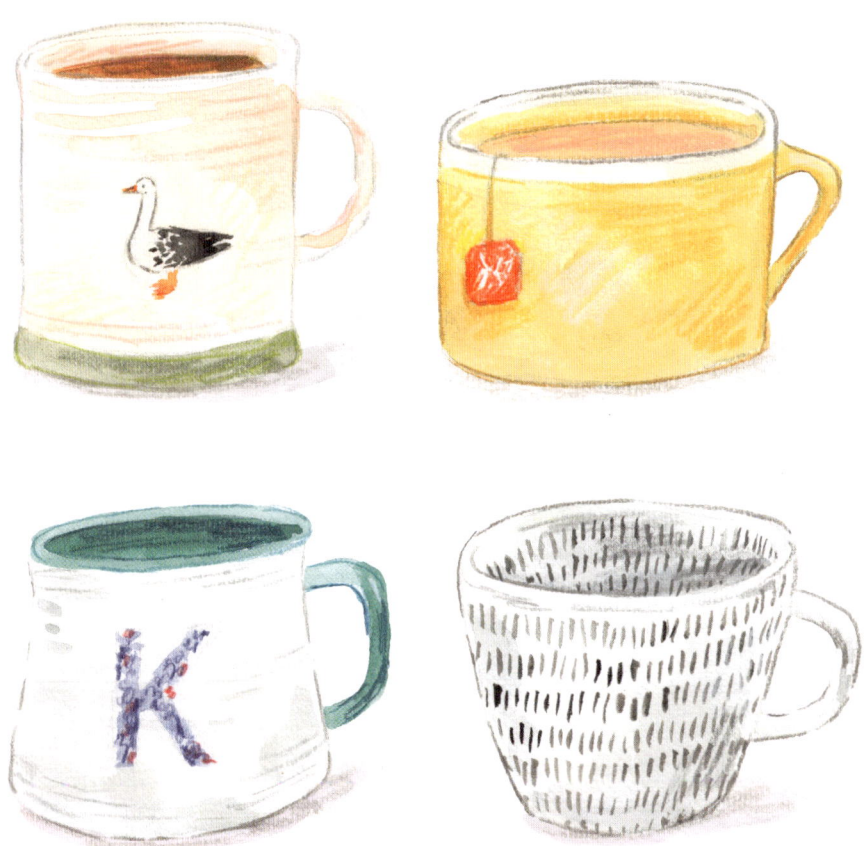

1. Start by using a grey pencil to draw the outline of your mug. Rather than doing one solid line, hold your pencil lightly as you sketch out the main shape. You can make multiple lines until you get the curves right, and these outlines will guide you to as to where to place colours in the next step.

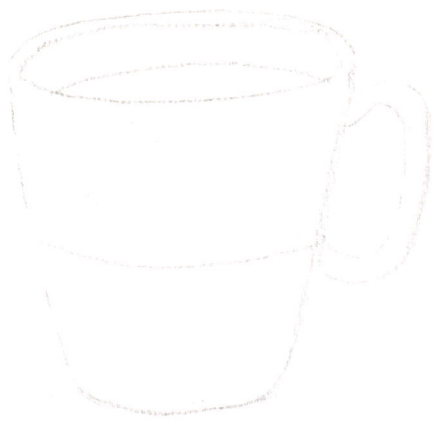

2. Mix up the various watercolour shades you need for your particular mug. Focus on the main colours and patterns and work on top of your sketched lines. Mix up a light grey with a bit of purple, and use a wet round brush to add a shadow to the base of the mug.

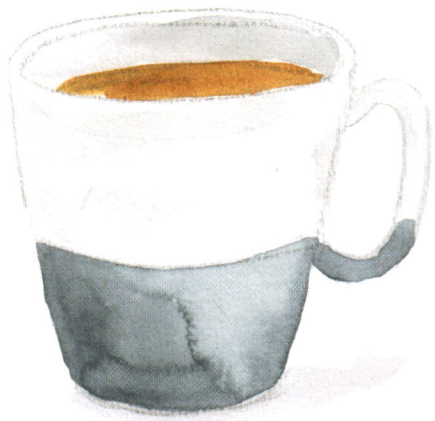

3. Lastly, it's time to add smaller details. Once your paint layer has dried, take some coloured pencils that are slightly darker than the watercolours you placed down. Add scribbly lines for texture and interest, as well as elements such as text or fine details. Finish by using a darker tone pencil to outline the final mug shape.

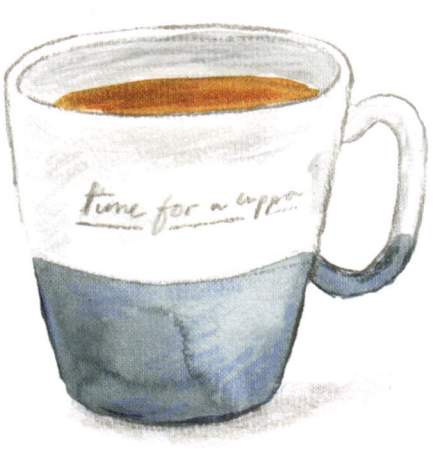

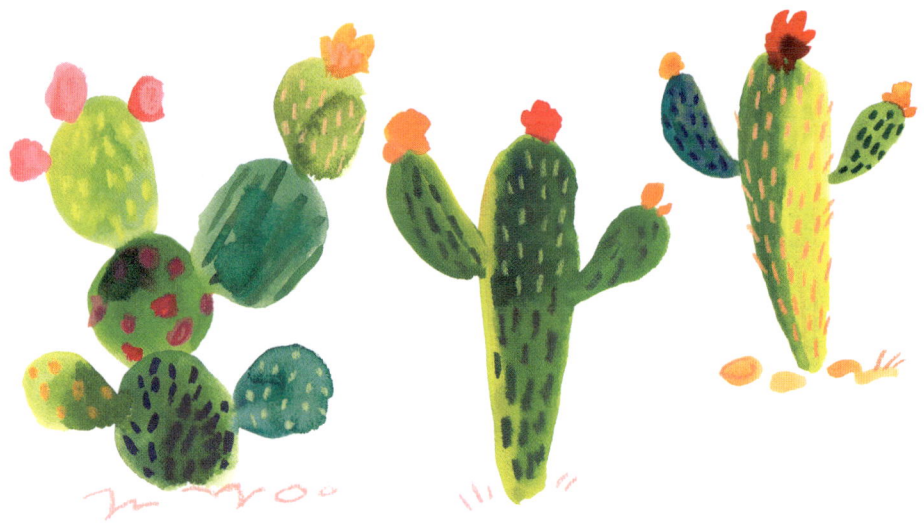

Cacti

This is a really fun project, perfect for playing with wet mediums like ink, and great for filling a sketchbook page with vibrant, eye-catching colours! Cacti are ideal subjects for drawing from your imagination, and for playing with pattern and colour too.

MATERIALS: acrylic ink, round brush, coloured pencils or wax pastels

1. Mix up a light green shade in acrylic ink, using the round brush, and paint a shape for the main trunk of the cactus.

2. Create dimensionality by adding a darker green brushstroke to one side. You don't have to wait for the first layer to dry for this step; using the wet-on-wet technique will create softer blending.

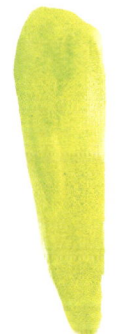

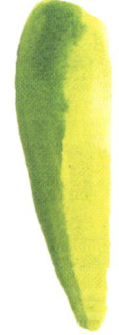

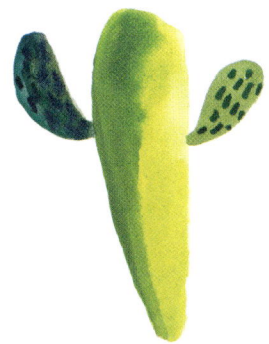

3. Now for the arms. Mix up different shades of green to add interest and variety, and paint in two organic shapes, one on either side of the main trunk.

4. Time to start adding patterns. You can be playful here and use unusual markings, or stick to a familiar cactus pattern of stripes and spikes. On the left arm you can see where the ink underneath was still wet when I applied the next layer so the marks are not as defined, whereas on the right they are clearer because the ink had already dried.

5. Use your inks to mix up reds, pinks or oranges to add the cactus flowers, and don't forget to add the suggestion of ground. I like to do this with wavy lines and ovals to represent stones.

6. It's time for the fun part! Grab your coloured pencils or wax pastels and add further patterns once the ink layers have completely dried. Use contrasting colours such as pink or blue for a whimsical touch.

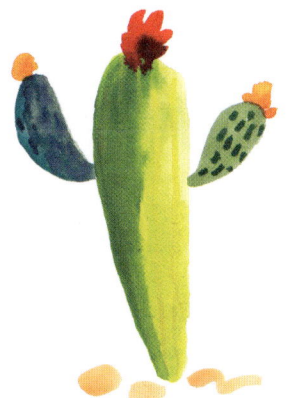

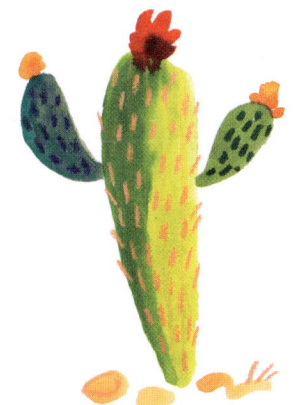

Wildflowers

Wildflowers are often overlooked but can add a huge amount of colour to nature scenes. I love painting them because of their organic shapes, and I'm always photographing them when out on a walk to reference later. Even weeds like dandelions or bindweed can be an effective subject to paint in your sketchbook.

I'm using gouache for this project, but watercolours would also work well.

MATERIALS: coloured pencils, gouache, round brush

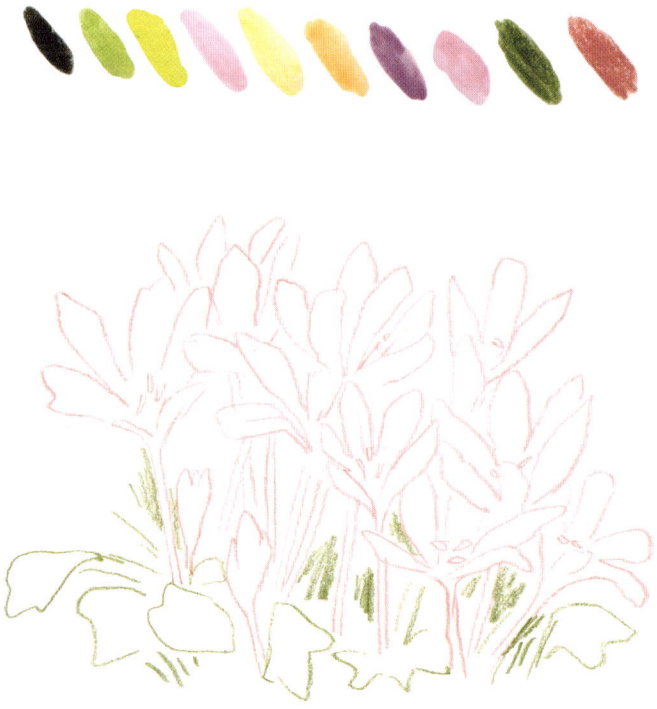

1. Start by sketching the outlines of the flowers and leaves. Instead of using a graphite pencil to erase later, I'm using coloured pencils that correspond to the colour of the area I'm referencing. The lines will be visible in the final painting, so they add definition but don't detract from the colour or subject.

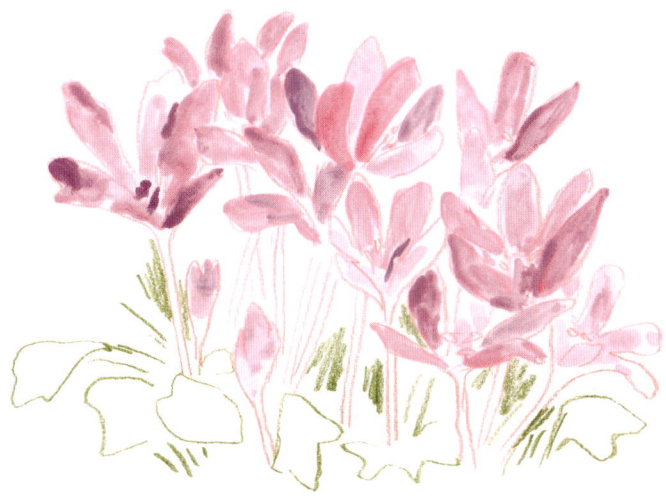

2. Mix up the colour of your flower, using gouache and your round brush. We'll be adding this first to keep it nice and clean before adding the greens later. Mix up different colour tones by adding white or using more or less water on your brush; you want lots of variation in the petals rather than one block colour. You can also alter the tone slightly, for a touch of realism, in this case adding a bit more pink to the purple for some of the petals.

Use the length of the bristles on your brush, rather than the tip, to place down your paint, and don't worry about staying within the lines or filling in every white space.

3. Continue in this way, mixing up different values of your petal colour and filling in any gaps. Then mix up a yellow for the stamens of the flowers, as well as a light green to fill in the stems.

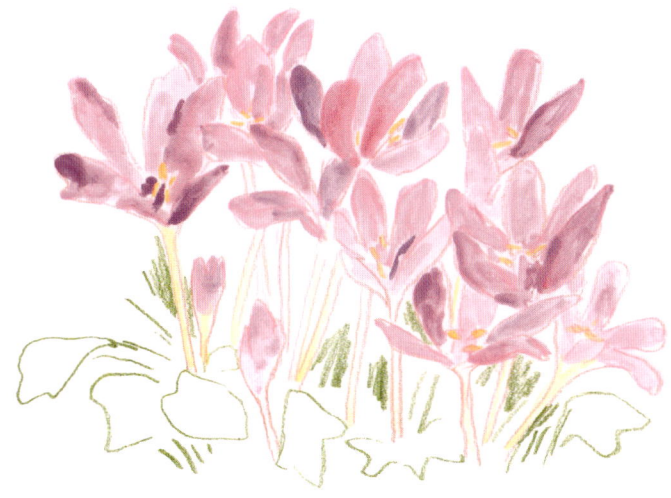

4. Now it's time to add the rest of the greens. In the same way as the petals, mix up various shades as you fill in the leaves. Go back and forth continuously to your palette to mix in more yellow or green to vary the tone. You can also go outside of the leaf lines you drew earlier to suggest more ground or foliage around the base of the flower. This creates a more organic feel.

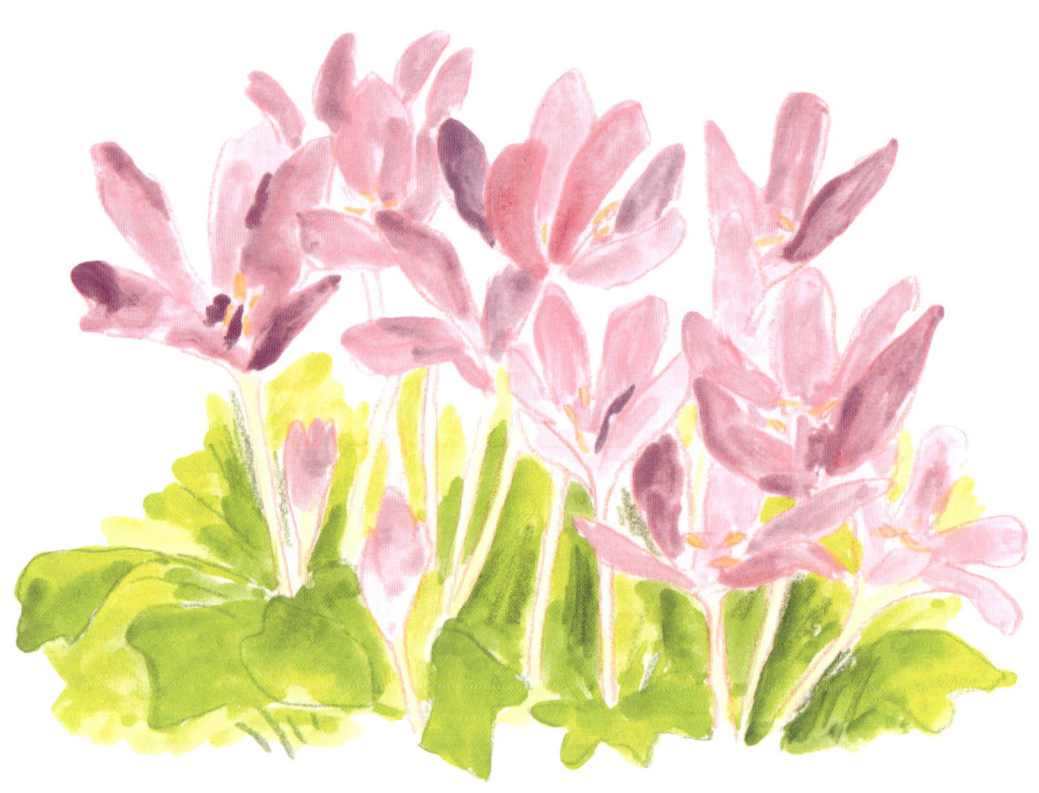

5. Once your paint layers have dried, it's time to use your coloured pencils to add contrast in a darker tone. This is a really pivotal step in the painting as it stops the subject from looking flat and boring.

Use a darker tone that matches the colour of your flowers to outline some of the petals again, and to add some lines in the middle of the petals for texture. For the foliage, use a dark green to colour around the leaves and define the base of the stems, and a mid-tone colour to add the leaf veins.

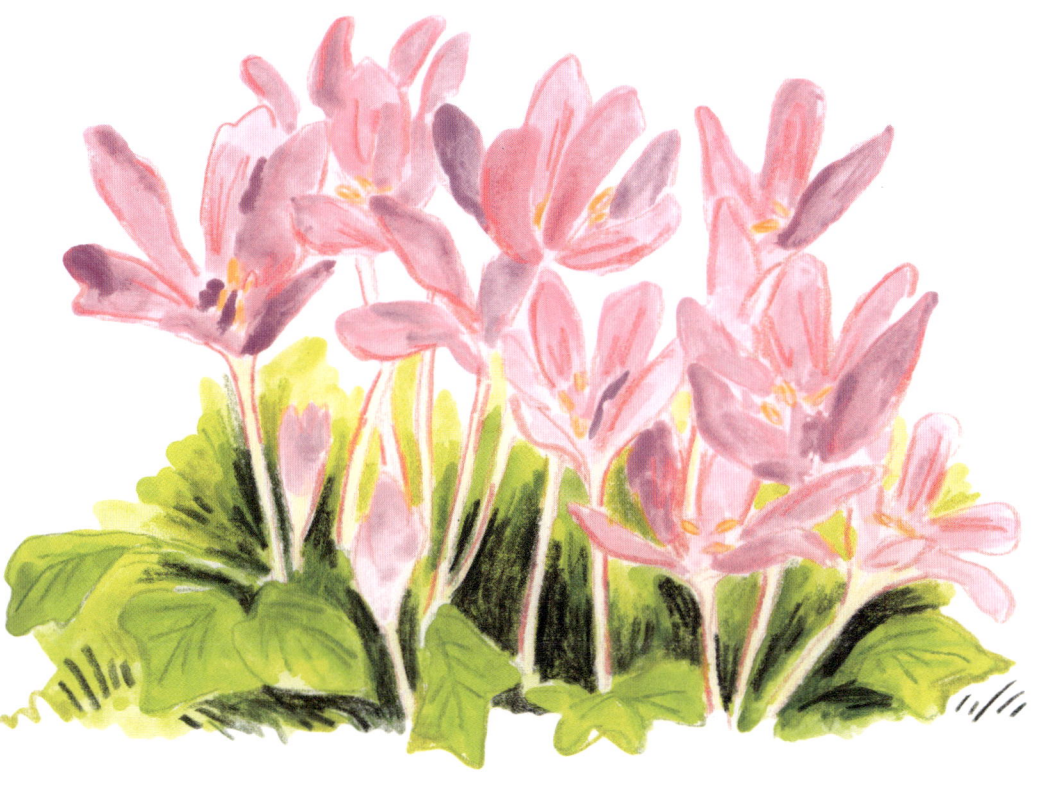

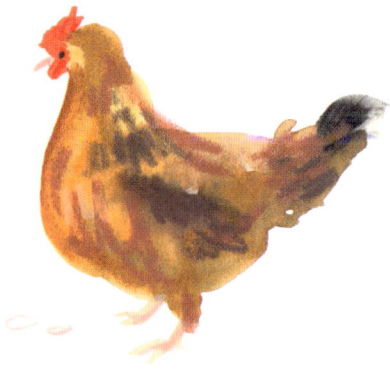

Chickens

Just like the butterfly project, this will easily fill a double page spread in your sketchbook. You can pick any animal here – I've drawn frogs, ducks, bugs and parrots in this way, and here I'm painting chickens!

Using a wet medium like gouache or watercolour means you can create some interesting effects with the paint blending, or you can use dry mediums if you'd prefer to work faster. The pages are very easy to fill because the individual elements are quite small, and you can build them all up in layers rather than painting them one at a time.

MATERIALS: gouache, round brush, coloured pencils

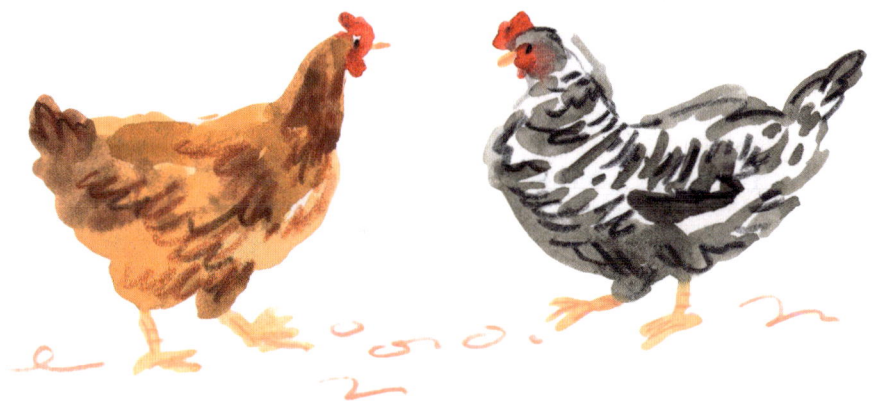

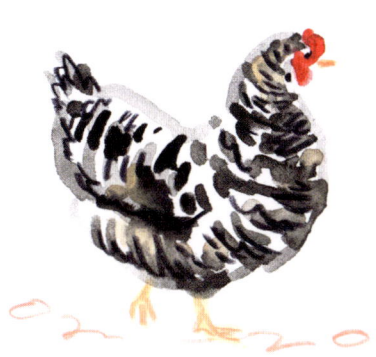
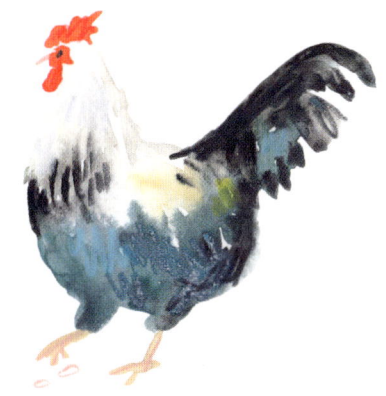

1. Start painting your chicken from the tail using a light-tone gouache and a round brush. Depending on the pattern of the chicken, you can start with small, short brushstrokes, or with a swipe of your brush to create the shape along the spine. If you're filling your page with chickens, do this for each of them before moving on to the next step. It keeps them cohesive in colour, but you can still create variation by painting the chickens in different poses.

2. Next, fill in the rest of the chicken shape using a different tone. By changing tone you add texture and shading to the chicken. Define the rest of the body of your chicken by adding more shapes, such as the belly, neck and head.

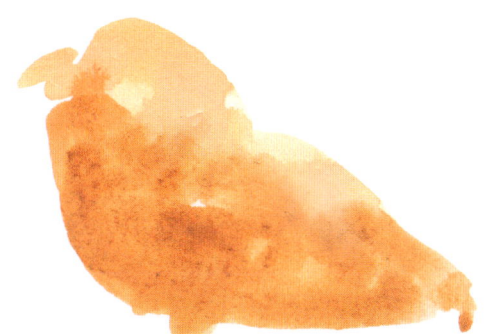

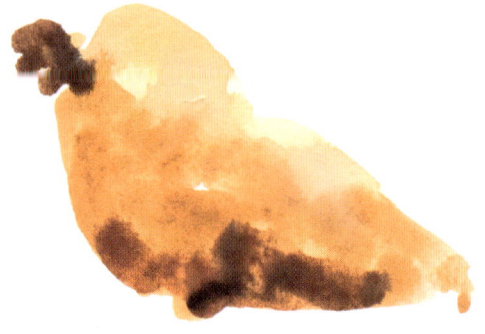

3. Mix up a darker tone again to add further texture and shade. Add some looser brushstrokes for the tail feathers, followed by a shadow along the bottom half of the chicken.

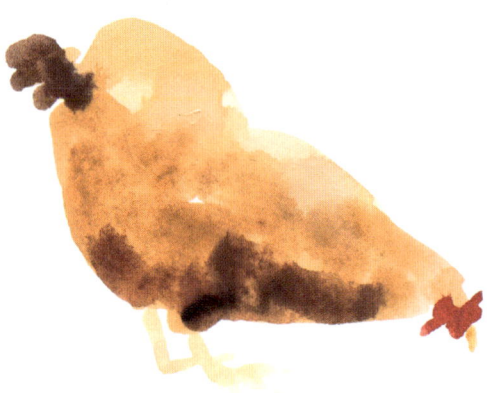

4. Use a red shade and the tip of your brush to add the chicken's comb and wattles around the head. It doesn't have to be too accurate, just a suggestion of red works fine here. Mix a light cream or beige shade to paint in the beak and legs. You can simplify these shapes, but if they are too small for your brush, you can add it with pencil in the last step.

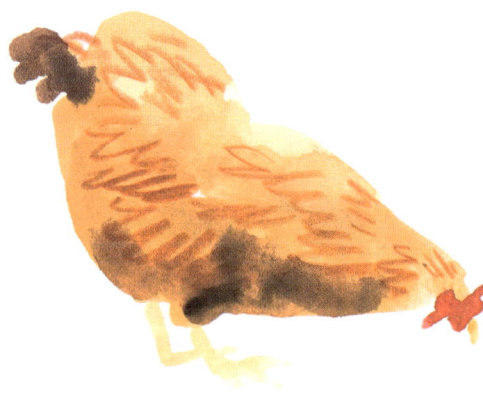

5. Once your paint layer has dried, take a mid-toned coloured pencil that is slightly darker than the base layer of your chicken. Use scribbly lines and uneven marks to suggest the texture of ruffled feathers: you want the chicken to look feathered rather than flat, so change the angle of your lines depending on the position of your chicken. Work along the chicken, varying the direction of the feathers and mimicking the way they grow naturally.

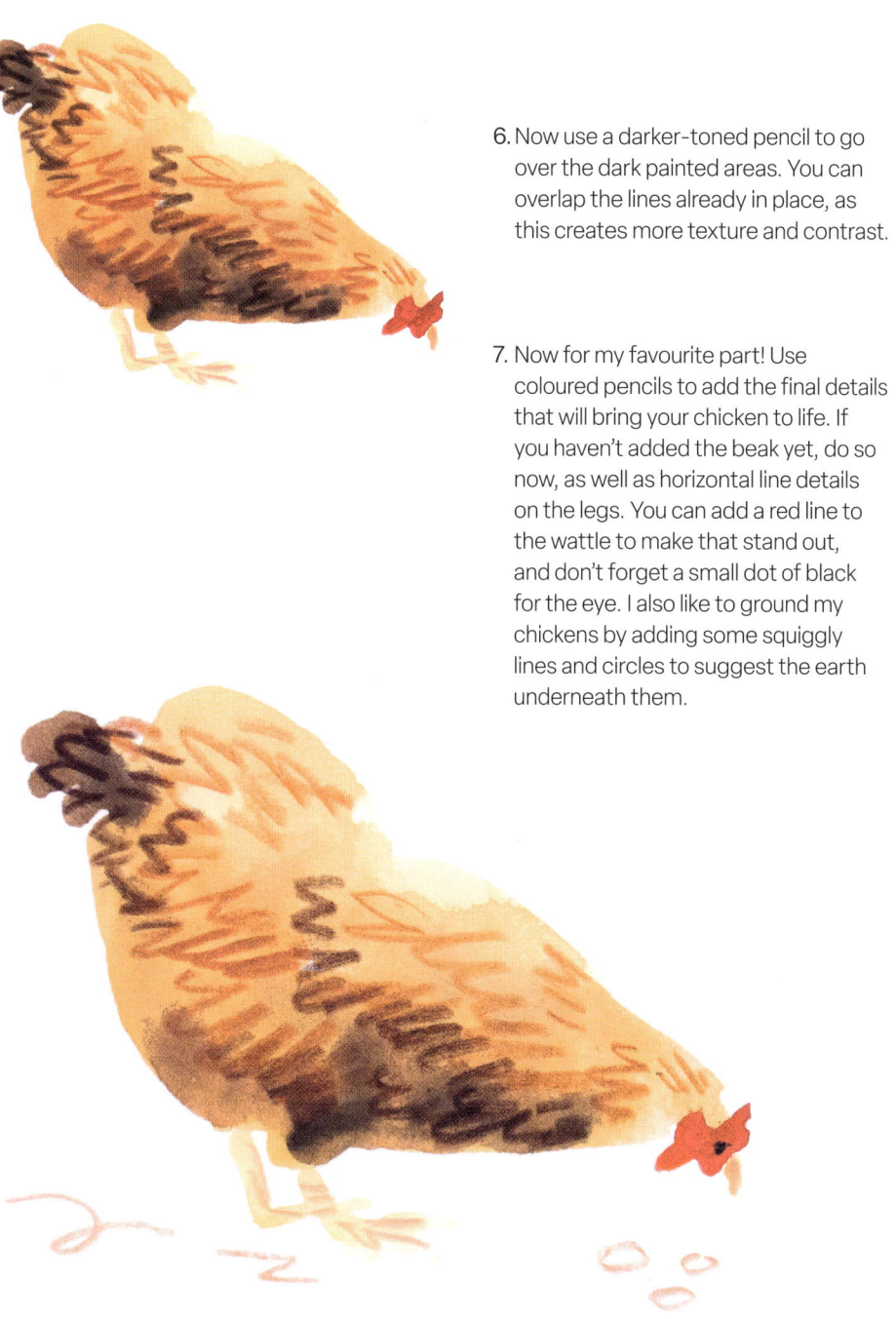

6. Now use a darker-toned pencil to go over the dark painted areas. You can overlap the lines already in place, as this creates more texture and contrast.

7. Now for my favourite part! Use coloured pencils to add the final details that will bring your chicken to life. If you haven't added the beak yet, do so now, as well as horizontal line details on the legs. You can add a red line to the wattle to make that stand out, and don't forget a small dot of black for the eye. I also like to ground my chickens by adding some squiggly lines and circles to suggest the earth underneath them.

Urban sketching

Urban sketching can be seen as quite a daunting project because most urban views are extremely detailed. Here, we're going to be simplifying shapes and details to make the scenes much more manageable and stylized. You can use the techniques in this project with any medium, but here I'll be using brush pens.

Urban sketching can also be done on location, so once you've practised a few times it could be a fun way to draw from life and test your skills outside.

MATERIALS: brush pens, coloured pencils

  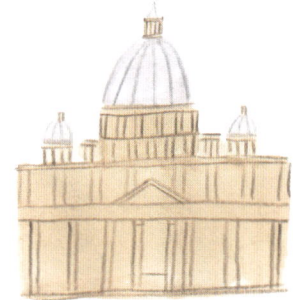

1. First, simplify the buildings you see into their very basic building blocks. Start by using squares or rectangles and filling in the biggest shapes using a neutral shade brush pen. Greys, beiges and soft pastel colours work best for buildings in urban scenes.

2. Now add the smaller shapes on top. Some buildings will simply be made up of one big rectangle, while others will have extra architectural elements. I've added in smaller squares and domes. It helps to do this as the second step, because you can sit them on top of the main shape from Step 1.

3. Now to add linework with coloured pencil. This is the step that really makes your shapes start to look like buildings. There may be lots of detail on the reference you're using, so focus on the lines that stand out the most. You don't want to get carried away trying to include every line, so just keep the forms relatively simple. For example, there were lots of lines on the building I'm drawing, but I have used longer lines to span the building rather than lots of small ones – this shows there's still a lot going on but it's readable as a detailed facade.

4. Here's where you add smaller details, such as windows and other elements that fill out the space. I like to use a dark tone for the windows, to make them stand out, and the same brown I used in Step 3 to add a few more basic shapes. I've added smaller lines and little squares and rectangles, as well as some dots on the dome to highlight the decoration of the structure.

5. All buildings can be drawn in this way. Here, I've filled in around the finished building with various shades and pastel colours. I'm using squares and rectangles again and different browns for the rooftops.

6. With a few more details added to each building, the busy urban scene is finished! Using coloured pencils that are the same colour as the base shape but darker in tone means they sit well together but the details still stand out. I've also added other elements, such as background and sky and the suggestion of people.

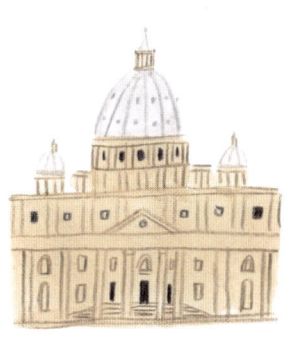

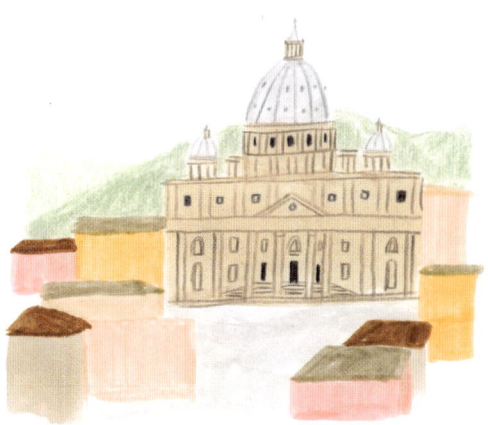

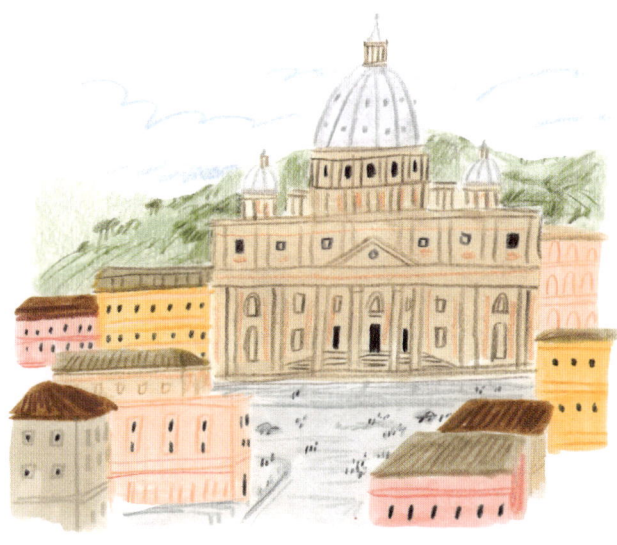

Fish

Fish are really fun to include in your sketchbook! I like to intensify the saturation of the fish's colours and go brighter than in real life. You can use a variety of materials for this project, and in this example I'm using gouache as my base.

This is one of my favourite subjects to paint on a timer, too. Drawing against the clock is a great way to loosen up and avoid overcomplicating or overthinking your marks. Have a go and see if you can paint or draw three fish in twenty minutes! You might be surprised just how fast you can work when there's a time limit.

MATERIALS: coloured pencils, gouache, round brush

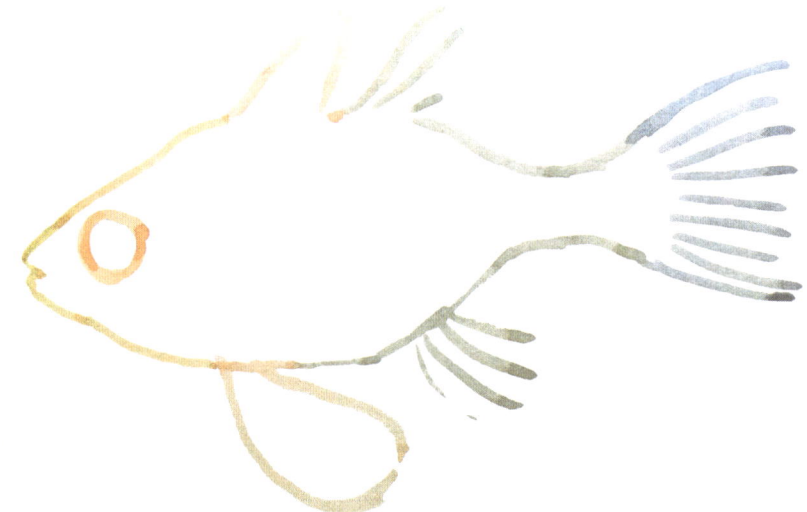

1. Start with the head of your fish. You can use a coloured pencil to sketch the base shape of your fish first or go straight in with gouache and a round paintbrush like I have here. Pick a neutral colour or one that matches the colour of your fish. The eye and the mouth add a lot of personality to the fish and are a great place to start.

2. Outline the rest of the fish. Include the fins, body and tail – you can use one colour for this or multiple. I wanted the fins to be different colours to reflect the shades on my reference photograph. For thinner fins, use long, thin brushstrokes to suggest the lines, rather than outlining, as it gives a softer effect.

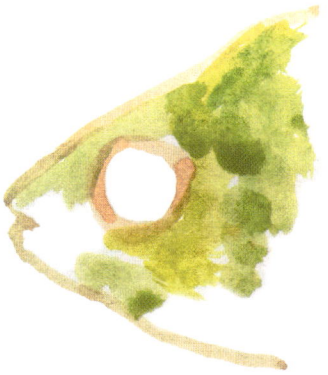

3. Mix up different shades and apply them to the fish with small, short strokes. Use the tip of a round brush and apply in a dabbing motion to add texture and mimic the scaly texture of the fish.

4. Work your way along the fish and mix up the different colours on the body. Some fish may be grey so you can add purple, blue or green tones for a bit more vibrancy. You can also add colour to the fins at this stage, and patterns too.

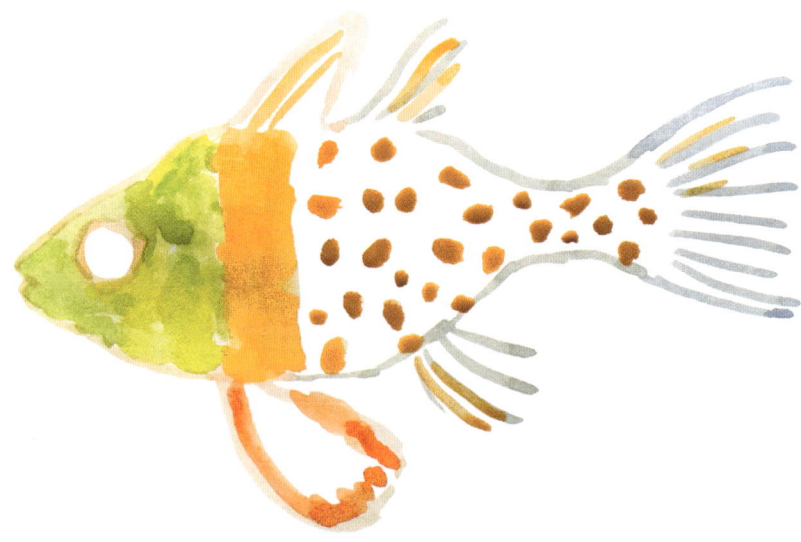

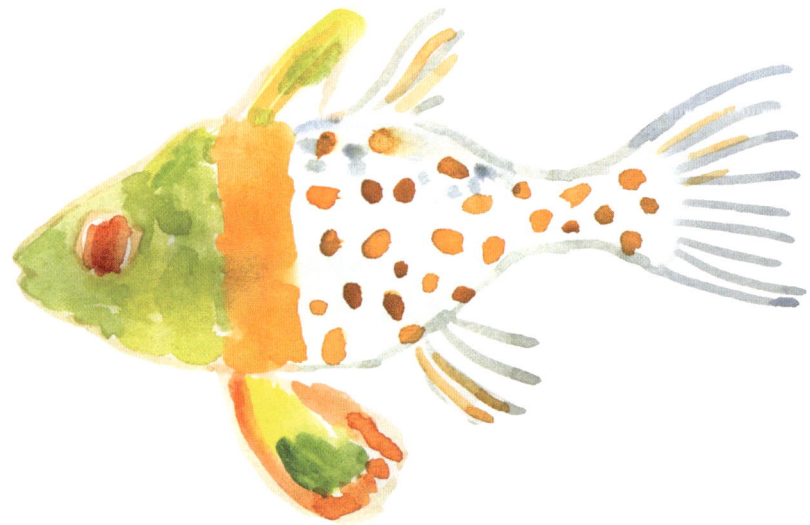

5. Continue filling in the areas of your fish. I find it easier to mix up whichever colour I need for the area I'm focusing on, rather than working in a specific order, such as from light to dark. Fish are an extremely forgiving subject, so enjoy the process! You can see here I've filled in more of the fins and added the eye colour and some shading using watery gouache along the top edge.

6. Now let's add some pencil details. If you're working to the timer, you can do all three fish at this stage, as by the time you've completed the paint layer on the third one, the first one should be dry and ready for your details.

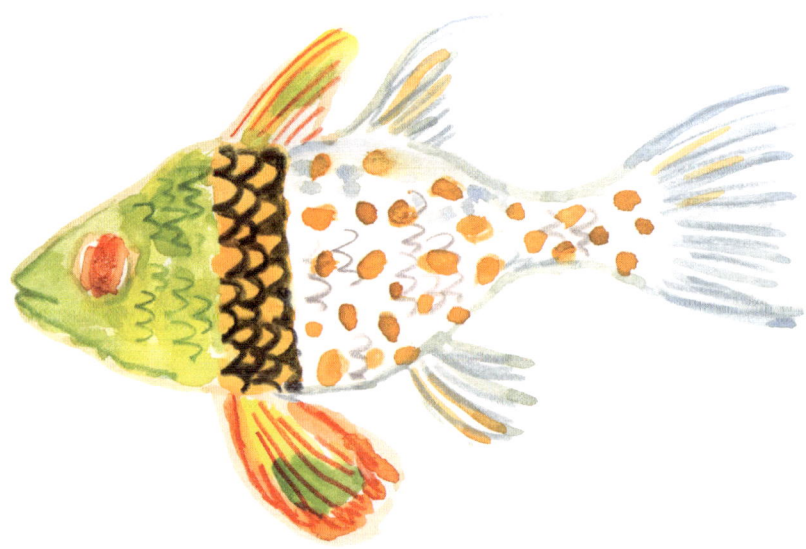

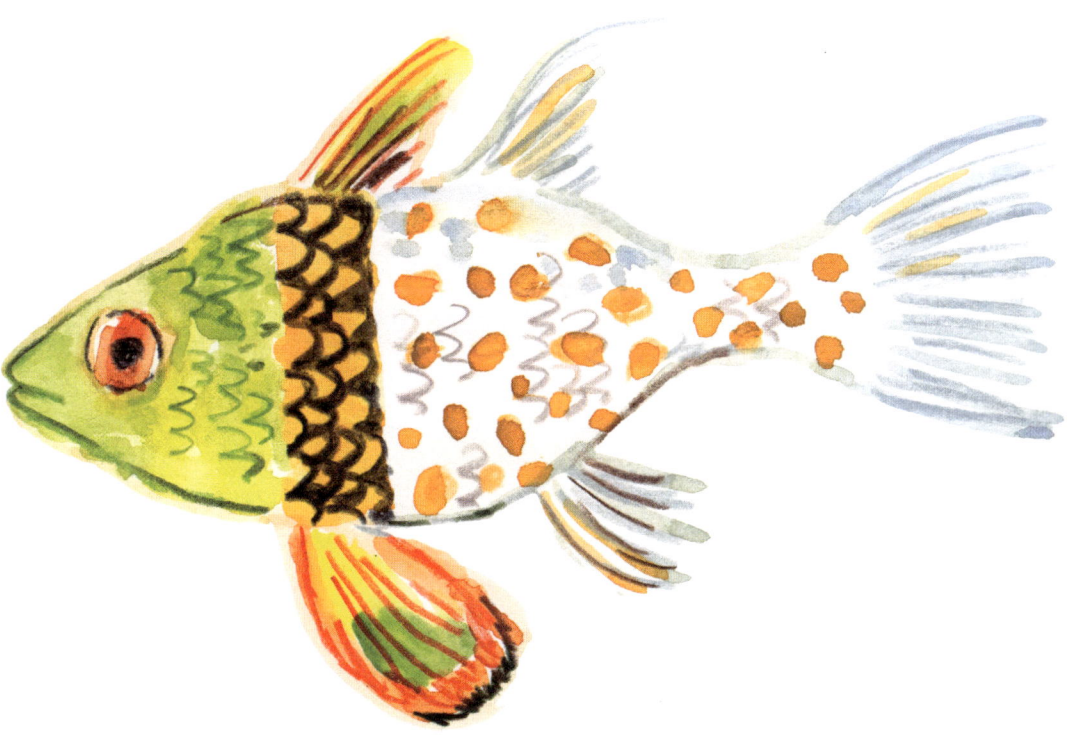

You can use lots of different shades of coloured pencils, and can literally pick any colour as fish are iridescent in the water. I like to add a scale effect using sideways scalloped lines – just make sure the open end of your scallop is facing the head of the fish. Be sure to keep them all in this direction rather than at differing angles. I leave some gaps between the scales as otherwise the fish can look a bit too busy.

7. Finally, add the darkest tone and your finishing touches. Outline various areas of your fish, like the head and the eye, and add the iris. The outlines really help make the fish feel complete.

Sunset

Sunsets are beautiful and add colour to your sketchbook. You can use bright paints, inks or pens to replicate the colours, or softer mediums like pastels or pencils to capture the atmosphere. Here, I'll show you how to use soft pastels and blend them to create an ethereal feeling. You can use your own photographs to work from, or there are plenty to be found on copyright-free sites if you search for 'sunrise' or 'sunset'.

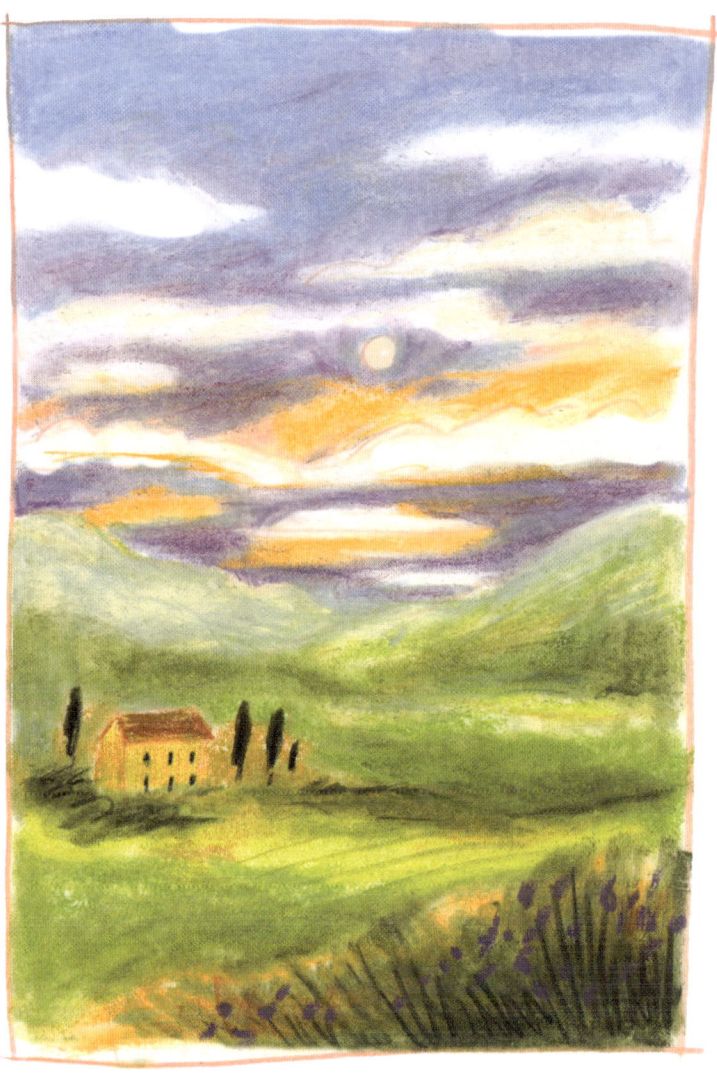

MATERIALS: coloured pencils, soft pastels, pastel blending tools or eyeshadow applicators, eraser, fixative spray

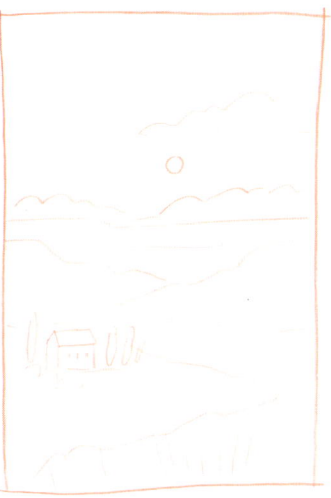
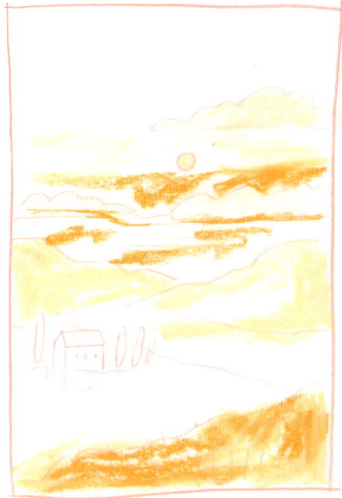
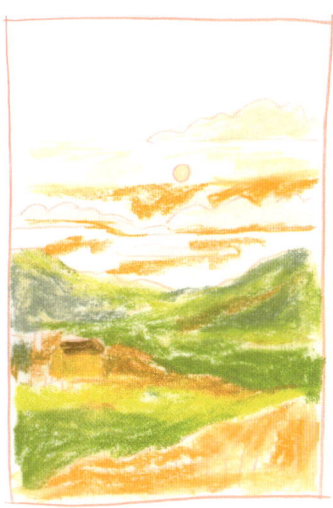

1. Let's start by sketching the basic elements of the landscape. Use a mid- or light-tone pencil rather than a dark tone so it blends better with the pastels you will lay on top. Focus on the bigger shapes first and then move onto adding smaller shapes such as trees or buildings.

2. Use your lightest pastel shades to start building your scene in layers. I've used a white, a light yellow and a light orange. You can be messy at this stage, so it's okay if you go over your sketched lines. This is the base you're going to be building on top of with other colours. I'd like my sunset to have a warm atmosphere, so that's influencing the colours I'm using.

3. Now start adding other colours. Add more pastel on top of your sketch and even over some of the colours you laid down in Step 2. You're not blending until Step 6, so don't worry about leaving any white space or gaps showing from the paper underneath.

   Use light and medium tones again as you add the pigment to your page.

4. Now onto that colourful sky. I'm using purples and pinks to go alongside the orange I added in Step 2. Again, I'm keeping my application quite scribbly and not worrying about the paper showing through.

5. Add darker tones of the colours you've already applied, such as dark purple or dark green. Use these on top of the original colour below but apply it in short, sharp strokes as you don't want to completely cover up the layer underneath. Use the short edge of the pastel to get this effect and the corner of the pastel for smaller details like trees or grass.

6. And now for the transformation! Using your blending tools, start blending the colours slowly by applying the sponge in small circles. I find it helpful to have multiple blending tools, one for each area of colour, as it stops things getting muddy. Work from the top down and be careful where you lay your hand as it will smudge easily. Don't smudge or blend any areas that you'd like to be more defined (like the small trees next to the house in my drawing).

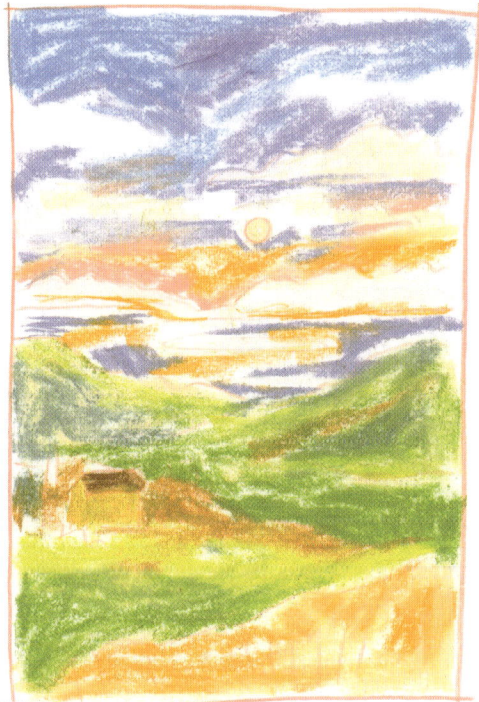
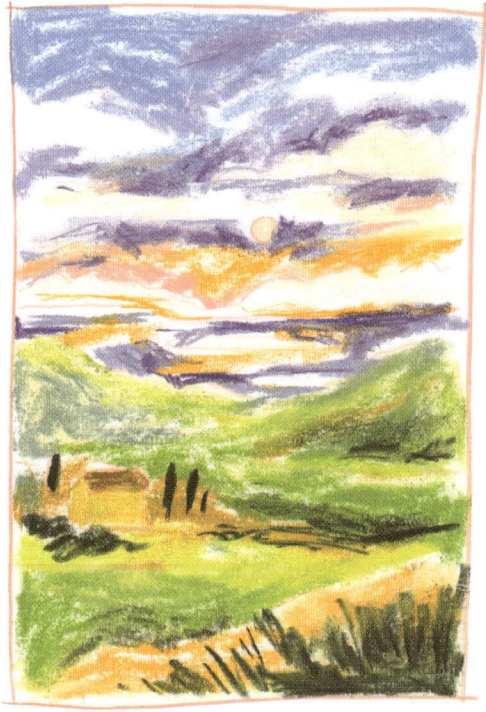

7. Time to neaten things up and finish with a final touch of pastel and pencil. Here's where you can evaluate how your drawing is looking and add any more colour. I wanted to add a blue to the sky to intensify the colour, as well as a bit more purple to increase richness. I also wanted to create more of a sense of distance with the mountains, so I applied a lighter colour over the green. It helps to push things back and away from the viewer's eye, and is a great technique to learn.

If you have areas that you wanted to be white but that are looking unclean due to smudging, you can use an eraser. I used a small eraser to bring back the white of my clouds, and this made a big difference to the sky. I also used dark coloured pencils to create tiny details like tree trunks, windows and the flowers in the foreground.

To seal your pastel drawings and stop them from smudging or transferring once you've finished, apply a fixative spray in thin layers to keep it in place.

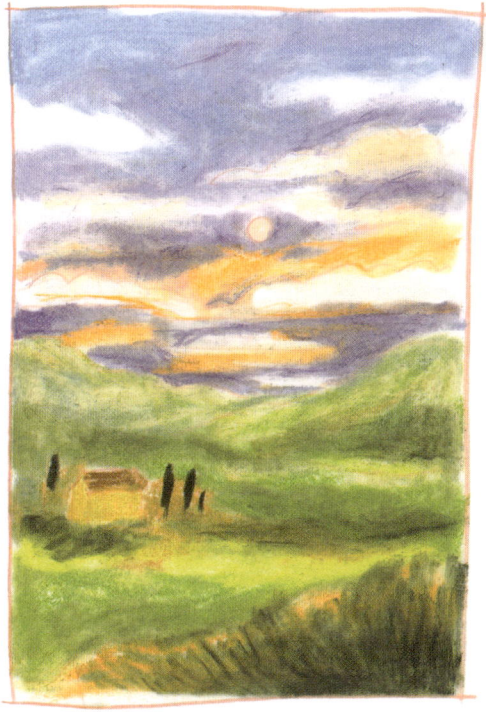
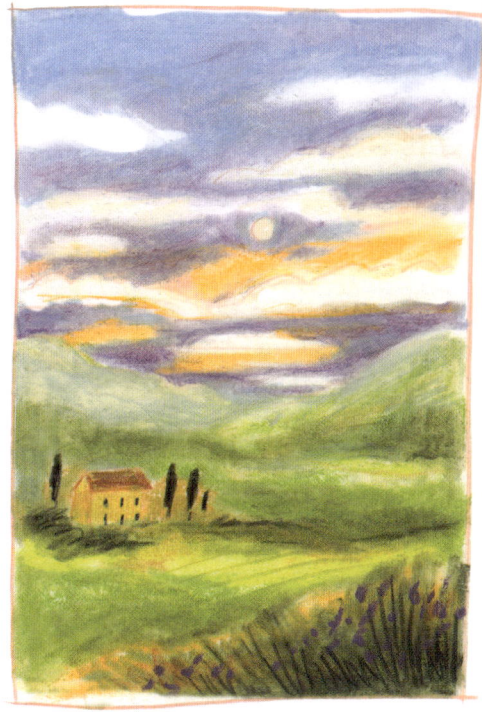

Coastal landscape

Coastal landscapes are some of my favourite views to paint. I recommend gouache or watercolour for this one as they really lend themselves well when painting water. I'll also share a technique I use for adding movement and interest when illustrating water, and how you can build up the full painting in sections.

MATERIALS: gouache, round brush, coloured pencils, wax pastels

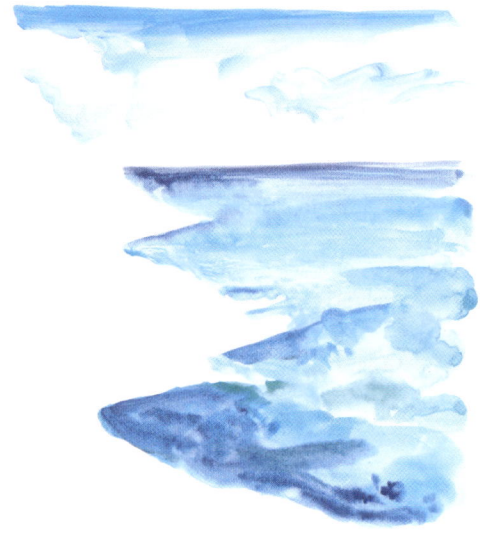

1. Start with your blue tones as these can often become dirty after mixing other colours on your palette. Applying them first keeps them uncontaminated. Use lots of water on your round brush when applying your gouache to the page as it creates softer blends and is helpful for painting water.

Use various shades of blue for the water rather than just one, so continuously mix up different tones on your palette. Apply a darker blue to the water's edge nearest to land and also in the distance on the horizon.

2. We'll tackle the lightest tone next for the coast or cliffs. Use short strokes with your brush loaded with a beige/light ochre colour to create lots of texture to mimic the rocky landscape, again applying with varying amounts of water to adjust the tones. I've also added some rocks in the foreground using this same colour so I don't need to mix it again later on.

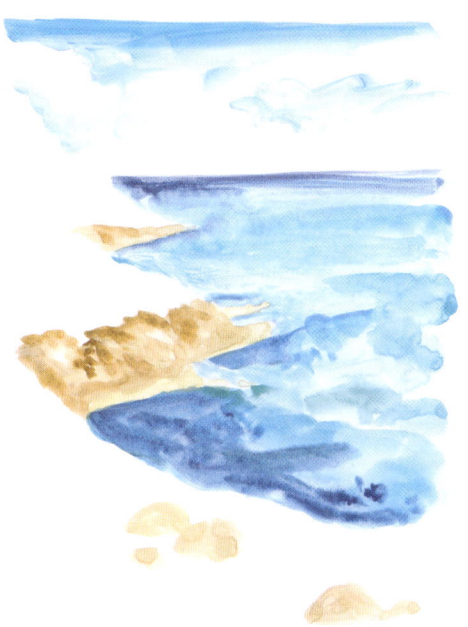 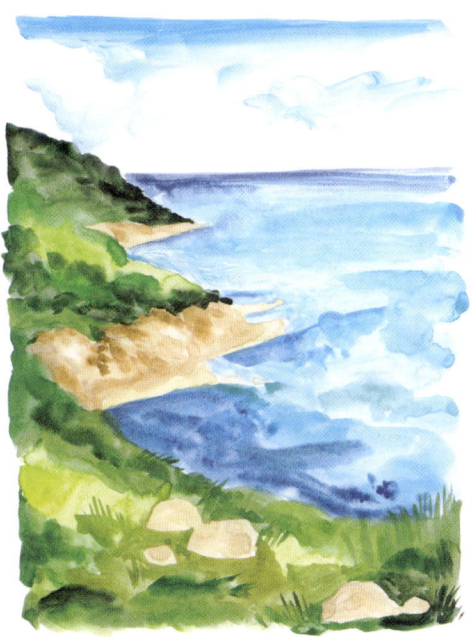

3. Now move on to the greens. Start with your lightest shade of green and apply it all over the land area. Then mix progressively darker shades of green and add them on top to suggest foliage and groups of trees or bushes. You don't need to let each step dry for this because the wet-on-wet effect works well for the differing greens. Finish with your darkest greens and use the tip of your brush to add grass textures, and thicker paint for individual blades. Add these in different directions in the foreground of your image only as we want the marks to be softer further away in the landscape.

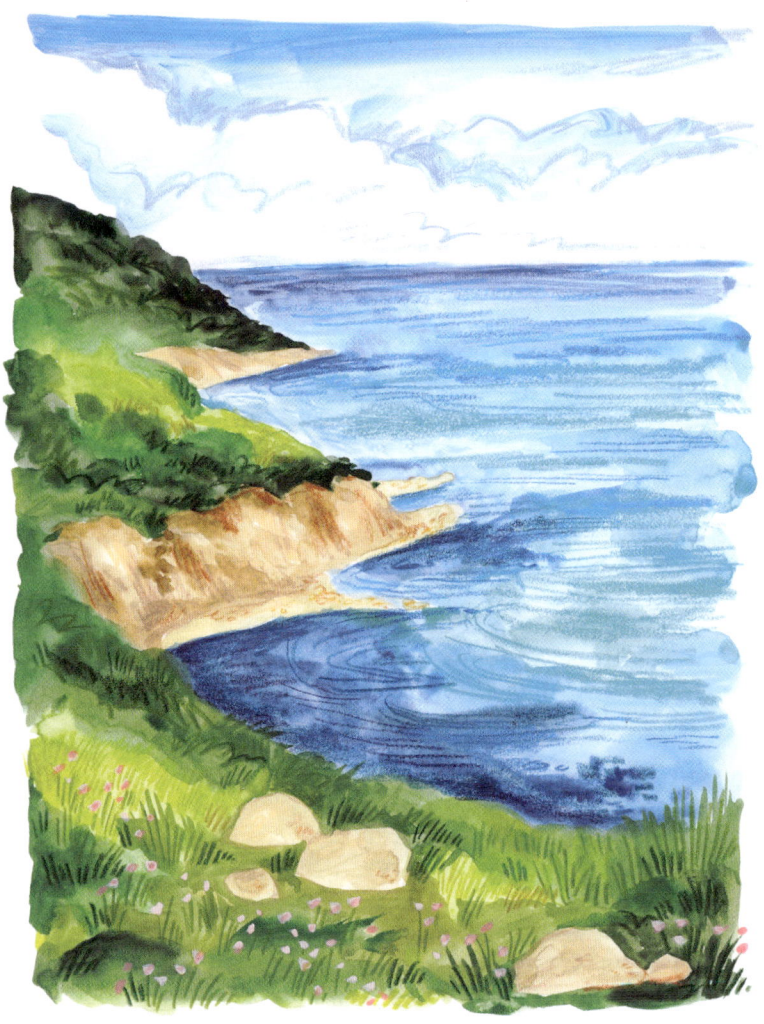

4. My favourite part – coloured pencils!
Once your paint layers have dried, it's
time to add details and linework to your
painting. Using different shades of
blue pencil, draw horizontal lines on top
of your water to suggest movement
and waves. These can be straighter
towards the horizon and more curved
as you work your way to the foreground
of the scene. Use a darker blue as you
draw them closer to the coastline.

Add scribbly marks and bouncy lines
on top of your bushes and forests
in the distance using a variety of
greens. In the foreground, use
lots of short lines to draw in grass,
again using lots of different greens
because this adds interest and
texture. You can subtly vary the
angle of your lines here to mimic the
grass growing in different directions.

I've also added some pink blobs in the foreground too. Creating a suggestion of wildflowers like this is a great way to add a pop of colour. Pink, purple, yellow or even white work wonderfully in landscapes like this.

5. Time for the final pops of colour. I'm using wax pastels here in pink, lime green and a lavender/blue shade. Apply these sporadically throughout the landscape over lines you've already drawn or on the edges of elements to highlight them. It can help to define edges like the top of the cliff face as well as highlighting more colour in the grass or waves.

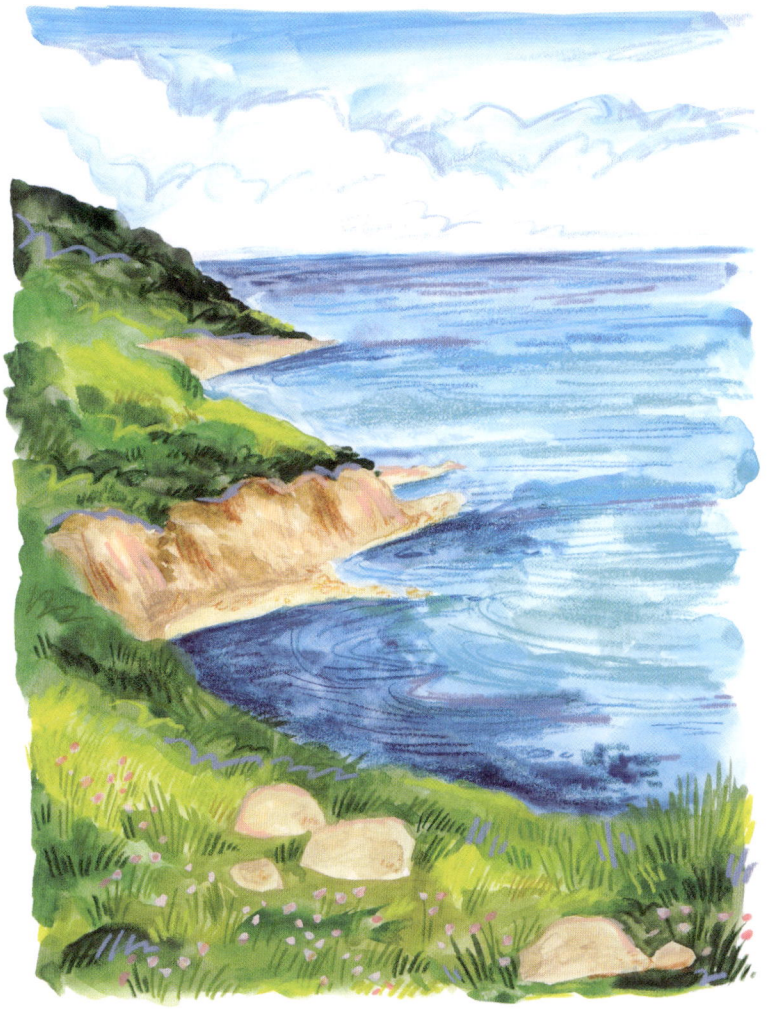

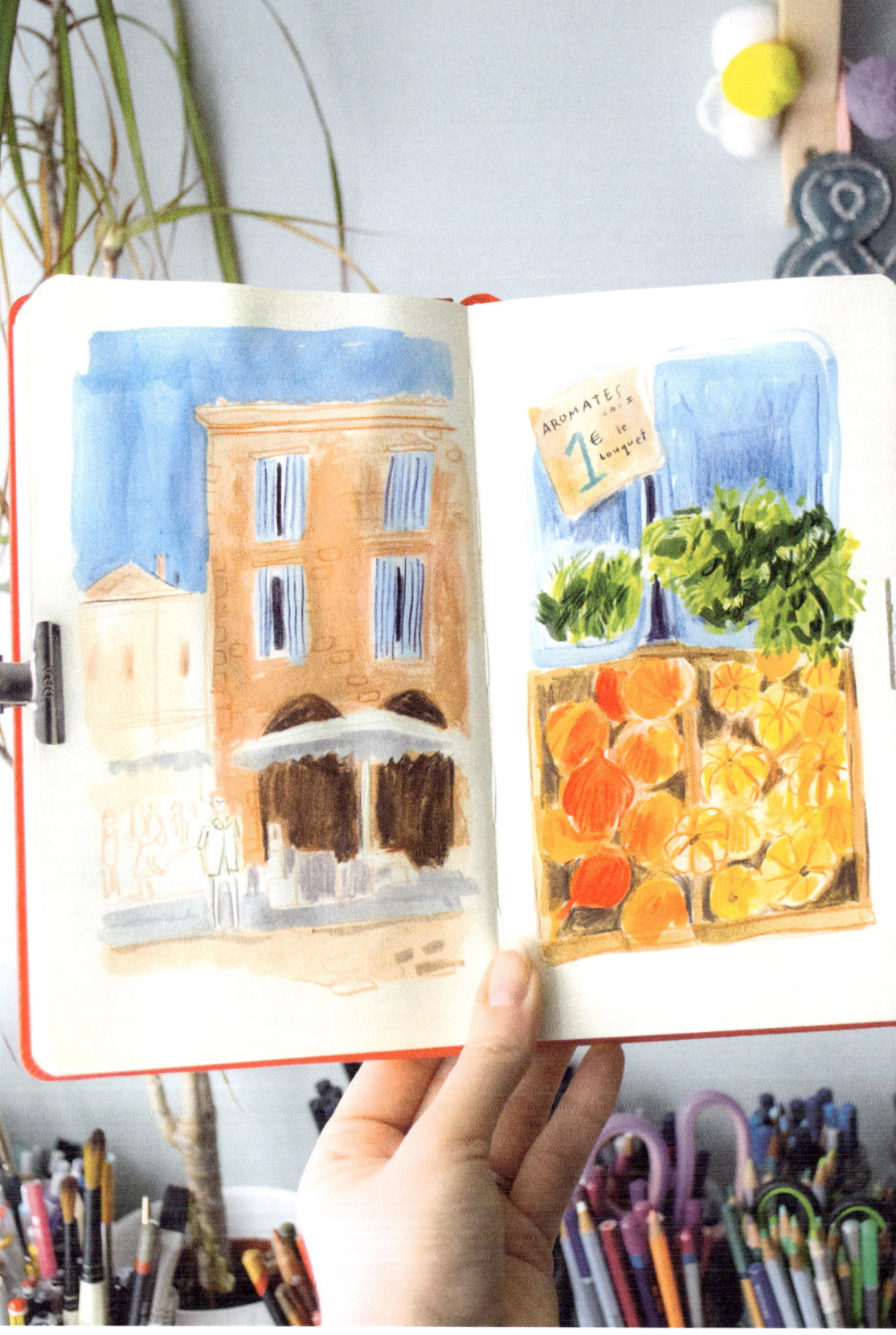

Now it's your turn

The projects and techniques in this book are great starting points for getting creative, but the real journey begins now.

As I mentioned in the introduction, this book is about giving you the confidence and the inspiration to fill your sketchbook with colour and joy. Now you've reached this point and maybe completed a few of the projects, it's time to continue exploring your creativity.

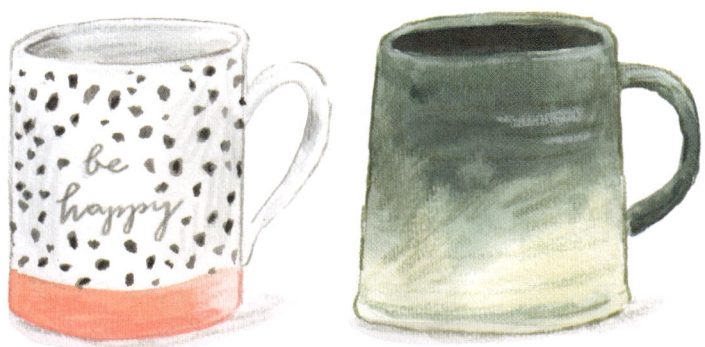

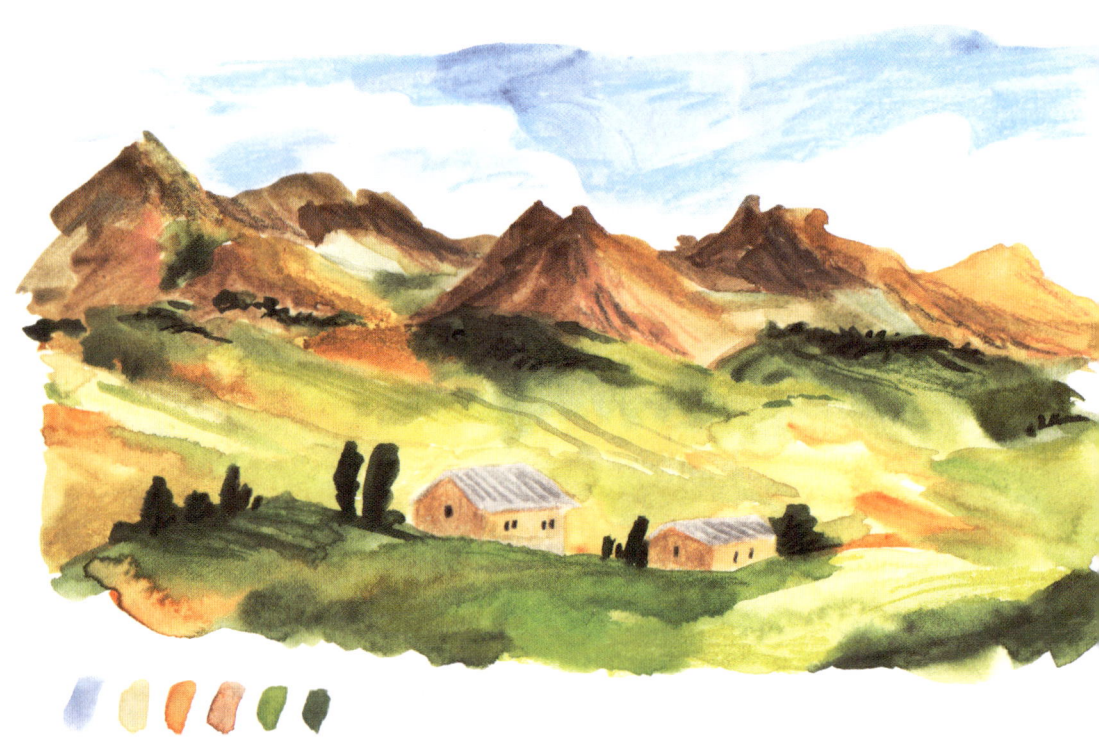

Inspiration

There will be days when you're totally stuck for ideas of what to draw, and there will be days when your motivation is non-existent. This is all completely normal and you're just as much of an artist whether you draw every day or every month. My biggest tip for creating is that inspiration often comes once you've simply made a start. Giving yourself just five minutes to open your sketchbook and scribble with some pencils is an amazing gateway to drawing because usually once you've started, you'll be unstoppable! The biggest barrier to entry is often our minds holding us back, whether that's due to perfectionism, overthinking, self-doubt or limiting beliefs.

It's okay if you don't like the work you've created. That's where you learn the most, and you'll be surprised how much it might affect your art down the line because you know what not to do. Art isn't about creating masterpieces and beautiful art we love all the time. It's the act of creating that's important.

Style

Style is a subject that comes up time and time again. The big secret is that it's not a goal but a journey, and one that's constantly evolving and changing. There will never be a moment when you feel like you've hit the style jackpot and that's the end of the process. As an artist, you always want to be exploring and trying new things, using new materials that change your style in subtle ways, and continually playing in your sketchbook – that is where the joy comes from.

So don't worry if you don't have a 'style', because everything you create is yours whether there's a cohesive style or not. The more you create, the more you'll learn what you like, what makes your heart sing and what feels like you. You won't develop a creative practice without drawing, and you won't feel those incredible highs of painting something you love without messing up a few times first. It's all part of your journey as an artist.

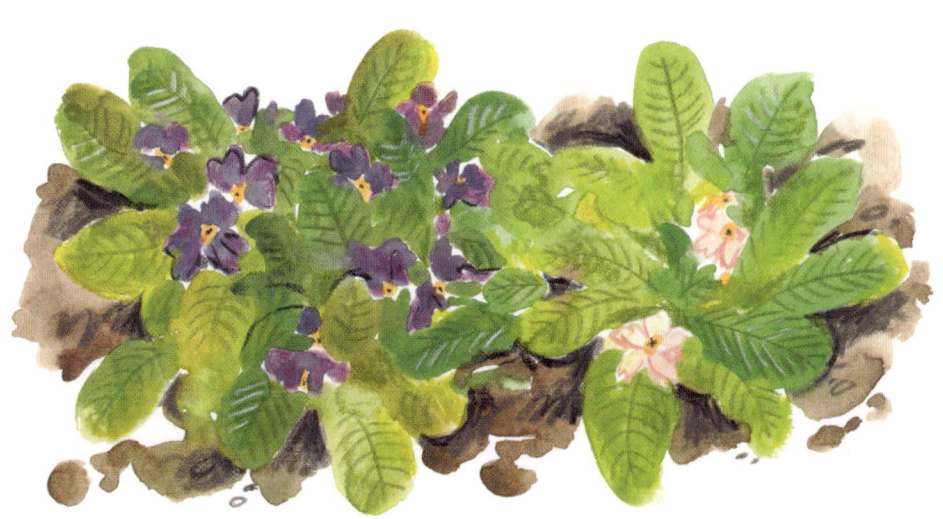

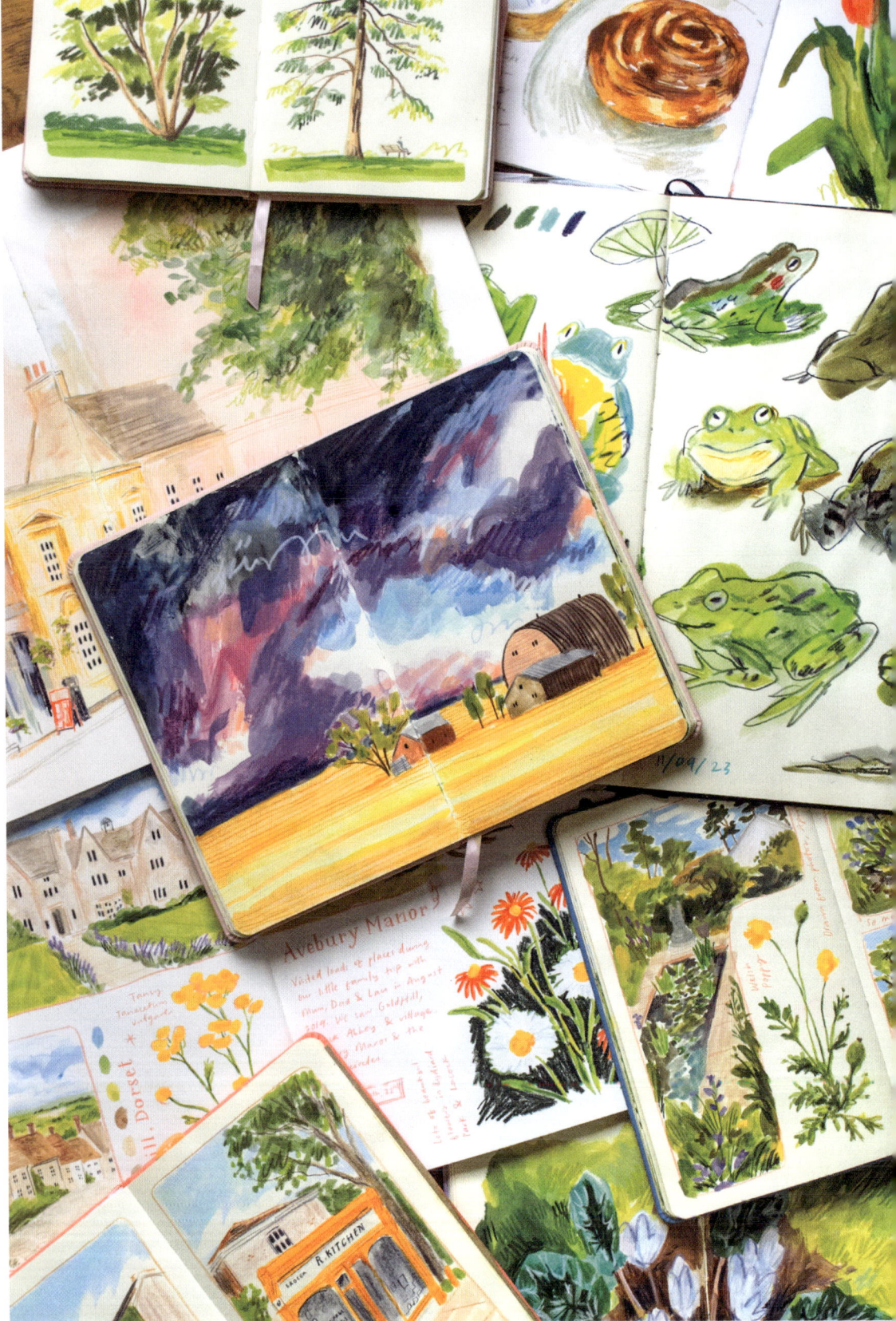

Prompt list

For those times when you do open your sketchbook and are at a loss as to what to draw, when you look at a blank spread and wonder what to fill it with, I have a few ways to tackle this lack of inspiration.

I might flip through my other work and older sketchbooks to see if there's anything that inspires me to get creative. This could be a colour combination I spot that I'd like to use again, or a particular topic I'd like to explore more. Another option is to pick through my personal prompt list, which gives me a limited amount of choice. Sometimes it's easier to be told what to do!

So here I'm sharing some ideas and prompts for filling your own sketchbook. Pick and choose any that take your fancy – you don't have to work through them in order. Use them as a starting point and see where your creativity takes you.

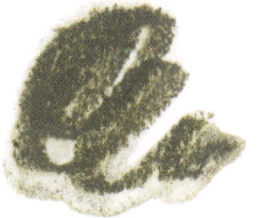

* Do you know a friend who loves to travel? Ask if they'll share their photos from a recent trip with you and draw from them.

* Scour through old photo albums (borrowing some from relatives is a lovely way to get connection in your work) and draw from what you see.

* Create a narrative by drawing out some panels on your spread and painting an animal in each panel as they move across a changing background landscape.

* Use a reference photo to draw an initial sketch and map out the main features and composition with pencil. Add paint and other mediums to finish it off without looking at the photo again. If you can't remember some things, use your imagination to fill in the gaps rather than peeking at the original image.

* Look outside your window and draw the view you see.

* Pick out something near you and practise your observational drawing skills. Draw it from multiple angles, such as above and below.

* Grab your favourite book and create a new cover inspired by a favourite scene from the book.

* Pick out an item in your home and use it as colour palette inspiration. Paint something using just those colours.

* Hop onto Google Maps and drag your pin to a country you'd love to visit. Click into the street view and draw what you find.

* If you have an art material that you've been unsure how to use, give it a go. See how many marks you can make with it – it doesn't have to be a finished drawing, just a mark-making exercise.

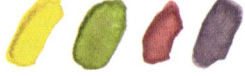

* Grab two paint colours and see how many different shades you can mix with them by varying the amount of each colour.

* Use a mirror to draw a self-portrait.

* Pick three materials from your art supplies and create something with the limited colours.

* Draw everything that you usually carry in your bag and annotate them on a spread.

* Decorate your sketchbook cover.

* Cut up a magazine and use collage to create a landscape.

* Head to your kitchen cupboard and draw the label of a jar.

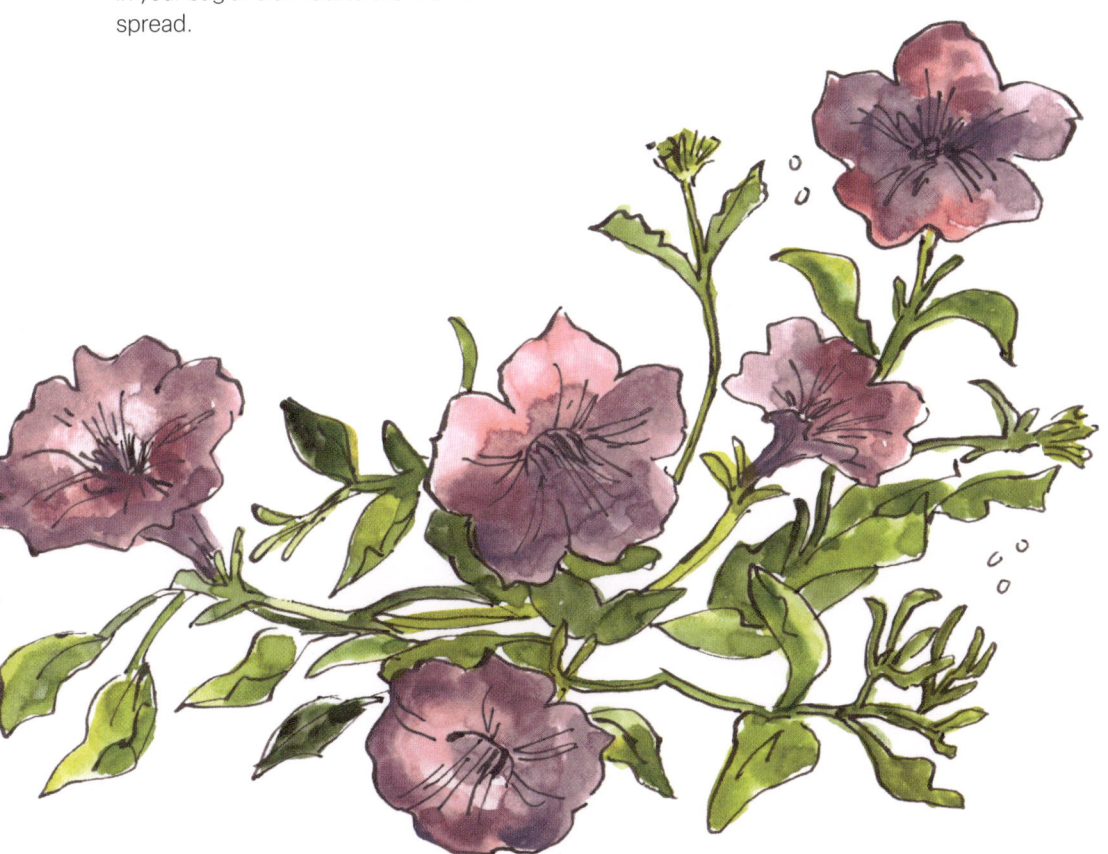

Resources

REFERENCES

WEBSITES
Pexels.com
Unsplash.com
Google.com/maps
Mapcrunch.com

BOOKS
The Natural History Book, DK Books
   (DK Books)
A Colour Guide to Familiar Wild Flowers,
*   Ferns and Grasses*, Bohumil Slavik
   (Octopus Books)
The Oxford Book of Trees, A.R. Clapham
   (Peerage Books)
Old English Villages, Laurence Fleming,
   Ann Gore and Clay Perry (Weidenfeld
   & Nicolson)
Birds: An Introduction to General
*   Ornithology*, James Fisher and Roger
   Tory Peterson (Aldus Books Ltd)

SKETCHBOOKS
Royal Talens Art Creation
Strathmore 500 Series Mixed Media
Clairefontaine Goldline Mixed Media

GOUACHE
Winsor & Newton Designers Gouache
Daler-Rowney Designers' Gouache
Pēbēo Studio White Gouache

WATERCOLOUR
Kuretake Gansai Tambi Watercolours

ACRYLIC
Daler-Rowney System3 Acrylic Paint and
Acrylic Ink
Royal Talens Amsterdam Acrylic Paint
Montana Acrylic Markers and Ink Refills

COLOURED PENCILS
Caran d'Ache Luminance Colour Pencils
Derwent Drawing Pencils

PAINTBRUSHES
Daler-Rowney Graduate Round Brush,
size 12, 10 and 6
Derwent Push Button Waterbrushes
Artway Mop Brushes

WAX PASTELS
Caran d'Ache Neocolor™ II

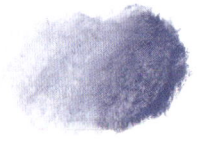
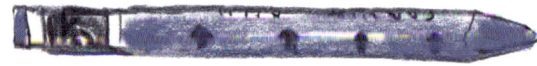
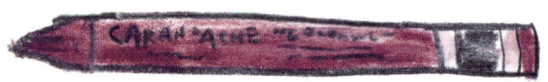
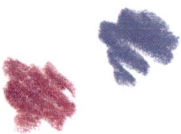

OTHER MIXED MEDIA

Derwent Inktense Blocks
PanPastels
POSCA Paint Pens
Sennelier Oil Pastels

PATREONS

Some drawings in this book were
created during online drawing sessions.
I recommend checking out these artists
with online communities:
Emma Carlisle
Sarah Dyer
TJ Marston
Beth Spencer

SOCIAL MEDIA

Connect with me online! I post a new
YouTube video every week sharing my
creative process, and I share work on
Instagram too.
youtube.com/@KatieMoody
instagram.com/katie_moody

For tutorials and drawing sessions with
me and our creative community, join me
on Patreon.
patreon.com/KatieMoody

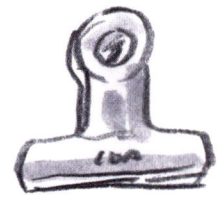

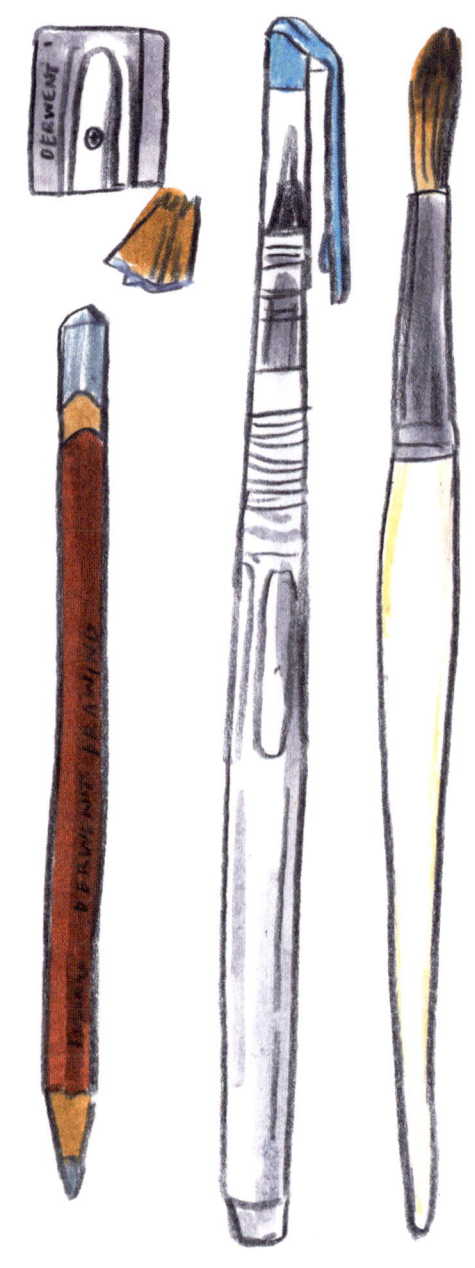

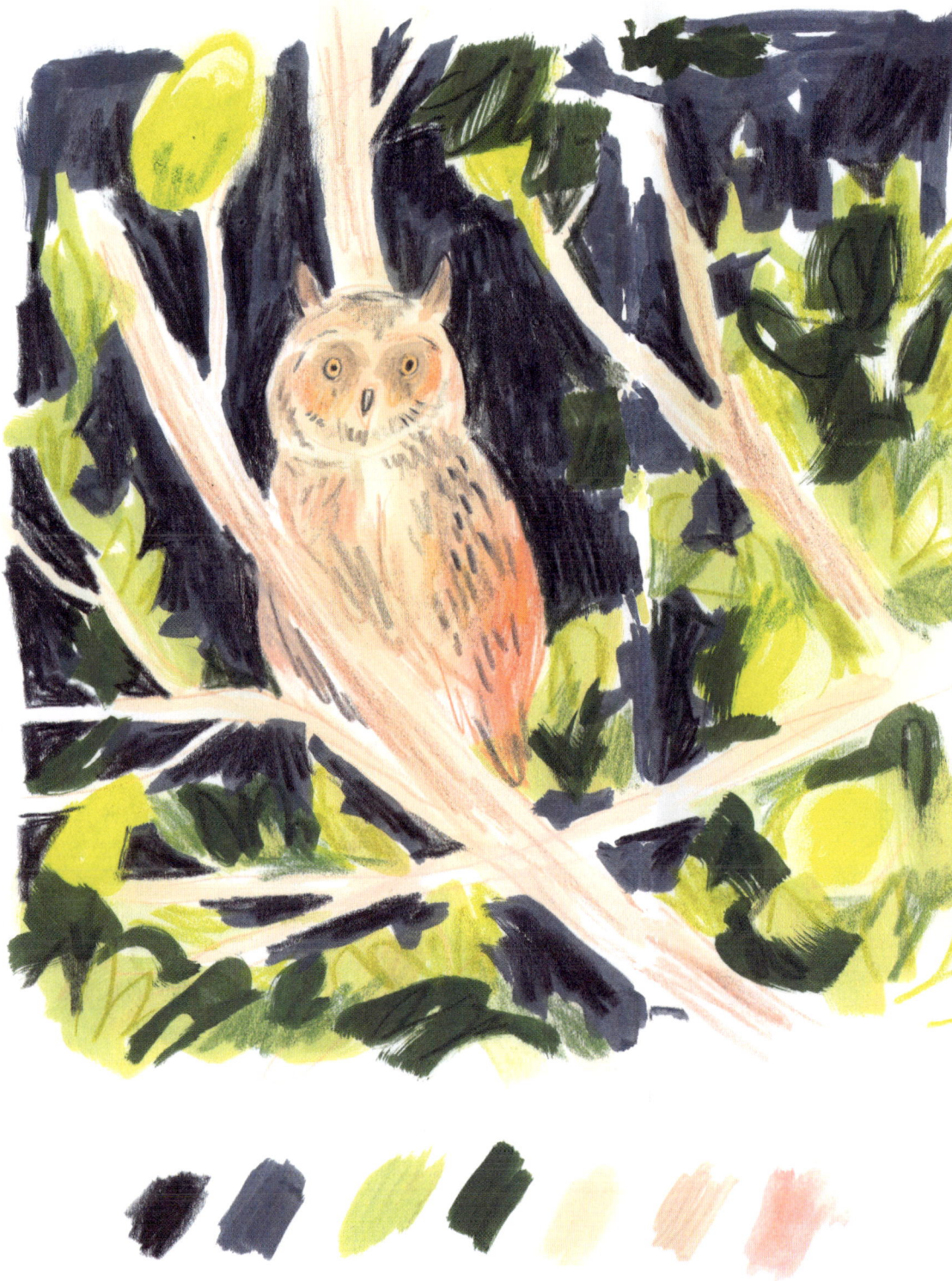

Index

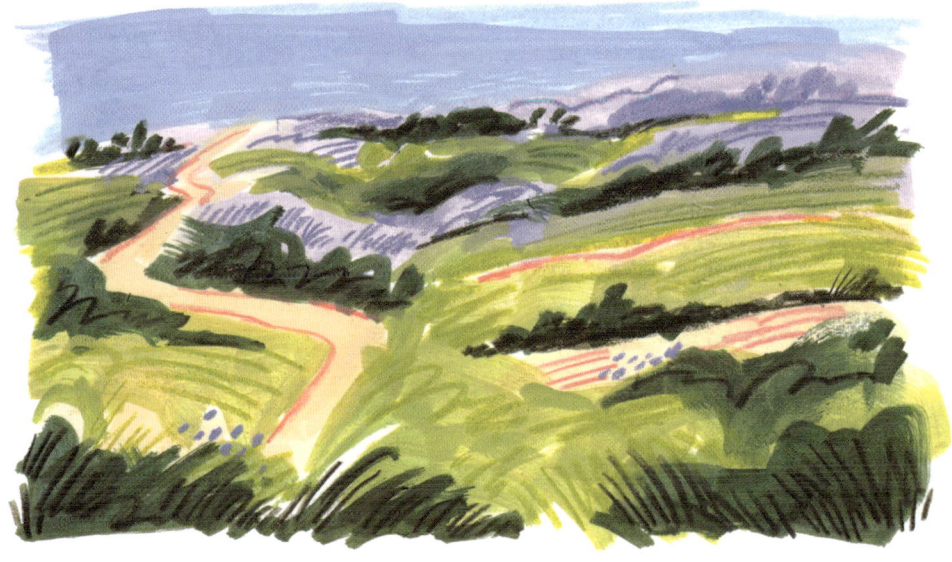

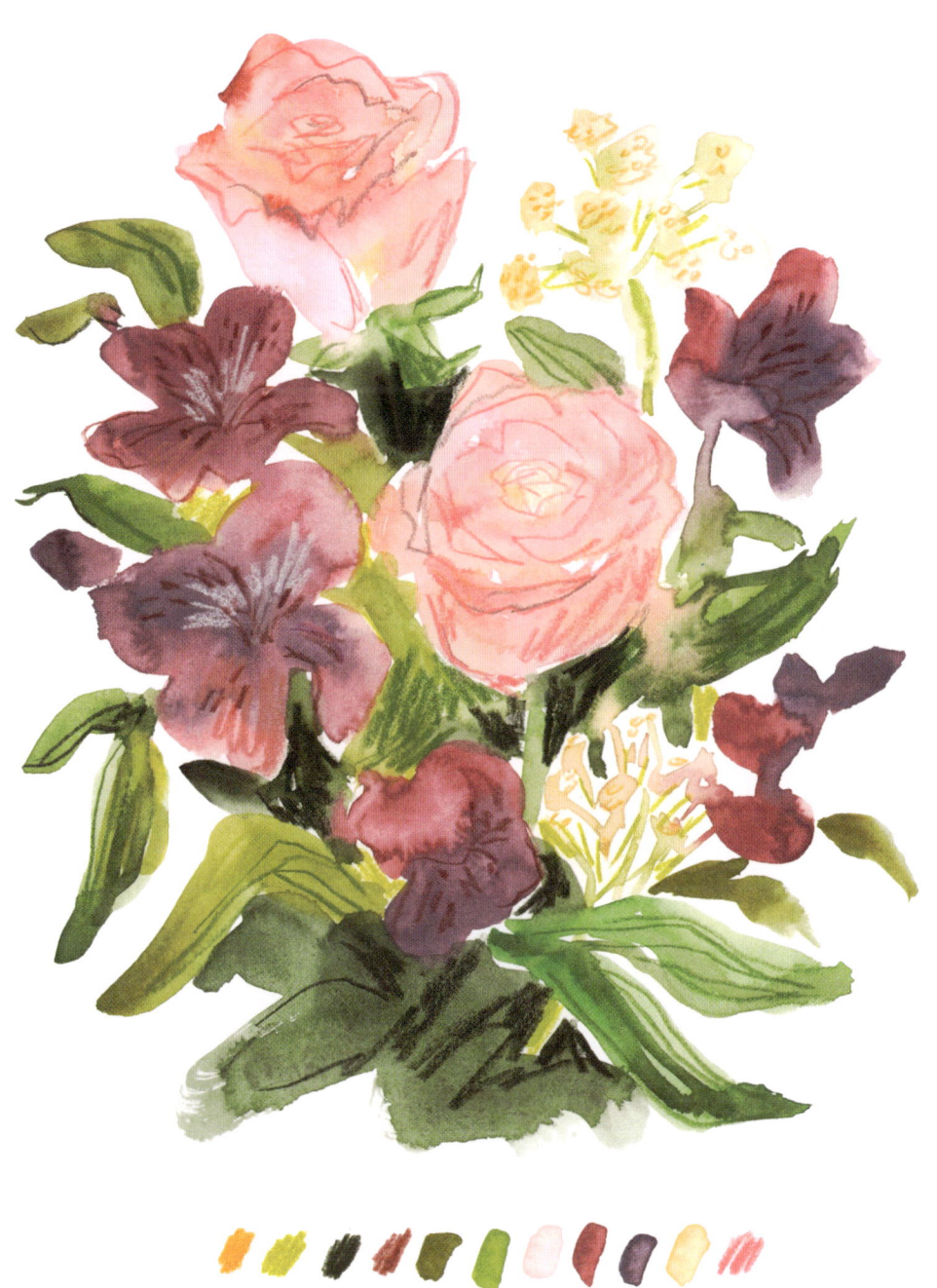

Acknowledgements

This book wouldn't have happened without Monica Perdoni, so a huge thank you to Monica for getting in touch and believing in this project! I'm so grateful to the whole team at Leaping Hare for all of their work and for bringing this book to life.

I wouldn't be writing this book without the support of my amazing online community, in particular my patrons, who have supported me in becoming a full-time artist and finding my purpose.

To my incredible husband, Mitch – your constant encouragement and love allowed this project to come to fruition. Without you, I would never have had the courage to put my art into this book. You believe in me more than I believe in myself and I couldn't do life without you.

Lastly, to my wonderful family and friends. I can't thank them enough for always cheering me on and checking in.

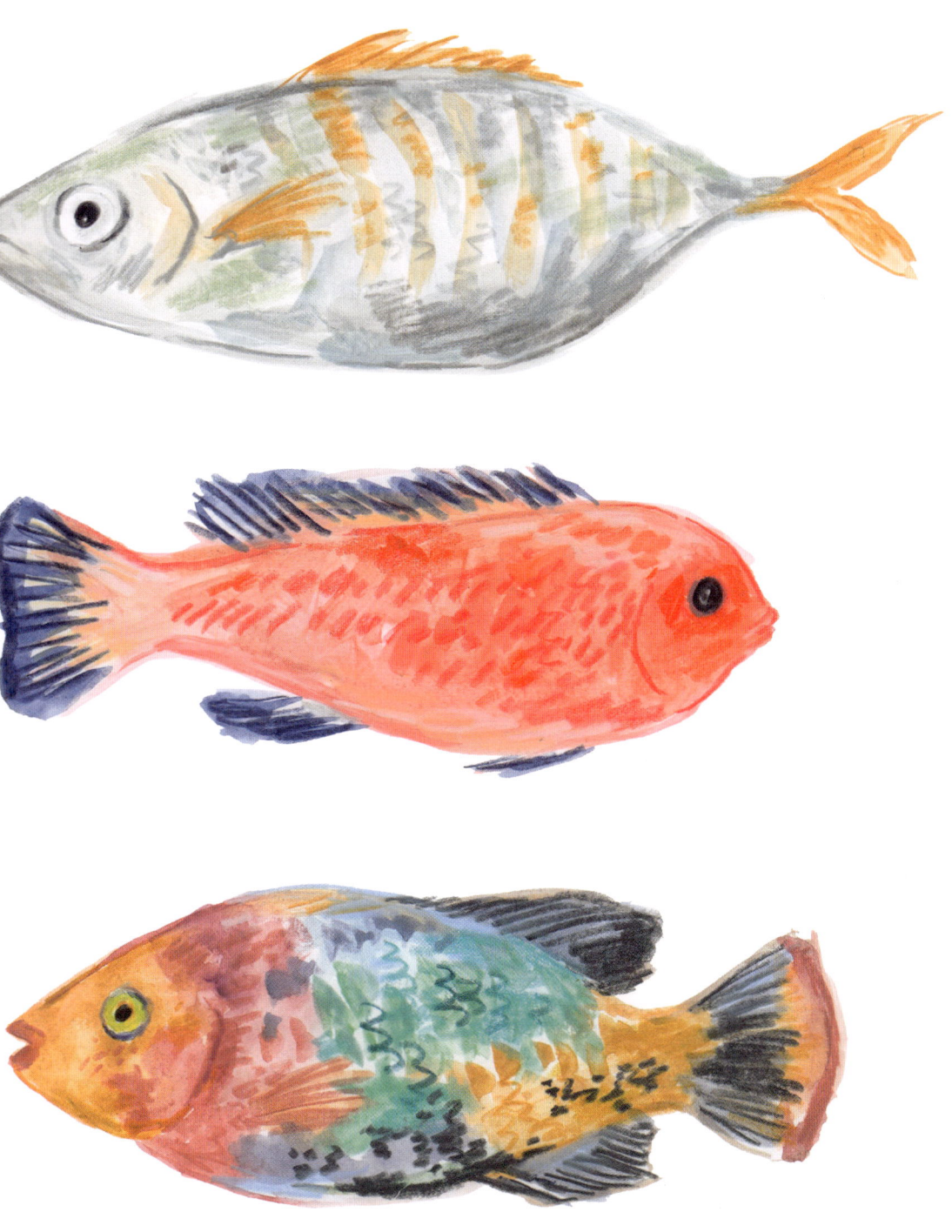

Quarto

First published in 2025 by Leaping Hare Press
an imprint of The Quarto Group.
One Triptych Place, London, SE1 9SH
United Kingdom
T (0)20 7700 9000
www.Quarto.com

EEA Representation, WTS Tax d.o.o., Žanova ulica 3, 4000 Kranj, Slovenia

A catalogue record for this book is available from the British Library.

ISBN 978-1-83600-067-9
EBOOK ISBN 978-1-83600-068-6

10 9 8 7 6 5 4 3 2

Book Design by Nicki Davis
Editorial Director Monica Perdoni
Senior Designer Renata Latipova
Senior Editor Charlotte Frost
Senior Production Controller Rohana Yusof

Printed in China

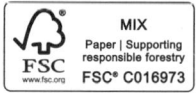